THE COMPLETE GUIDE
FOR MORTGAGE MATHEMATICS
With Financial Tables
and Lotus Templates

W9-AHB-595

Paul R. Goebel
Norman G. Miller

Prentice Hall, Englewood Cliffs, NJ 07632

Library of Congress Cataloging-in-Publication Data

Goebel, Paul R.
  The complete guide for mortgage mathematics with financial tables
and Lotus templates / Paul R. Goebel, Norman G. Miller.
    p.   cm.
  Includes index.
  ISBN 0-13-159393-5 (pbk.)
  1. Business mathematics--Real estate business--Problems,
exercises, etc. 2. Interest--Problems, exercises, etc.--Computer
programs. 3. Lotus 1-2-3 (Computer program) 4. Interest--Tables.
I. Miller, Norman G. II. Title.
HF5716.R4G62 1991
332.8'0285'5369--dc20   90-44265
                                                   CIP

Editorial/production supervision: *Anthony Calcara*
Cover design: *Richard Puder Design*
Manufacturing buyer: *Ilene Levy / Ed O'Dougherty*

 © 1991 by Prentice-Hall, Inc.
A Division of Simon & Schuster
Englewood Cliffs, New Jersey 07632

Printed in the United States of America

10 9 8 7 6 5 4 3 2 1

ISBN 0-13-159393-5

Prentice-Hall International (UK) Limited, *London*
Prentice-Hall of Australia Pty. Limited, *Sydney*
Prentice-Hall Canada Inc., *Toronto*
Prentice-Hall Hispanoamericana, S.A., *Mexico*
Prentice-Hall of India Private Limited, *New Delhi*
Prentice-Hall of Japan, Inc., *Tokyo*
Simon & Schuster Asia Pte. Ltd., *Singapore*
Editora Prentice-Hall do Brasil, Ltda., *Rio de Janeiro*

CONTENTS

Chapter 3
Mortgage Instruments   68

Chapter 4
Seller and Non-Traditional Financing   95

Chapter 5
Lotus Templates   111

Chapter 6
Financial Tables   137

Index   196

PREFACE

The Complete Guide for Mortgage Mathematics with Financial Tables and Lotus Templates is an up-to-date reference for use by lenders, real estate practitioners, investors, and students of real estate finance. The mathematical formulations included here will provide the user with sufficient information to handle virtually all situations relating to mortgage mathematics, as well as provide a base for further manipulations of specific situations as it becomes necessary. As real estate finance continues to adjust to changing market conditions, it will be necessary to modify the existing methodology of mortgage calculations. But the basic foundations, as provided in this text, will remain constant.

Chapter 1 is intended to introduce the basic mathematics associated with the time value of money. A clear understanding of the time value of money is essential to all of us, whether a financial analyst, lender, borrower, investor or consumer. Lending and borrowing alternatives are becoming more complex than ever and these concepts are necessary to properly evaluate the true cost of borrowing or lending. Since the material in Chapter 1 is elementary, the reader who is familiar with time value of money concepts may wish to start with Chapter 2 after briefly reviewing the material in Chapter 1.

A calculator is an essential tool to both the first chapter as well as the rest of the book. In order to use the full formulas from Chapter 1, the calculator should have a "power to the *n*" key and at least one memory. For those who have a financial calculator, it is suggested that you work along with the examples to more fully understand what the calculator is doing. Throughout the book the Hewlett Packard model 12C was used as a demonstration calculator for the solving of problems. Other calculators, such as the Texas Instrument or Sharp financial lines, will also perform the basic calculations, although the key strokes for working the problems will differ slightly from those illustrated here. If you have a basic understanding of how your particular calculator works, you should have little difficulty in working through the example and sample problems. Additionally, for those desiring to use the computer programs included, you will need an IBM or IBM-compatible machine (with a DOS operating system) with at least 640k memory and a 5 1/4" or 3 1/2" disc drive.

The material in Chapter 3 deals with various mortgage instruments, beginning with the legal aspects of a mortgage contract. After discussing the different types of mortgages, the specifics of fixed rate and variable rate mortgages are detailed. Next, interest variable mortgage mechanics are explored in detail, followed by a discussion of the different types of variable balance mortgages. Graduated payment mortgages are next discussed, with an explanation of growing equity, shared appreciation, reverse annuity and open ended home equity mortgages completing the chapter.

Chapter 4 deals with various types of seller financing, including buydown, wraparound and other non-traditional mortgages. While brief, this chapter incorporates a number of concepts detailed in the previous chapters. As this is the revised edition of this text, it is felt that a more detailed discussion of the different types of mortgage instruments will aid the reader in the understanding of the mortgage mathematics.

Chapter 5 contains the materials explaining and illustrating the Lotus computer templates that again incorporate the concepts developed in Chapters 1 and 2. Chapter 6 contains the computer tables that were generated using the mortgage mathematics developed in Chapters 1 and 2.

The authors wish to acknowledge with great appreciation the programming assistance of Steve Strickland on the Chapter 6 Tables. In addition, the authors wish to thank Robert Ritchey for assistance with the macros on the computer templates. All errors and omissions are the sole responsibility of the authors.

Paul R. Goebel   Norman G. Miller
Texas Tech University   University of Cincinnati
Lubbock, Texas   Cincinnati, Ohio

CHAPTER 1

FUNDAMENTAL TIME VALUE OF MONEY MATHEMATICS

Introduction

Understanding the time value of money, not just in concept but mathematically as well, is probably the *single most important financial concept and tool* necessary to make sound financial decisions. The key concept is that a dollar is worth more today than a dollar to be received at some time in the future. Whether money is received 100 years from now or one day from now, it is still worth less than if received today. The following are three primary reasons for this concept:

(1) The receipt of money in the future is less certain than if held today. Although receipt of the money in the future might be quite certain, there still exists a chance that the money will *not* be received, and this *risk* should be compensated.

(2) Inflation, if it is expected to occur, even at low rates like three or four percent, means money received in the future will purchase less than today. This lost purchasing power deserves compensation, so that one can expect to at least stay even in terms of real (today's) purchasing power.

(3) Money can be invested. "Opportunity cost" is the return one could expect by investing money in some interest bearing instrument over a given time period at a given risk level. For example, a one-year U.S. Treasury bill might yield 8%, or $80 per year on a $1,000 investment. So even at low or no risk, one who has $1,000 today would want at least $1,080 one year from today to make up for the forgone return.

Money, to most of us, has no utility in itself. However, a certain amount of money may need to be held in cash or in checking or similar accounts just so that it will

1

be available as needs arise. This is called *liquidity* need, which explains why not all of our money must be invested and why some investments are of shorter maturity or duration than others. Beyond the liquidity need, all extra money should be invested to earn a return for one or more of the reasons listed above. The return, or yield, expected and required becomes higher as the perceived risk increases.[1] This required return also becomes higher given expected inflation or uncertainty of inflation, or greater opportunity costs based on available alternative investments, or a longer term of investment because of the greater uncertainty of longer periods in terms of both inflation and opportunity costs.[2] The higher the return expected, then the greater is the future value or the less is the present value of a given dollar. Once the appropriate yield, or rate of return, is known, one can then develop the time value of money formulations.

Time Value of Money Formulations

The time value of money formulations are the mathematical relationships between present value, yield, and future values. The two central relationships involve compounding a present value into future value and discounting a future value back to a present value:

> Present Value -------> compounds to --------> Future Value

or

> Future Value --------> discounts to --------> Present Value

The mathematical relationships for a single sum will next be developed.

A.   Future Value of a Single Sum

The future value [FV] of a single sum investment [PV] compounded at a given yield [i] for each period [n] from the present to the future is:

$$\$FV = (1 + i)^n\ (\$PV) \tag{1-1}$$

The single sum $\$PV$ is invested at the present time ($n=0$), and the investment will generate a return for each and every period until the investment term is over. The interest rate must be appropriate for the given period.

Example 1:

What is the future value of $1 invested at an annual yield of 10% per year for two years?

---

[1]Yield and return will be used interchangeably throughout this text.

[2]This is also known as *interest rate risk* as it relates to the term structure of interest rates.

$$\$FV = (1 + .10)^2 \ (\$1)$$

$$= (1.10)(1.10)(\$1)$$

$$= \$1.21$$

As can be seen, the $1 investment will grow to $1.21 after 2 years, based on a 10% annual rate of interest. Note that the compounding period in Example 1 is *annual*, which means that *10% is paid* at the end of *each year* for both years of the investment period. If the interest rate were to be paid monthly, then monthly compounding would be required and the answer would be different. Let us look at that situation next.

Example 2:

What is the future value of $1 invested at a yield of 10%, *compounded monthly*, for two years?

$$\$FV = (1 + .10/12)^{2 \times 12} \ (\$1)$$

$$= (1 + .008333)^{24} \ (\$1)$$

$$= 1.220391 \ (\$1)$$

$$= \$1.2204$$

Note that to convert the relationship to monthly compounding, the annual rate of return must be divided by 12 and the term n must be converted to the total number of months of the investment period.

The result shows that with monthly compounding the $1 investment grows to $1.22, which is of course greater than the $1.21 earned with annual compounding. The difference in the answers in Examples 1 and 2 may seem insignificant, but when the effects of compounding on larger dollar amounts are carried out for many years, the differences can be substantial. This is shown in Table 1-1 below, where a $10,000 initial investment is compounded at 10% per year, both annually and monthly.

TABLE 1-1 Annual Versus Monthly Compounding Comparison

Investment	Annual Compounding Future Value in Year			Monthly Compounding Future Value in Year		
	10	20	30	10	20	30
$ 10,000	$25,937	$67,275	$174,494	$27,070	$73,281	$198,374

Most mortgages involve monthly compounding. Table 1-1 should make it obvious that "correct" answers cannot even be approximated when the compounding term is simplified, such as using annual compounding when monthly compounding is appropriate.

The relationship between present value and future value based on the compounding of some yield for some period n can be expressed as a future value "factor". A factor indicates the value of the compounding on a per dollar basis and applies to any dollar amount. In other words, if $10,000 grows to $27,070 when compounded at 10% monthly for 10 years, then the relationship of $27,070 divided by $10,000, or 2.7070, will hold true for any dollar amount. This future value factor of 2.7070 will be used in the next example to illustrate this relationship.

Example 3:

How much will $100, $500, and $1,000 each be worth in 10 years when compounded monthly at 10%?

$$\text{Investment x FV Factor} = \$FV$$

$$\$100 \times 2.7070 \quad = \$ \ \ 270.70$$

$$\$500 \times 2.7070 \quad = \$1,353.50$$

$$\$1,000 \times 2.7070 \quad = \$2,707.00$$

Tables of future value factors can be developed which apply to any dollar amount. Prior to the development of inexpensive calculators with financial calculation capabilities, such tables were extremely valuable for solving such problems.

To illustrate the development and use of financial tables, Chapter 6 contains representative factors, with the first set of tables containing Future Value of Single Sum factors assuming monthly compounding. This table covers interest rates from 9.0% to 14.75% over terms of 1 year to 35 years. The factors in this, and every, table in Chapter 6 are derived by applying the appropriate formula, as developed in this chapter. To convert the future value table to present value factors, the inverse of the future value factor can be calculated. Present value factors are developed in the next section of this chapter.

Further Examples Solved with a Financial Calculator

Example C-1:

In this example, which is a repeat of Example 1, the use of a financial calculator will be introduced. The examples are set to work on virtually any financial calculator, such as a Hewlett Packard (HP) or Sharp or Texas Instruments (TI). While the model numbers and features will vary, the input keystrokes are fairly standardized. Throughout this book, the HP 12C will be used as a reference, with all key strokes tied to it. For specific calculator inputs that differ from those presented here, see the instruction manual provided with your calculator.

What is the future value of $1 invested at 10% per year for two years?

(1) Turn the calculator on and clear the calculator. On many calculators you must enter a financial mode, which requires "*2nd FIN*"" keystrokes on the Sharp or TI. Then clear the financial register, "*f FIN*" on the HP 12C, and set your display to the appropriate decimal place, "*f 4*" on the HP 12C for at least four places.

(2) Press "1 *CHS*" to change the sign to -1 on the display, which indicates an investment, or outlay, of $1. Then key "*PV*", which enters $1 as the present value. (On calulators other than an HP, the negative sign usually can be entered by inputting the number, then hitting a +/- key. Throughout the remainder of the text, the - sign will denote a process whereby a negative number should be entered.)

(3) Press "1 0" to display 10, then "*i*" to enter 10% as the interest rate.

(4) Press "2 *n*" to enter 2 compounding periods, corresponding to years in this example.

(5) Press "*FV*", and the display will show "*running*".

(6) The answer on the display should be 1.2100, which means that the $1 invested at 10% will grow to $1.21 over the two year investment period.

Example C-2 (a repeat of Example 2):

What is the future value of $1 invested at 10% compounded monthly for 2 years?

(1) After clearing the calculator, enter " - 1", and then "*PV*", as before.

(2) Press the "1 0 *enter*" keys for 10, and key in "*g i*" to input the monthly interest rate. An alternative would be to key "10 *enter* 12 *divide*" and then input the result as "*i*".

(3) Next press "2 *g n*" to enter the 24 compounding periods, where the HP 12C makes the conversion automatically. Alternatively, key in "2 *enter*", then "1 2 *x*" to derive the 24 monthly compounding periods, and press "*n*".

(4) Now press "*FV*", and the answer displayed should be 1.2204.

Try to repeat the problems in Example 3 using your financial calculator, if you need some more practice. The power of compounding present values into future values creates some pretty astonishing results, as the following examples indicate.

Example 4:

Assume the average price of a new car today is $13,500, and a new house is $92,400. What will the likely price of a new car be in 45 years, if the only expected price change is an average of 6% annual inflation?

$$\$FV = (1 + .06)^{45} \ \$13,500$$

$$= (13.7646) \ \$13,500$$

$$= \$185,822$$

Interpreted literally, a person who is 20 years old today will pay twice the current price of an average new house just to buy a car when he reaches 65 years of age, assuming inflation rates average 6% annually. In fact, if inflation averaged 4.367%, he would pay almost exactly the same price for an average new car in 45 years as the average price of a new house today. The following illustrates the proof:

$$\$FV = (1 + .04367)^{45} \ \$13,500$$

$$= (6.8445) \ \$13,500$$

$$= \$92,401.23$$

Example C-4 (a repeat of Example 4):

(1) Enter " - 13,500 *PV*" as the initial investment.

(2) Enter "6 *i*" as the inflation rate.

(3) Key in "45 *n*" for the time period.

(4) Then hit "*FV* to derive 185,822.

(5) To calculate the second part of the example, first enter "- 13,500 *PV*".

(6) Next enter "45 *n*" and "92,401.23 *FV*".

(7) Finally, hit "*i*". The calculator will then solve for *i* and display 4.367.

Example 5:

What would $25 grow to at 7% per year for 200 years?

$$\$FV = (1.07)^{200} \ \$25$$

$$= (752{,}931.62) \, \$25$$

$$= \$18{,}823{,}290.54$$

This is correct, almost $19 million! This is a dramatic illustration of the time value of money.

Example C-5 (a repeat of Example 5):

(1) Enter " - 25 *PV*" for the initial investment.

(2) Enter "7 *i*" for the interest rate.

(3) Enter "200 *n*" for the investment period.

(4) Finally hit "*FV*" to derive the answer of $18, 823,290.54.

B. Present Value of a Single Sum

In Example 3, it was shown that $100 will grow to $270.70 in 10 years at 10% compounded monthly. This same relationship can be restated in present value terms. The present value of $270.70 when discounted at 10% per year, compounded monthly, is $100. For each dollar received in 10 years the present value relationship or factor is the *inverse* of the future value factor. This is illustrated by reformulating equation (1-1):

$$\$FV \;\; = (1 + i)^n \, (\$PV) \qquad\qquad (1\text{-}1)$$

where $(1 + i)^n$ is the future value factor. Dividing each side by $(1 + i)^n$ results in:

$$\left(\frac{\$FV}{(1 + i)^n} \right) = \$PV \qquad\qquad (1\text{-}2)$$

and dividing each side by $\$FV$ results in:

$$\left(\frac{1}{(1 + i)^n} \right) = \frac{\$PV}{\$FV} \qquad\qquad (1\text{-}3)$$

where $\dfrac{1}{(1 + i)^n}$ is the present value factor. Finally, multiplying each side by $\$FV$ yields the present value, as follows:

$$\$PV = \left(\frac{1}{(1 + i)^n} \right) (\$FV) \qquad\qquad (1\text{-}4)$$

Equation (1-4) is merely a variation of equation (1-2), which more clearly separates out the present value factor, the portion in brackets. The use of this equation will now be demonstrated.

Example 6:

How much is $1,000 to be received in 5 years worth today if discounted at 13.0% per year?

$$\$PV = \left(\frac{1}{(1 + i)^n}\right) (\$FV)$$

$$= \left(\frac{1}{(1 + .13)^5}\right) (\$1,000)$$

$$= .54276 \, (\$1,000)$$

$$= \$542.76$$

Again, one must be concerned with the effects of monthly or annual discounting of a required rate of return. Example 6 can be recalculated using monthly discounting, as shown in Example 7.

Example 7:

How much is $1,000 to be received in 5 years worth today when discounted at an annual rate of 13.0%, with monthly discounting?

$$\$PV = \left(\frac{1}{(1 + .13/12)^{5 \times 12}}\right) (\$1,000)$$

$$= \left(\frac{1}{(1 + .010833)^{60}}\right) (\$1,000)$$

$$= (.523874) \, \$1,000$$

$$= \$523.87$$

Monthly discounting will always result in a lower present value than annual discounting (unless the discount rate is zero) just as monthly compounding will always result in a higher future value than annual compounding. Present value factors with monthly compounding are tabulated in the second set of tables in Chapter 6, from 9.0% to 14.75% from 1-35 years.

To use this table, multiply the given future dollar sum by the present value factor to derive the present value. Notice in the table under 13% and in the row corresponding to the 5th year that the factor is .52387, which is the precalculated equivalent of the factor in Example 7. A further example is provided using the Present Value of a Single Sum tables in Chapter 6.

Example 8 (using tables):

How much is $10,000 to be received in 10 years worth today when discounted at an annual rate of 9.0% with monthly discounting?

$$\$PV = \text{(factor from Table 2, 9\%, 10 years)} \$10,000$$

$$= (.40794) \$10,000$$

$$= \$4,079.40$$

Example C-6 (a repeat of Example 6):

(1) Key in " - 1,000 *FV*" for the future value of the investment.

(2) Key in "5 *n*" for the time period of the investment.

(3) Press "13 *i*" for the interest rate.

(4) Then press "*PV*" and the display will show $542.76.

This solution indicates the present value of $1,000 to be received in 5 years, when a 13.0% annual discount rate is assumed, is $542.76.

Example C-7 (a repeat of Example 7):

(1) Key in " - 1,000 *FV*" to input the future value of the investment.

(2) Press "5 *g n*" to convert the years to equivalent months.

(3) Press "13 *g i*" to convert the 13% annual interest rate to a monthly rate.

(4) Finally, press "*PV*" and the display will show $523.87.

Three points should now be clear. One is that the further away money is to be received in terms of time (or the larger is *n*) the less it is worth today. Another point is that the higher the assumed discount rate (or *i*), the less it is worth today. The third point is that the greater the number of compounding periods used, the less it is worth today.

C. Future Value of an Annuity

An "annuity" by definition is an *equal amount* to be paid or received at the end of each and every period. The future value of an annuity is found through the same type of procedure as for the future value of a single sum. The mathematical expression for calculating future value of annuity factors is:

$$FVAF = \frac{(1 + i)^n - 1}{i}$$ (1-5)

One can remember this relationship by noting that $(1 + i)^n$ is the future value of a single sum factor from which 1 is subtracted, and then the result is divided by i. Note that i is the same on the numerator and denominator side and should be adjusted for the appropriate period, monthly, annual or other. The equation for valuing the future value of an annuity is then:

$$\$FV = \left(\frac{(1 + i)^n - 1}{i}\right) (\$ANN)$$ (1-6)

In this equation, it is assumed that the payment, or annuity, is either deposited or received at the *end* of the period. That is called an *ordinary annuity*. For a payment to be received or made at the *beginning* of the period, termed an *annuity due*, then an adjustment must be made to the formula.[3] Since most calculations in real estate involve ordinary annuities, the annuity due formulation will not be used further.

Example 9:

What is the future value of $50 to be received at the end of each year for 20 years at an annual rate of 12%, with annual compounding?

$$\$FV = \left(\frac{(1 + .12)^{20} - 1}{.12}\right)(\$50)$$

$$= \left(\frac{(9.6463 - 1)}{.12}\right)(\$50)$$

$$= \left(\frac{8.6463}{.12}\right)(\$50)$$

$$= 72.052 \ (\$50)$$

$$= \$3,602.62$$

The Future Value of an Annuity Factor in this example is 72.052. This factor could be used to solve a similar problem of any size annuity ($ANN) if the interest rate and term are the same. Future Value of an Annuity Factors have been tabulated in the

---

[3]The adjustment needed to convert an ordinary annuity to an annuity due is to simply multiply the equation, or factor, by $(1 + i)$, which effectively adds one more compounding period.

third table of Chapter 6, assuming monthly compounding, for 9.0% to 14.75% from 1-35 years. As before, to use this table simply multiply the given annuity by the table factor to solve for the future value of an annuity. The use of the Future Value of an Annuity table is used in the next example.

Example 10 (using tables):

What is the future value of $920 to be received at the end of each month for 20 years at an annual rate of 12.0%, with monthly compounding?

$$\$FV \; = \text{(Future Value of Annuity Factor) (\$}ANN)$$

$$\$FV \; = 989.255 \; (\$920)$$

$$= \$910,114.60$$

Example C-10 (a repeat of Example 10):

(1) Key in " - 920 *PMT*" as the annuity amount.

(2) Press "20 *g n*" for the monthly term over the 20 years.

(3) Press "12 *g i*" for the monthly interest rate.

(4) Finally, press "*FV*" and $910,114.94 will be displayed as the answer.

This answer is $.34 different from the one in Example 10 due to rounding of the factor in Example 10 to three decimal places. If the factor were carried out to more decimal places, the answer would start to converge to the one from the calculator example. In dealing in large numbers or long periods of time, one should carry out calculations to at least four decimal places. This is done automatically by financial calculators regardless of whether the numbers are displayed.

As with the prior sections on present and future values of a single sum, the annuities are very sensitive to earning returns on an annual or monthly basis (or any compounding period). As shown, to convert the years to months, multiply *n* by 12 as before, and to convert *i* to a monthly rate, divide by 12. This is again illustrated in the next example. It should be noted that the formulas in this text can be modified to accomodate any number of compounding periods, except for continuous compounding, by making the adjustments of multiplying the years by the compounding periods and dividing the interest rate by the number of compounding periods.[4]

Example 11:

---

[4]The formula for calculating continuous compounding is $i=e^{rt}$.

What is the future value of $50 to be received at the end of each month for five years at an annual rate of 12.0%, compounded monthly?

$$\$FV \ = \ \left(\frac{(1 + .12/12)^{5 \times 12} - 1}{.12/12}\right) (\$50)$$

$$= \left(\frac{(1 + .01)^{60} - 1}{.01}\right) (\$50)$$

$$= 81.6697 \ (\$50)$$

$$= \$4,083.48$$

Example C-11 (a repeat of Example 11):

(1) After clearing the financial registers, enter " - 50 *PMT*".

(2) Enter "12 *g i*" for the monthly interest rate.

(3) Enter "5 *g n*" for the time period, in this case months.

(4) Press "*FV*" to get the answer of $4,083.48.

D. Present Value of an Annuity

The present value of an annuity is equal to the sum of the present values of a single sum for each period, discounted back to the present from the time received or paid back. As in a future value of an annuity, if an equal amount is to be received each period, then a mathematical expression can be used to simplify the process:

$$PVAF \ = \frac{1 - \dfrac{1}{(1 + i)^n}}{i} \tag{1-7}$$

The annuity factor again contains the present value of a single sum, $\dfrac{1}{(1 + i)^n}$, but the simplification allows the application of the expression to the stream of payments one time, as opposed to using the present value of a single sum on each payment for each period. The equation for calculating the present value of an annuity is:

$$\$PV \ = \left(\frac{1 - \dfrac{1}{(1 + i)^n}}{i}\right) (\$ANN) \tag{1-8}$$

Example 12:

What is the present value of an annuity of $100 each year for 5 years, with annual discounting at 10.0%, with each payment received at the end of each year?

To solve this as an individual stream of payments would require:

$$\text{Total } \$PV \ = \ \left(\frac{1}{(1 + .10)^5}\right) (\$100) \quad \text{(discounted from the end of year 5)}$$

$$+ \left(\frac{1}{(1 + .10)^4}\right) (\$100) \quad \text{(discounted from the end of year 4)}$$

$$+ \left(\frac{1}{(1 + .10)^3}\right) (\$100) \quad \text{(discounted from the end of year 3)}$$

$$+ \left(\frac{1}{(1 + .10)^2}\right) (\$100) \quad \text{(discounted from the end of year 2)}$$

$$+ \left(\frac{1}{(1 + .10)^1}\right) (\$100) \quad \text{(discounted from the end of year 1)}$$

$$= 3.790787 \, (\$100)$$

$$= \$379.08$$

Discounting the individual payments back to the present in this manner is obviously tedious, especially if a large number of compounding periods are present. In solving this problem using the mathematical expression for the present value of an annuity, the procedure becomes much less complicated:

$$\$PV \ = \ \left(\frac{1 - \dfrac{1}{(1 + .10)^5}}{.10}\right)(\$100)$$

$$= \left(\frac{(1 - .62092132)}{.10}\right) (\$100)$$

$$= \left(\frac{.37907868}{.10}\right) (\$100)$$

$$= 3.79079 \, (\$100)$$

$$= \$379.08$$

Obviously, the processes yield the same result, but just as obvious is the fact that by using the present value of an annuity expression, considerable time can be saved.

Example 13:

What is the present value of an annuity of $750, received at the end of each month for 30 years, at a discount of 12.5% with monthly compounding?

$$\$PV = \left(\frac{1 - \dfrac{1}{(1 + .125/12)^{30 \times 12}}}{.125/12} \right) (\$750)$$

$$= \left(\frac{1 - \dfrac{1}{(1.01041667)^{360}}}{.01041667} \right) (\$750)$$

$$= (93.69808)(\$750)$$

$$= \$70,273.55$$

Example C-13 (a repeat of Example 13):

(1) After clearing the financial registers, enter " - 750 *PMT*".

(2) Enter "30 *g n*" for the the compounding periods, in this case 360 months.

(3) Enter "12.5 *g i*" for the monthly compounding rate of interest.

(4) Then press "*PV*" to get the answer, which again should be $70,273.56.

As before, the difference between the two answers is due to rounding, where, if the example using the formula carried the decimal places out further, the answers between the two examples would be the same.

The fourth table in Chapter 6 contains present value of annuity factors, with monthly compounding, for 9.0% to 14.75% and 1-35 years. The use of this table is illustrated next.

Example 14:

What is the present value of an annuity of $920, received at the end of each month for 30 years at a yield of 12.0%, with monthly compounding?

$$\$PV = (\text{Table Factor})(\$ANN)$$

$$= (97.2183)(\$920)$$

$$= \$89,440.84$$

E.   Solving for the Present Value of Unequal Flows

When unequal cash flows are involved, or if lump sums are received in addition to an annuity, the format for performing present value calculations requires combining present value of a single sum and present value of annuity equations. The calculation process is cumulative, summing present dollar values from various sources received in the future to the same point in time at the present.

Example 15:

What is the present value of a bond which pays a coupon rate of $90 paid once per year at the end of the year, and then $1,000 at maturity in exactly 10 years to an investor who requires a 13.0% annual yield?

The solution involves summing together the present value of the annuity, which is the $90 each year over 10 years, with the present value of a single sum, represented by the $1,000 to be received in 10 years. The general solution format is indicated below:

$$\$PV = (\$PV \text{ of Annuity of } \$90 \text{ for } n = 10, i = .13) + (\$PV \text{ of Single Sum of } \$1,000 \text{ for } n = 10, i = .13)$$

$$= \left(\frac{1 - \frac{1}{(1 + .13)^{10}}}{.13} \right) (\$90) + \left(\frac{1}{(1 + .13)^{10}} \right) (\$1,000)$$

$$= (5.4262435)\,(\$90) + (.29458835)\,(\$1,000)$$

$$= \$488.36 + \$294.59$$

$$= \$782.95$$

Example 16:

What is the present value of $1,000 per year, received at the end of the 6th, 7th, 8th, 9th and 10th years of an investment when an annual yield of 10.0% is required?

There are two ways this problem could be solved. One method is to use the present value of a single sum factor for years 6 through 10, discounted back to the present at the 10%. This involves several calculations. Another method would be to use the present value of an annuity for five years at 10%, and then take the present value of that sum as a single sum from the end of year 5 back to the present. These methods are demonstrated in turn.

Method 1:

$$\$PV \; = \; \left(\frac{1}{(1 + .10)^6}\right) (\$1,000) \qquad \text{from year 6}$$

$$+ \; \left(\frac{1}{(1 + .10)^7}\right) (\$1,000) \qquad \text{from year 7}$$

$$+ \; \left(\frac{1}{(1 + .10)^8}\right) (\$1,000) \qquad \text{from year 8}$$

$$+ \; \left(\frac{1}{(1 + .10)^9}\right) (\$1,000) \qquad \text{from year 9}$$

$$+ \; \left(\frac{1}{(1 + .10)^{10}}\right) (\$1,000) \qquad \text{from year 10}$$

$$= \$2,353.78$$

In this method the factor that is applied in each year is the present value of a single sum, where each $1,000 payment is thus discounted back to the present to find the total value.

Method 2:

$$\$PV \; = \; \left(\frac{1}{(1 + .10)^5}\right) \left(\frac{1 - \dfrac{1}{(1 + .10)^5}}{.10}\right) (\$1,000)$$

$$= (.62092)\,(3.79079)\,(\$1,000)$$

$$= \$2,353.78$$

In method 2, the present value of an annuity factor for 5 years (years 6-10) is first applied to the $1,000 series of payments, and then the product is further discounted back to the present using the present value of a single sum. One can see that method 2 is easier to use than method 1, and is possible as long as annuities are involved.

Example C-16 (a repeat of Example 16):

    (1) Clear all financial registers, then enter " - 1,000 *PMT*" for the annuity.

    (2) Enter "10 *i*" for the percent interest.

    (3) Enter "5 *n*" for the compounding period.

    (4) Press "*PV*" to derive $3,790.79, which is the value of the annuity stream.

(5) Next press "*ENTER*", then "*f FIN*" to again clear the financial registers.

(6) Now press "*FV*", which will enter the previously saved $3,790.79 as the future value of a single sum.

(7) Then enter "10 *i*" for the discount rate.

(8) The year in which the annuity will be received is entered as "5 *n*".

(9) And finally, press "*PV*" to get the discounted value of - $2,353.78.

Example 17:

What is the present value of $1,000 to be received at the end of year 2, $1,500 to be received at the end of year 3, and $2,500 to be received at the end of year 5, with a required annual rate of return of 15%?

$$\$PV = \left(\frac{1}{(1+.15)^2}\right) \$1,000 + \left(\frac{1}{(1+.15)^3}\right) \$1,500 + \left(\frac{1}{(1+.15)^5}\right) \$2,500$$

$$= \$756.14 + \$986.27 + \$1,242.94$$

$$= \$2,985.35$$

Example C-17 (a repeat of Example 17):

The easiest way to solve this with a calculator is to use the memories to hold two of the above answers and then sum all three together. One approach would be as follows:

(1) Clear all registers, and key in " - 1,000 *FV*" for the first payment.

(2) Enter "15 *i*" for the discount rate.

(3) Enter "2 *n*" for the compounding period.

(4) Press "*PV*" to get $756.14, then hit "*STO* 1" to put the number in memory.

(5) Enter " - 1,500 *FV*" for the second payment.

(6) Enter "3 *n*" for the period (the interest rate does not change).

(7) Enter "*PV*" to get $986.27, which is put in memory with "*STO* 2".

(8) The last payment is input with " - 2,500 *FV*".

(9) Enter "5 *n*" for the compounding period (the interest rate does not change).

(10) Press "*PV*" to get $1,242.94.

(11) The final answer is derived by pressing "*ENTER*" to set the $1,242.94, then "*RCL* 2 +" to add the second payment, then "*RCL* 1 +" to add the first payment. The final answer of $2,985.35 will then be displayed.

F.   Solving for the Future Value of Unequal Sums or Yields

The process of solving for the future value of unequal sums is essentially the same as for present value calculations except that one must compound rather than discount. Some examples will demonstrate the method.

Example 18:

What is the future value of $500 to be received at the end of each year at 8.0% for 10 years, and to be reinvested as a lump sum at that time for 10 more years at 10.0%?

$$\$FV \ = \left(\frac{(1 + .08)^{10} - 1}{.08}\right)(\$500)\,(1 + .10)^{10}$$

$$= \$7,243.28\,(1.10)^{10}$$

$$= \$18,787.21$$

Example 19:

What is the future value of $5,000 yielding *monthly* returns with annual stated rates of 10.0% the first year, 12.0% the second year and 14.0% the third year, at the end of the three years?

$$\$FV \ = (\$5,000)(1 + .10/12)^{12}\,(1 + .12/12)^{12}\,(1 + .14/12)^{12}$$

$$= (\$5,000)\,(1.10471)\,(1.12683)\,(1.14934)$$

$$= \$7,153.61$$

Example C-19 (a repeat of Example 19):

(1) Clear all registers, then enter " - 5,000 *PV*" for the initial investment.

(2) Press "10 *g i*" for the initial monthly interest rate.

3) Press "1 *g n*" to enter the first 12 month compounding period.

(4) Press "*FV*", which will provide the value at the end of year 1 of $5,523.57.

(5) Next press "*ENTER PV*" to reenter the year 1 value as the next *PV*.

(6) Press "12 *g i*" to change the interest rate to 12% for year 2.

(7) Press "*FV*", which will provide the value of - $6,224.09 at the end of year 2.

(8) Next press "*ENTER PV*" to reenter the final *PV*.

(9) Press "14 *g i*" to set the third year interest rate.

(10) Finally, press "*FV*" to derive the final answer of $7,153.61.

G.   Solving for Yields or Rates of Return

Any time the present value *and* future values are known over a definite time period, the yield or return may be derived. Stated another way, any time present and future values are known, expected yields may be calculated. The procedure is mathematically direct in the case of single sums or annuities, but when unequal sums or annuities are combined the solution procedure is iterative, involving trial and error.

(1) Single Sum Yields

Recall that:

$$\$FV = (1 + i)^{n} \$PV \qquad \text{from equation (1-1), and}$$

$$\$PV = \frac{1}{(1 + i)^{n}} \$FV \qquad \text{from equation (1-4).}$$

Therefore, equation (1-1) may be rearranged as follows:

$$\frac{\$FV}{\$PV} = (1 + i)^{n} \qquad \text{and taking the } n\text{th root of each side results in}$$

$$\sqrt[n]{\frac{\$FV}{PV}} = (1 + i) \qquad \text{and subtracting 1 from each side results in}$$

$$\sqrt[n]{\frac{\$FV}{\$PV}} - 1 = i \qquad \text{which leaves } i \text{ by itself, and is the yield sought.}$$

The use of this equation will be demonstrated next.

Example 20:

$1,000 will accumulate to $10,000 over 20 years at what rate of return per year, assuming annual compounding?

$$\sqrt[20]{\frac{\$10,000}{\$1,000}} - 1 = i$$

$$\sqrt[20]{10} - 1 = i$$

$$1.12202 - 1 = i$$

$$.12202 = i$$

$$\text{or} \quad 12.202\% = i$$

Testing the result:

$$(\text{Future Value of Annuity Factor}) (\$PV) \quad = \$FV$$

$$(1 + .12202)^{20} (\$1,000) = \$FV$$

$$= \$10,000.28$$

The slight difference in the answers is due to rounding.

(2)   Annuity Yields

Recall that for known future values and annuities:

$$\$FV = \left(\frac{(1 + i)^n - 1}{i}\right)(\$ANN) \qquad \text{from equation (1-5).}$$

Rearranging equation (1-5) results in:

$$\frac{\$FV}{\$ANN} = \frac{(1 + i)^n - 1}{i} \tag{1-5a}$$

Unfortunately i cannot be separated out from the right hand side in Equation (1-5a). When $\$FV$, n, and $\$ANN$ are known values, a trial-and-error method is required to solve for i. This is shown next.

Example 21:

The future value of an annuity of $100 per month is $33,653.66 after 10 years. What is the annual rate of return? (Note that monthly compounding is assumed, so the monthly i will first be solved and multiplied by 12 to derive the annual rate of return.)

(1) Set up the relationship for a future value of annuity factor, where the factor necessary is calculated as:

$$\frac{\$33,653.66}{\$100} = 336.5366$$

(2) Next, solve for i:

$$336.5366 = \left(\frac{(1 + i)^{120} - 1}{i}\right)$$

(Note n must be the number of months in 10 years.)

(3) To solve the problem, select an arbitrary interest rate, say 10%, and calculate the future value of an annuity:

$$= \frac{(1 + .10/12)^{120} - 1}{.10/12}$$

$$= 204.84$$

(4) Since 204.84 is far below the desired 336.5366, we need to try a higher interest rate to yield a higher future value of an annuity factor. Try 20% next:

$$= \frac{(1 + .20/12)^{120} - 1}{(.20/12)}$$

$$= 376.0953$$

(5) Since 376.0953 is too high, we must now use a lower yield. We could continue the trial and error procedure choosing say 19%, where we would find a future value of an annuity factor of 352.8703, which is closer but still too high. At 18%, we get an annuity factor of 331.2882, which again is closer but is too low, indicating the answer must be between 18 and 19%. Trying 18.25% gives us:

$$= \frac{(1 + .1825/12)^{120} - 1}{(.1825/12)}$$

$$= \frac{6.11816047 - 1}{.01520833}$$

$$= 336.53658$$

which is exactly the result desired. Therefore, the true yield is 18.25%.

Example C-21 (a repeat of Example 21):

(1) Clear all registers, then enter "- 100 *PMT*" for the monthly annuity.

(2) Enter "33,653.66 *FV*" for the required present value of the annuity stream.

(3) Enter "10 *g n*" to enter the 120 compounding periods.

(4) Press "*i*" to solve for the monthly yield rate. Finally, press "*ENTER* 12 *x*" to convert the answer to an annual yield, which will be 18.25%. Note that the running time took longer in this example because of the iterative trial and error procedure used internally by the calculator.

Another method of solving Example 21 would be with the use of the financial tables in Chapter 6. Looking in the Future Value of an Annuity table under the 10 year row, scan across the interest rate columns until 336.5366 is found. After finding this number, or the closest number to it, see what the corresponding annual rate is. In this example, 18.25% is right on the money. For such problems, tables provide a reasonably quick alternative, although in cases when the interest rate is not exact, interpolation will be necessary to get an exact solution. When that is the case, then a financial calculator will be more accurate and quicker.

Present value of an annuity yields are solved in the same manner based on the following relationship:

$$\$PV = \left(\frac{1 - \frac{1}{(1 + i)^n}}{i} \right) (\$ANN) \qquad \text{from equation (1-6)}.$$

Rearranging equation (1-6) results in:

$$\frac{\$PV}{\$ANN} = \frac{1 - \frac{1}{(1 + i)^n}}{1} \qquad\qquad (1\text{-}6a)$$

As in the situation involving the future value of an annuity, when $\$PV$, n and the $\$ANN$ are known, then i can be solved using the trial-and-error process with equations, a financial calculator, or tables.

Example 22:

The present value of an annuity of $500 to be received at the end of each month for 30 years is $50,490.18. What is the annual rate of interest being earned, assuming monthly compounding?

(1) Set up the relationship for a present value of annuity factor, where the necessary factor is calculated as:

$$\frac{\$50{,}490.18}{\$500} = 100.98036$$

(2) Next, solve for i:

$$100.98036 = \left(\frac{1 - \dfrac{1}{(1 + i)^{360}}}{i} \right)$$

(3) To solve the problem, select an initial interest rate, say 10%:

$$100.98036 = \left(\frac{1 - \dfrac{1}{(1 + .10/12)^{360}}}{.10/12} \right)$$

$$= 113.95082$$

(4) The result of 113.95082 is obviously too high, so a higher discount rate must be used to lower the present value. If we were to try 12% the result would be 97.21833, which is of course too low. Trying 11% results in a factor of 105.00635, indicating the exact yield is between 11 and 12%. Using a rate of 11.5% provides an annuity factor of 100.98037, which is the desired answer, meaning the yield earned on this investment is 11.5%

Example C-22 (a repeat of Example 22):

(1) After clearing all registers, enter "- 500 *PMT*" for the annuity amount.

(2) Enter "30 *g n*" for the 360 compounding periods.

(3) Enter "50,490.18 *PV*" for the required present value amount.

(4) Finally, press "*i*" to solve for the monthly interest rate. Then press "*ENTER* 12 *x*" to convert this rate to an annual yield, which should be 11.5%.

Tables may again be used to find a given present value factor (or one closest to the desired factor), which will result in an approximate yield solution. In Example 22, a present value of annuity factor of 100.98036 is desired. The interest rate is not known, but the term is. In the Present Value of an Annuity Table from Chapter 6, scan across the 30 year row until 100.98037 is found. This occurs at the column corresponding to 11.5%. In this manner tables might save time in searching for approximate answers.

(3)   Effective Yields or The Internal Rate of Return

An effective yield is the actual yield when all expected sources of returns and costs are considered. The **Internal Rate of Return** (IRR) is "that yield or rate of return at which the present value of all future returns will be exactly equal to the initial investment." The IRR is solved through a trial-and-error method by using the following equation.

$$\$PV = \frac{\$Returns_1}{(1 + IRR)^1} + \frac{\$Returns_2}{(1 + IRR)^2} + \cdots + \frac{\$Returns_n}{(1 + IRR)^n} \qquad (1\text{-}8)$$

With this generalized relationship, the $Returns need not be annuities or equal values, but the *same* IRR value must be used for discounting future returns.

Example 23:

For an initial investment of $1,000, an investor will receive $300 at the end of year 1, $400 at the end of year 2, and $500 at the end of year 3. What is the annual IRR (or effective yield)?

(1) Set up the relationship:

$$\$1,000 = \frac{\$300}{(1 + IRR)^1} + \frac{\$400}{(1 + IRR)^2} + \frac{\$500}{(1 + IRR)^3}$$

(2) Try an arbitrary guess, such as 10%:

$$= \frac{\$300}{(1 + .10)^1} + \frac{\$400}{(1 + .10)^2} + \frac{\$500}{(1 + .10)^3}$$

$$= \$272.73 + \$330.58 + \$375.66$$

$$= \$978.97$$

(3) The result of $978.97 is very close, but is still below the desired result. A lower IRR will produce a higher present value, so try 9.25%:

$$= \frac{\$300}{(1 + .0925)^1} + \frac{\$400}{(1 + .0925)^2} + \frac{\$500}{(1 + .0925)^3}$$

$$= \$274.60 + \$335.13 + \$383.45$$

= $993.18

(4) This result is still too low, so try 8.8%:

$$= \frac{\$300}{(1 + .088)^1} + \frac{\$400}{(1 + .088)^2} + \frac{\$500}{(1 + .088)^3}$$

$$= \$275.74 + \$337.91 + \$388.22$$

$$= \$1,001.87$$

(5) This answer is very close to the initial investment, indicating that the IRR is just over 8.8%, approximately 8.89%. The issue of accuracy required is an investment decision issue, although for most investment decisions, the above result would suffice.

Unfortunately, the trial-and-error process of solving for an IRR is a tedious one if performed manually. Many calculators, such as the HP 12-C (and most programmed computers), can solve for the IRR with an internally automatic search routine. Thus, the calculators available today ease the burden of repetitious trials for IRR solutions.

Example C-23 (a repeat of Example 23):

(1) Clear all financial registers, then enter "-1,000 *g CF_o*", which enters the initial investment.

(1) Clear all financial registers, then enter "-1,000 $g\ CF_o$", which enters the initial investment.

(2) Enter "300 $g\ CF_j$" to enter the first year return.

(3) Next enter "400 $g\ CF_j$" to input the second year return.

(4) To enter the third year return press "500 $g\ CF_j$".

(5) Key "*f IRR*" to solve for the IRR. The display will show 8.89633947, which will round to 8.9%.

Example 24:

What is the IRR for a 30 year mortgage of $100,000 with monthly payments of $952.32 based on an 11.0% contract rate, when the loan must be prepaid in full at the end of 12 years and the lender charges $13,100 in prepaid interest charges at the time the loan is issued? (Hint: The mortgage balance remaining at the end of the 12th year is $89,415.87.)

(1) To solve this problem, first set up the problem parameters. The PV is $100,000, less the $13,100 which the lender is charging at the time of loan

origination, so the actual net investment is $86,900. For 12 years, there is a monthly annuity of $952.32, and then at the end of the 12th year the entire balance is paid off. The mortgage balance at the end of the 12th year is $89,415.87, which is a single sum.

(2) Using both a present value of an annuity factor and the present value of a single sum, with both yields replaced by the IRR, results in:

$$\$86,900 = \left(\frac{1 - \dfrac{1}{(1 + IRR)^{144}}}{IRR}\right)(952.32) + \frac{\$89,415.87}{(1 + IRR)^{144}}$$

Note that the IRR above is monthly and must be multiplied by 12 to derive the annual rate of return. Note also that the mortgage balance is multiplied by the present value of a single sum factor $\dfrac{1}{(1 + IRR)^{144}}$, which is the same as dividing by just $(1 + IRR)^{144}$.

(3) Through trial and error, a monthly IRR of 1.1041667% is derived, which multiplied by 12 is 13.25%. Testing this result provides:

$$\$86,900 = \left(\frac{1 - \dfrac{1}{(1.011041667)^{144}}}{.011041667}\right)(\$952.32) + \left(\frac{\$89,415.87}{(1.011041667)^{144}}\right)$$

$$= 71.935661 \, (\$952.32) + \frac{\$89,415.87}{4.861203}$$

$$= \$68,505.77 + \$18,393.77$$

$$= \$86,899.54$$

(4) Taking into consideration rounding errors, this answer is essentially equal to the $86,900 net investment, thus confirming that the IRR in this example is 13.25%.

Unfortunately, most financial calculators do not allow for enough separate monthly inputs to solve many mortgage type effective yield calculations. This is where tables developed via computers are most valuable. For such problems, Table 8 in Chapter 6 would help one get into the range of the IRR immediately. The use of these tables will be developed in Chapter 2.

Mortgage Related Financial Terminology

Once the time value of money concepts as discussed in the first part of this chapter are understood, then one may solve any type of financial calculation typically required by a lender. Some definitions are useful as a starting point.

Contract Rate: The interest rate quoted which is used to determine the actual mortgage payments based on the full initial mortgage value.

Mortgage Payment: Mortgage payments generally include both interest (a return on investment) and principal (a return of investment). An **interest only** loan would include no principal repayment. The mortgage payment is calculated from the contract rate, term of the loan and mortgage balance.

Mortgage Constant: The proportion of each dollar of the original mortgage loan which must be paid each period over the life of the loan to pay off all interest required while completely repaying the principal balance by the end of the mortgage term. Mortgage constants are precalculated in Table 5 of Chapter 6. A monthly mortgage constant of .01050 would require a monthly payment of $1.05 for each $100 borrowed over the entire term of the loan. Thus, mortgage constants are multiplied by the initial full loan amount to derive the monthly payment.

Loan-to-Value Ratio: The ratio of the mortgage loan (in dollars) over the lesser of the purchase price or the appraised value of the property. Typical loan-to-value ratios are 75, 80, 90, and sometimes 95 percent. The higher the loan-to-value ratio, the riskier the loan is from the lender's perspective. Furthermore, lenders are restricted by regulation as to the percentage of assets they can put into the high loan-to-value mortgages.

Points: One "point", also referred to as a **discount point**, is one percent of the original mortgage loan (not the purchase price). So for a $50,000 loan, one point would be $500. Points are used to change the effective yield on mortgage loans. They are paid in addition to the typical closing costs, such as credit check, appraisal, title search, and so forth. Points and closing costs are paid at the time the mortgage loan is actually originated and closed.

Effective Yield: An effective yield is the actual yield to the lender including the effects of points or prepaid interest, mortgage payments and any balances or other returns due in the future. It is the yield the lender actually expects to receive. The effective yield equals the contract rate when there are no points or other charges, but if there are any points involved the effective yield will exceed the contract rate. Early prepayment of a mortgage involving point charges will increase the effective yield. The earlier the prepayment, the greater the impact of points on the effective yield. Prepayment penalties, as defined below, may also increase the effective yield. The effective yield is the same as the IRR on a mortgage loan, as defined earlier in this chapter.

Annual Percentage Rate: The annual percentage rate (APR) is an effective yield calculated with the effects of points but without any prepayment assumption. Full term is assumed for the life of the mortgage. The APR must be disclosed to the borrower on a truth in lending statement under Regulation Z and the Truth in Lending Act.

Refinance Risk: The risk to a lender that borrowers will pay off mortgages earlier than expected with the possibility of forcing reinvestment at lower yields. The longer the fixed-interest-rate-period before mortgage interest rates are adjusted, the greater is this risk if market rates are declining, offset somewhat by prepayment penalties. Fixed interest rate mortgages have the greatest refinance risk, with five year adjustable rate mortgages bearing slightly less risk, and one year adjustables the least refinance risk.

Prepayment Penalty: A financial penalty for early repayment of the principal portion of a mortgage loan. Generally this penalty is a percentage of the mortgage balance. Partial repayment is usually allowed without penalty, and in the case of a residential single family property, penalties may automatically be waived upon sale. Prepayment penalties reduce the refinance risk to a lender, which result in a sudden surge in mortgage payoffs, when market interest rates drop.

Call Year: A loan which is callable is one where a remaining mortgage balance is due in the call year. Such a mortgage is also referred to as a **balloon mortgage** or note.

Amortization Term: The term used to calculate mortgage payments. The maximum term over which repayment would be made if there were no call year.

Interest Rate Index: All variable rate mortgages contain an "index" by which the contract rate, and subsequent interest rates, are adjusted. The interest rate adjustment may be a relative adjustment, up or down in the same proportion as the index, or an absolute-plus-percentage adjustment. In the latter case, the adjustment of the contract rate is in equal absolute size as the index, up or down, with a predetermined spread above the index, such as 1.5 to 2.5% (150 to 250 basis points). Typical indexes include U.S. Treasury bills and notes, but just about any publicly known and market based index may be used. Shorter term indexes (i.e., 1 year T-bills) tend to be more volatile than long term based indexes.

Wraparound Mortgage: A second mortgage which is set up so as to include servicing of the mortgage payments for the first mortgage in the note. This arrangement helps to protect the second mortgage holder from an unexpected foreclosure.

Specific Mortgage Types: For other specific mortgage types and amortization alternatives, see Chapter 3.

Time Value of Money Problems and Solutions

Problems Using Formulas

1. What is the present value of $10,000 to be received 5 years from now if one expects an 8.0% annual yield?

2. Repeat problem 1 above using monthly compounding.

3. You lend someone $1,000 today in return for a promise to be repaid $1,311 exactly four years from now. What annual rate of return are you expecting?

4. How many years would it take for $1,000 to grow to $10,804 at 12.0% per year?

5. Someone offers to buy your car for $7,000 or to rent the car for $1,000 per year for 5 years, and then buy it for $5,000. If you assume 10.0% to be the appropriate return on the "loan", which is the better offer?

6. You borrow $2,000 today to be paid off annually over 4 years at 10%. What are the annual payments?

7. Repeat problem 6 above with a monthly payment and monthly discounting. Are the total of each year's monthly payments more or less than the annual payments?

8. How much can someone accumulate in the future if he deposits $100 every month into an investment account which yields 12.0%, compounded monthly, for 25 years?

Solutions to Problems Using Formulas

1. $$\$PV = \left(\frac{1}{(1 + .08)^5}\right) \$10,000$$

    $$= (.680583) \$10,000$$

    $$= \$6,805.83$$

2. $$\$PV = \left(\frac{1}{(1 + .08/12)^{5 \times 12}}\right) \$10,000$$

    $$= (.671210) \$10,000$$

$$= \$6,712.10$$

With Tables: Look in Table 2 for the present value of a single sum factor, with monthly compounding, under the 8.0% column in the 5 year row. The factor is .67121, which when multiplied by the future value of $10,000 produces the same answer as above.

3.   One approach to solving this problem is to set up the following known relationships:

Present Value = Future Value (Present Value of Single Sum Factor)

$$\$1,000 \ = \$1,311 \left(\frac{1}{(1 + ?\%)^4} \right)$$

Then dividing both sides of the equation by $1,311 results in:

$$\frac{\$1,000}{\$1,311} = \frac{1}{(1 + ?\%)^4}$$

$$.76277651 = \frac{1}{(1 + ?\%)^4}$$

We can then take the inverse of both sides, which creates the future value of a single sum factor:

$$\frac{1}{.76277651} = (1 + ?\%)^4$$

$$1.311 = (1 + ?\%)^4$$

And taking the 4th root of both sides:

$$\sqrt[4]{1.311} = (1 + ?\%) \qquad \text{which results in:}$$

$$1.0700 = (1 + ?\%)$$

$$1.07 - 1 = ?\%$$

$$.07 = ?\% \qquad \text{or 7\% annual rate of return.}$$

4.   Set up the relationship which is known using either the future value or present value factor. In this case the future value factor is used.

$$\$1,000 \ (1 + .12)^n = \$10,804$$

$$(1 + .12)^n = \frac{\$10,804}{\$1,000}$$

$$(1.12)^n = 10.804$$

At $n = 21$ the above holds true, thus the answer is 21 years.

5. You have a choice between $7,000 now or an annuity of $1,000 per year plus a single sum of $5,000 in 5 years. Discounting this second alternative at 10.0% results in:

$$\$PV = \$1,000 \ (\text{Present Value of Annuity Factor}) + \$5,000 \ (\text{Present Value of Single Sum Factor})$$

$$\$PV = \$1,000 \left(\frac{1 - \dfrac{1}{(1 + .10)^5}}{.10} \right) + \$5,000 \left(\frac{1}{(1 + .10)^5} \right)$$

$$= \$1,000 \ (3.7908) + \$5,000 \ (.62092)$$

$$= \$6,895.39$$

Take the $7,000 cash, since it is greater than the annuity plus the lump sum.

6. Set up the relationship using the present value of an annuity factor:

$$\$2,000 = \left(\frac{1 - \dfrac{1}{(1 + .10)^4}}{.10} \right) \$ANN$$

$$\$2,000 = (3.1698654) \ \$ANN$$

$$\frac{\$2,000}{3.1698654} = \$630.94 \qquad \text{which is the annual payment.}$$

7. The same procedure applies as in problem 6, except that the 10% must be divided by 12 to derive a monthly rate and the 4 years must be converted to 48 months. Then:

$$\$2,000 = \left(\frac{1 - \dfrac{1}{(1 + .10/12)^{4 \times 12}}}{.10/12} \right) \$ANN$$

$$\$2{,}000 \ = (39.42816) \ \$ANN$$

$$\frac{\$2{,}000}{39.42816} = \$50.73 \qquad \text{which is the monthly payment.}$$

Note that (12 x $50.73) = $608.70 which is less than the annual payment derived in problem 6. This is because even during the first year, the principal begins to be paid down, requiring less total interest.

8.   Setting up the future value of an annuity factor:

$$\$FV \ = \left(\frac{(1 + .12/12)^{25 \times 12} - 1}{.12/12}\right) \$100$$

$$= (1{,}878.8466) \ \$100$$

$$= \$187{,}884.66$$

Problems Using the Calculator

1.   What is the present value of $15,000 to be received in exactly 10 years with an annual rate of return of 12%?

2.   Repeat problem 1 with monthly compounding, and then with daily compounding.

3.   What will a single deposit of $29,000 accumulate to if invested for 7 years at 18% with monthly compounding?

4.   What is the present value of $250 per month, received at the end of each month for 4 years to a lender who expects a 14% yield with monthly compounding?

5.   What is the annual yield on an investment which pays $1,000 at the end of each month for 10 years and originally required a $100,000 investment?

Solutions to Problems Using the Calculator

1.   (1) After clearing registers, enter "15,000 *FV*" for the future value.

      (2) Enter "10 *n*" for the 10 year period.

      (3) Enter "12 *i*" for the interest rate.

      (4) Press "*PV*" to derive -4,829.60 for a present value of $4,829.60.

2.   (1) After clearing registers, enter "15,000 *FV*" for the future value.

(2) Enter "10 *g n*" for the monthly 10 year period.

(3) Enter "12 *g i*" for the 12% interest rate, compounded monthly.

(4) Press "*PV*" to derive the present value of $4,544.92.

For daily compounding, the procedure is exactly the same:

(5) Clear the registers, then enter "15,000 *FV*".

(6) Key in "10 *ENTER* 365 *x n*" to put in the total days over 10 years.

(7) Key in "12 *ENTER* 365 ÷" for the daily interest rate.

(8) Press "*PV*" to derive $4,518.80 as the present value.

Note the difference between the answers to problems 1 and 2 based on the compounding assumptions. The greater the number of compounding periods, the less is the present value needed to achieve the same future value.

3.   (1) Clear the registers, then enter "- 29,000 *PV*" for the initial deposit.

       (2) Enter "7 *g n*" for the 7 year investment period.

       (3) Key in "18 *g i*" for the 18% monthly compounding.

       (4) Finally, press "*FV*" to derive the answer of $101,285.10.

4.   (1) Clear the registers, then enter "- 250 *PMT*" for the monthly annuity.

       (2) Enter "14 *g i*" for the monthly interest rate.

       (3) Enter "4 *g n*" for the monthly investment period.

       (4) Finally, press "*PV*" to derive the present value of $9,148.64.

5.   (1) After clearing the registers, enter "1,000 *PMT*" for the monthly investment.

       (2) Enter "- 100,000 *PV*" for the initial investment.

       (3) Enter "10 *g n*" for the investment period.

       (4) Then press "*i*" to get the monthly rate of .31142.

       (5) Finally, press "*ENTER* 12 *x*" to put it on an annual basis of 3.737%.

The reason the return is so low is because the payments must include a return of principal, which is $100,000. Over 10 years $120,000 is the total being paid, spread out over 10 years, which is only $20,000 above the principal.

CHAPTER 2

MORTGAGE MATHEMATICS

Introduction

A mortgage is an investment, and like any other investment it must provide a sufficient expected return for the given risk level in order to attract capital. The sources of return for a mortgage investment include the mortgage payments allocated to principal and interest over the expected life, the remaining mortgage balance at the end of the expected term if a balloon mortgage is used, any prepaid interest or points charged at the time the loan is made and any prepayment penalties which might be due. All of these factors must be included in calculating the expected effective yield on a mortgage. From the borrower's perspective, all of these factors must be considered in order to estimate the effective cost of the loan. The calculations required for the above relationships follow.

Mortgage Mathematics Formulations

A. Mortgage Payments

A mortgage is analogous to the present value of an annuity, where the annuity is the mortgage payments. Recall equation (1-8) where:

$$\$PV = \left(\frac{1 - \frac{1}{(1 + i)^n}}{i} \right) (\$ANN) \qquad (1\text{-}8)$$

Substituting the mortgage for $\$PV$ and the mortgage payments for the $\$ANN$ results in:

$$\$\text{Mortgage} = \left(\frac{1 - \frac{1}{(1 + i)^n}}{i} \right) (\$\text{Mortgage Payments}) \qquad (2\text{-}1)$$

If the required yield i, the term n and the mortgage payments are known, then the value of the mortgage can be calculated. Most often, however, the mortgage loan, term and required yield are known and the mortgage payment is the unknown. Separating out the mortgage payments results in:

$$\left(\frac{(\$\text{Mortgage})}{\dfrac{1 - \dfrac{1}{(1 + i)^n}}{i}} \right) = \$\text{Mortgage Payments} \qquad\qquad \text{or}$$

$$(\$\text{Mortgage}) \left(\frac{1}{\dfrac{1 - \dfrac{1}{(1 + i)^n}}{i}} \right) = \$\text{Mortgage Payments}$$

Notice that the second component on the left side is the inverse of a present value of an annuity factor. It is also known as the **mortgage constant** and will be denoted by MC. Thus, the equation for calculating a mortgage payment, which as defined earlier in Chapter 1 includes both interest and principal repayment, becomes:

$$\$\text{Mortgage Payments} = (\$\text{Mortgage})\,(MC) \qquad\qquad (2\text{-}1a)$$

In calculating mortgage payments with a mortgage constant, the i is the annual contract rate of interest divided by 12 (for monthly payments), the mortgage is the full initial value of the mortgage before any points are considered, and n is the number of months over which the loan payments are calculated, known as the **amortization term.** An example will illustrate the use of the mortgage constant.

Example 25:

Find the monthly mortgage payments ($\$MP$) required for a mortgage of $150,000 with an annual contract rate of 9% and a 30 year amortization term.

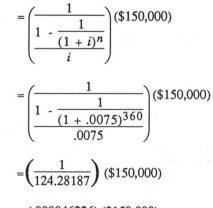

$$\$MP \ = MC\,(\$150{,}000)$$

$$= \left(\frac{1}{\dfrac{1 - \dfrac{1}{(1 + i)^n}}{i}} \right)(\$150{,}000)$$

$$= \left(\frac{1}{\dfrac{1 - \dfrac{1}{(1 + .0075)^{360}}}{.0075}} \right)(\$150{,}000)$$

$$= \left(\frac{1}{124.28187} \right)(\$150{,}000)$$

$$= (.008046226)\,(\$150{,}000)$$

$$= \$1,206.93$$

This is the amount that would be paid each month for the next 360 months (30 years). It includes the return of the $150,000 principal borrowed over the life of the loan, as well as providing the lender a return of 9% annual interest, compounded monthly. The mortgage constant of .008046227 is also available in rounded form (.00805) in Table 5 in Chapter 6. The monthly mortgage constant could be used to determine the mortgage payments for any size mortgage as long as the contract rate is 9% and the term 30 years. Other precalculated mortgage constants are shown in Table 2-1.

Table 2-1 serves to illustrate several points. First notice the rate of decrease in the mortgage constants, and thus mortgage payments, as the term is extended. Each 10 years added to the term has less of an impact on reducing the payments. As the interest rate increases, the relative decline in mortgage constants is even less as the term is extended. At a 20% interest rate, notice how little the impact is of going from 30 to 40 years, a .22% decline in the payment compared to a 5.25% decline at 8%. In general, when interest rates are 12% or above there is little benefit to borrowers in extending terms beyond 30 years. The relationship is asymptotic, where the mortgage payment can never be lower than the annual contract rate of interest, but approaches this boundary as the interest rate is increased and/or the term is lengthened.

TABLE 2-1   Sample Monthly Mortgage Constants

Annual Interest Rate	Amortization Term in Years				
	10	20	30	40	50
8.0	.012133	.008364	.007338	.006953	.006793
9.0	.012668	.008997	.008046	.007714	.007586
10.0	.013215	.009650	.008776	.008491	.008391
11.0	.013775	.010322	.009523	.009283	.009205
12.0	.014347	.011011	.010286	.010085	.010026
13.0	.014931	.011716	.011062	.010895	.010850
14.0	.015527	.012435	.011849	.011711	.011678
15.0	.016133	.013168	.012644	.012532	.012507
20.0	.019326	.016988	.016710	.016673	.016667

To further illustrate this last point, notice the relationship between the annual contract rate and the monthly mortgage constant multiplied by 12. Extracting a few examples from Table 2-1 and multiplying them by 12 to put them on an annual basis results in Table 2-2.

TABLE 2-2   Sample Annualized Monthly Mortgage Constants

Annual Interest Rate	Amortization Term in Years		
	10	30	50
8.0	.145596	.088056	.081516
10.0	.158580	.105312	.100692
12.0	.172164	.123432	.120312
15.0	.193596	.151728	.150084

Again, notice how little the benefit there is in moving beyond 30 years with respect to the potential for reducing payments. Also notice how extending the term brings the mortgage constant closer and closer to the contract rate (the asymptote) of interest under which the mortgage constant can never decline or the loan would never be paid off. A table of precalculated monthly mortgage constants, rounded to the 5th decimal place, is available in Chapter 6.

B.   Interest and Principal Separation in Mortgage Payments

The interest portion of each mortgage payment is always based on the outstanding mortgage balance at the beginning of the period. In Example 25, the mortgage payment is $1,206.93 and the mortgage balance begins at $150,000. A portion of the $1,206.93 will be used for the appropriate interest portion of the payment, and the rest of the payment will be applied to reducing the $150,000 principal balance. Each month the interest portion declines, slowly at first, as the mortgage balance declines. Some interest and principal separation examples will illustrate this point.

Example 26:

What is the first month's interest portion of a monthly mortgage payment of $1,206.93 with a 9.0% annual contract interest rate on a $150,000 loan for 30 years? Solve for the second and third months as well.

To solve this problem, first set up the known relationship:

$Interest Portion of Payment = Monthly Interest Rate ($Previous Month's Balance)

For Month 1:

$Interest = (.09/12) $150,000

= $1,125.00

and since the total mortgage payment is $1,206.93, the difference between the total payment and the portion going to interest is the portion going to principal reduction:

$$\$Principal = \$1,206.93 - 1,125.00$$

$$= \$81.93 \qquad \text{and the new mortgage balance will be:}$$

$$\$150,000 - 81.93 = \$149,918.07 \qquad \text{outstanding at the end of month 1.}$$

For Month 2:

$$\$Interest = (.09/12) \, \$149,918.07$$

$$= \$1,124.39$$

and the portion of the payment going to principal reduction is again calculated:

$$\$Principal = \$1,206.93 - 1,124.38$$

$$= \$82.54 \qquad \text{and the new mortgage balance will be:}$$

$$\$149,918.07 - 82.54 = \$149,835.53 \qquad \text{outstanding at the end of month 2.}$$

For Month 3:

$$\$Interest = (.09/12) \, \$149,835.53$$

$$= \$1,123.77$$

and the portion of the payment going to principal reduction is:

$$\$Principal = \$1,206.93 - 1,123.77$$

$$= \$83.16 \qquad \text{and the new mortgage balance will be:}$$

$$\$149,835.52 - 83.16 = \$149,752.36$$

The mortgage balance remaining, as well as the portion of the payment going to principal and interest in each month, can be calculated in a similar manner for each payment period of the loan. This is called an **amortization schedule**. Short cuts in calculating the separation of principal and interest are possible once the mortgage balance remaining is fully understood.

Example 27:

Calculate the total interest paid if a mortgage of $150,000 is paid over 30 years with monthly payments of $1,206.93.

$1,206.93 x 12 months x 30 years = $total of all payments

= $434,494.80

$434,494.80 - $Mortgage = $interest payments

$434,494.80 - $150,000 = $284,494.80

It is unlikely that anyone will actually pay the total interest which would be due over the 30 year period. Most mortgage loans are paid off in 7 to 12 years.

C.   Mortgage Balance Remaining

There is a simpler method of calculating the interest portion of mortgage payments during any given year than the method used in Example 26, which requires individual monthly calculations. It is simply to calculate the remaining mortgage balance at the end of each year. Knowing the remaining mortgage balance from one year to another allows one to calculate the principal portion repaid during that year, which when subtracted from the total mortgage payments made during the year leaves the interest portion paid.

To calculate the mortgage balance remaining, denoted *MBR*, at any point in time, again refer to equation (1-8). But this time the n in the present value of an annuity factor is the *remaining number of months* of the mortgage term. The annuity is the mortgage payment as calculated with the full term mortgage constant.

$$\$MBR = (\$PV) = \left(\frac{1 - \frac{1}{(1 + i)^n}}{i} \right)(\$ANN) \qquad \text{from (1-8)}$$

Example 28:

What is the remaining mortgage balance at the end of year 1, year 5 and year 10 of a 30 year mortgage of $150,000 at 9.0%? The monthly payments are again $1,206.93.

$$\$MBR \text{ end of year 1} = \left(\frac{1 - \frac{1}{(1 + .09/12)^{348}}}{.09/12} \right)(\$1,206.93)$$

$$= (123.43278)(\$1,206.93)$$

$$= \$148,974.72$$

where the 348 is the original term of 360 months less the 12 months paid on the loan.

$$\$MBR \text{ end of year } 5 = \left(\frac{1 - \frac{1}{(1 + .09/12)^{300}}}{.09/12} \right)(\$1,206.93)$$

$$= (119.16162)(\$1,206.93)$$

$$= \$143,819.74$$

where the 300 is again the original term of 360 months less the 5 years, or 60 months, paid on the loan.

$$\$MBR \text{ end of year } 10 = \left(\frac{1 - \frac{1}{(1 + .09/12)^{240}}}{.09/12} \right)(\$1,206.93)$$

$$= (111.14495)(\$1,206.93)$$

$$= \$134,144.18$$

After 10 years, or one third of the term, of paying \$1,206.93 each month, only \$15,855.82, or a little over 10% of the original loan, has been paid off!

The higher the interest rate or term, the lower the percentage repaid would be, and vice versa for lower interest rates and shorter terms. Using this procedure allows separation of principal and interest for a given year without the tedious procedure of calculating monthly breakdowns as used in Example 26.

Example 29:

What is the total interest paid during the first year of a 30 year, \$150,000 loan at 9.0% interest, with monthly payments of \$1,206.93?

Using the mortgage balance calculation from Example 28:

$$\$\text{Mortgage} - (MBR \text{ end of year } 1) = \$\text{Principal Repaid in year } 1$$

$$\$150,000 - \$148,974.72 = \$1,025.28$$

and to calculate the total interest paid in year 1:

$$\$\text{Total payments} - (\$\text{Principal Repaid in year } 1) = \$\text{Interest portion paid in year } 1$$

$$(12)(\$1,206.93) - \$1,025.28 = \$\text{Interest}$$

$$\$14,483.16 - \$1,025.28 = \$13,457.88$$

One can use a similar procedure to find the interest portion for any given year as long as the remaining mortgage balance is known for the beginning and end of the given year.

(1)   Alternative Mortgage Balance Remaining Calculation

Recall that the mortgage is merely the present value of an annuity for a lender based on the remaining term, or full term when the mortgage is new. Then, if a borrower pays a mortgage over only part of the full amortization term, the present value of the remaining payments divided by the present value of the full term mortgage is the remaining mortgage proportion to be paid off. This equation, where n is the full term of the mortgage and j is the number of periods actually paid, is:

$$MBR_j = \frac{\left(\dfrac{1 - \dfrac{1}{(1 + i)^{n-j}}}{i}\right)}{\left(\dfrac{1 - \dfrac{1}{(1 + i)^{n}}}{i}\right)} \tag{2-2}$$

which, through mathematical simplification, reduces to a shorter version:

$$MBR_j = \frac{\left(1 - \dfrac{1}{(1 + i)^{n-j}}\right)}{\left(1 - \dfrac{1}{(1 + i)^{n}}\right)} \tag{2-3}$$

where MBR_j is the percentage of the mortgage balance remaining in period j. Note that the remaining mortgage balance *in dollars* is simply the percentage remaining times the initial mortgage amount. Therefore, equation (2-3) would apply to any dollar sized mortgage.

A set of mortgage balance remaining factors has been calculated in Table 6 in Chapter 6 using equation (2-3).

Example 30:

What is the mortgage balance remaining on a $150,000 mortgage, at 9.0% with monthly payments, paid for 12 years of an original 30 year term?

Solving this problem using equation (2-3):

$$\$MBR_{144} = \frac{\left(1 - \dfrac{1}{(1 + .09/12)^{360-144}}\right)}{\left(1 - \dfrac{1}{(1 + .09/12)^{360}}\right)} (\$150,000)$$

$$= \frac{.800901}{.932114} (\$150,000)$$

$$= .859231 (\$150,000)$$

$$= \$128,884.68$$

Therefore, the mortgage balance remaining after paying on the mortgage for 12 years would be $128,884.68. The same solution could be arrived at by using the tables from Chapter 6 (a slight difference will result due to rounding):

$$\$MBR_{144} = (\text{Table Factor}, 9\%, 30 \text{ years}, 12 \text{ year prepayment}) (\$PV)$$

$$= .85923 (\$150,000)$$

$$= \$128,884.50$$

D.   Calculating the Annual Percentage Rate

When points are charged at the time a mortgage loan is made, the effect is to reduce the lender's net cash outflow or present value. But since the mortgage loan payments are based on the contract rate and the full mortgage loan, the effective yield is increased to the lender. The annual percentage rate (APR) is calculated like an effective yield, but with the assumption that the loan will be repaid over its full term. If a loan has a balloon payment where it must be paid off before the full term, then the APR would be based on the call year. The APR solution is another variation of equation (1-8).

$$\$PV = \$\text{Mortgage} - \$\text{Points} = \left(\frac{1 - \dfrac{1}{(1 + APR/12)^n}}{APR/12}\right) (\$ANN) \qquad (2\text{-}4)$$

where i has been replaced by APR and n is the number of months in the full mortgage term. To solve for the APR requires substitution of various yields above the contract rate of interest for the APR until both sides of the equation are equal.

Example 31:

What is the APR for a 30 year loan of $85,000 with 5.0 points charged at closing, and a contract rate of 12.5%? The monthly payments should be calculated first

based on the contract rate and \$85,000. The result is a monthly payment of \$907.17.
The *APR* is solved as:

$$\$PV = \$85,000 - (.05)(\$85,000) = \left(\frac{1 - \dfrac{1}{(1 + APR/12)^{360}}}{APR/12} \right) (\$907.17)$$

Using a trial and error procedure to solve for *APR*, try 13.0%:

$$\$80,750 \stackrel{?}{=} \left(\frac{1 - \dfrac{1}{(1 + .13/12)^{360}}}{.13/12} \right) (\$907.17)$$

$$\stackrel{?}{=} 90.39961 \, (\$907.17)$$

$$\neq \$82,007.81$$

Since the \$*PV* at 13.0% is less than the \$80,750 actually lent, we need to try a
higher rate, say 13.25%:

$$\$80,750 \stackrel{?}{=} \left(\frac{1 - \dfrac{1}{(1 + .1325/12)^{360}}}{.1325/12} \right) (\$907.17)$$

$$\stackrel{?}{=} 88.82781 \, (\$907.17)$$

$$\neq \$80,581.93$$

This amount is very close, but too low. This means the *APR* is under 13.25%,
and with further calculations the actual *APR* is found to be 13.22%.

Example C-31 (a repeat of Example 31):

(1) Clear all registers, then enter "85,000 *PV*" for the contract mortgage amount.

(2) Enter "12.5 *g i*" for the monthly interest rate.

(3) Enter "30 *g n*" for the term.

(4) Press "*PMT*" to calculate the payment of - \$907.17.

(5) Next key in "85,000 *ENTER* 5 % -" to subtract out the points and get the
    actual amount advanced, \$80,750, and press "*PV*".

(6) Press "i", and when 1.10168 is displayed press "12 x" to annualize the interest rate, which is the desired *APR*, 13.22%.

Lenders are sufficiently close at 1/8th of one percent for disclosure purposes and so 13.25% would be a conservative and sufficient disclosure of the *APR* to the borrower. The *APR* in Example 31 would have been the same for any sized mortgage of similar term, contract rate and point charges. This generalized relationship can be expressed by substituting $1.00 for the mortgage loan and the mortgage constant, *MC*, for the mortgage payment (per dollar of mortgage). The equation to provide an *APR* for a given mortgage amount is:

$$\$PV = \$\text{Mortgage} - (\text{Points})(\$\text{Mortgage}) = \left(\frac{1 - \dfrac{1}{(1 + APR/12)^n}}{APR/12} \right)(\$ANN)$$

and the equation to provide a generalized *APR* for a given interest rate, term and points is:

$$\$PV = 1 - (\text{Points})(1) = \left(\frac{1 - \dfrac{1}{(1 + APR/12)^n}}{APR/12} \right)(MC) \qquad (2\text{-}5)$$

One can also separate out the *points* portion of equation (2-5) above and use this relationship to solve for the appropriate point charges, expressed as a decimal, to bring a given contract yield, r, up to a desired *APR*. This is shown below:

$$\text{Points} = 1 - \left(\frac{1 - \dfrac{1}{(1 + APR/12)^n}}{APR/12} \right)(MC) \qquad (2\text{-}6a)$$

where *MC* is the mortgage constant based on the contract rates, or:

$$\text{Points} = 1 - \left(\frac{1 - \dfrac{1}{(1 + APR/12)^n}}{APR/12} \right) \left(\frac{1}{1 - \dfrac{1}{(1 + r/12)^n}} \right) \qquad (2\text{-}6b)$$

Example 32:

How many points would a lender need to charge to bring a 12.0% contract rate loan up to an *APR* of 12.5% for a 30 year term monthly payment mortgage?

$$\text{Points} = 1 - \left(\frac{1 - \dfrac{1}{(1 + .125/12)^{360}}}{.125/12}\right)\left(\frac{1}{1 - \dfrac{1}{\dfrac{(1 + .12/12)^{360}}{.12/12}}}\right)$$

$$= 1 - \left(\frac{.97602}{.01042}\right)\left(\frac{1}{.97218/.01}\right)$$

$$= 1 - 93.69808\ (.01029)$$

$$= 1 - .96379$$

$$= .03621 \text{ or } 3.621 \text{ "points"}$$

Example C-32 (a repeat of Example 32):

(1) After clearing the registers, enter "1 *CHS PV*" for the initial $1.00 investment.

(2) Then enter "12 *g i*" for the interest rate.

(3) Enter "30 *g n*" for the term of the loan.

(4) Next press "*PMT*" to calculate the payment per dollar of the mortgage loan, which will be .01029.

(5) Then enter "12.5 *g i*" to reset the rate for the desired yield, leaving the payment alone.

(6) Now recalculate the $PV by pressing "*PV*", to derive .96379.

(7) Finally, press "*CHS ENTER*", then "1 +" and the residual will be .03621, which is equal to the decimal form of the answer of 3.621 points.

(1) Rules of Thumb for Point Calculations

An old rule of thumb used in the 1960s and 1970s, and unfortunately still in existence in a number of published materials, is that "8 discount points equal a one percentage point change in yield (*APR*)." This rule is not a bad approximation of the effect of point charges on APRs over very limited ranges. Specifically, when contract rates are in the 8% to 9% range and the amortization term is 25 years, this rule will produce the anticipated effect. Over the 9% to 10% range for a 30 year amortization term, the rule also works. But for all other typical interest rate and term combinations, the old rule of thumb will be incorrect and misleading. APRs have been precalculated incorporating points in Table 7 of Chapter 6.   With the availability of calculators, precalculated tables and computer programs, there is no need for using inaccurate rules of thumb!

E.   Calculating the Effective Yield (IRR) with Assumed Prepayment and Prepayment Penalties

The contract rate *APR* and *IRR* are only equal when no points or prepayment penalties are involved, and therefore all returns come through the interest portion of the mortgage payments. Whenever points are involved, the earlier the loan is paid off the greater is the impact on effective yield. To calculate the effective yield, or IRR, one solves for equation (1-8) where the returns include mortgage payments (or annuity) plus the mortgage balance and any prepayment penalties in the year of payoff. The number of years must be converted to months for monthly payments. Recalling equation (1-8):

$$\$PV = \frac{\$Returns_1}{(1 + IRR)^1} + \frac{\$Returns_2}{(1 + IRR)^2} + \cdots + \frac{\$Returns_n}{(1 + IRR)^n}$$

Now replacing $\$PV$ with the Mortgage Loan less Points, and converting the return stream into an annuity, and the mortgage balance plus prepayment penalties in month n as a single sum, results in:

$$\$Mortgage - \$Points = \left(\frac{1 - \dfrac{1}{(1 + IRR/12)^n}}{IRR/12}\right)(\$ANN) + \left(\frac{\$MBR}{(1 + IRR/12)^n}\right) +$$

$$\left(\frac{\$MBR\ (\%\ Prepayment\ Penalty)}{(1 + IRR/12)^n}\right) \tag{2-7}$$

where the mortgage payments are based on the full term of the loan and n is the expected prepayment year.

Example 33:

What is the effective yield for a $150,000 mortgage at a 9.0% contract rate for 30 years resulting in mortgage payments of $1,206.93 monthly, with 3.5 points charged at closing and a 1% prepayment penalty, if the loan is prepaid after one year?

The MBR at the end of year one is $148,974.72 (from Example 28), and with a 1% prepayment penalty the total due at the end of one year is $150,464.47. (Note that the *APR* is 9.40%, resulting from the lender charging the 3.5 discount points, but the *IRR* will be much higher.)

The net mortgage loan is:

Net Mortgage Loan   = $150,000 - .035 ($150,000)

= $150,000 - $5,250

$$= \$144,750$$

and the desired equality is:

$$\$144,750 = \left(\frac{1 - \dfrac{1}{(1 + IRR/12)^{12}}}{(IRR/12)} \right) (\$1,206.93) + \left(\frac{\$150,464.47}{(1 + IRR/12)^{12}} \right)$$

Solving for the *IRR*, try 14.0%:

$$= \left(\frac{1 - \dfrac{1}{(1 + .14/12)^{12}}}{(.14/12)} \right) (\$1,206.93) + \left(\frac{\$150,464.47}{(1 + .14/12)^{12}} \right)$$

$$= 11.13746 \, (\$1,206.93) + \$130,913.57$$

$$= \$13,442.13 + \$130,913.57$$

$$= \$144,355.70$$

Since we need to raise the present value, try a lower *IRR*, say 13.75%:

$$= \left(\frac{1 - \dfrac{1}{(1 + .1375/12)^{12}}}{(.1375/12)} \right) (\$1,206.93) + \left(\frac{\$150,464.47}{(1 + .1375/12)^{12}} \right)$$

$$= 11.15206 \, (\$1,206.93) + \$131,237.52$$

$$= \$13,459.76 + \$131,237.52$$

$$= \$144,697.28$$

This present value is still slightly lower than the $144,750 desired, which means that the true *IRR* is slightly less than 13.75%. In fact, the actual *IRR* can be calculated to be 13.71%. Note that the *IRR* of 13.71% is much higher than the contract rate of 9.0%, which dramatically illustrates the effect of point charges and prepayment penalties on effective yields, especially if they are paid off quickly. The longer the time before prepayment, the closer the *IRR* is to the contract rate when point charges are involved. When no point charges and no prepayment penalties are involved, the *IRR*, the contract rate and the *APR* are the same, even if prepayment occurs at any time.

Example C-33 (a repeat of Example 33):

(1) Enter "150,000 *PV*" as the mortgage amount.

(2) Enter "30 *g n*" for the monthly term.

(3) Enter "9.0 *g i*" for the annual interest rate, on a monthly basis.

(4) Press "*PMT*" to get the monthly payment of - $1,206.93.

(5) Next key in "12 *n FV*" to get the *MBR* at the end of the first year, which is
    - $148,975.20.

(6) Press "*ENTER*" then "1.01 *x* " to calculate the payoff including the penalty,
    for -$150,464.96, and press "*FV*" to enter it as the ending balance.

(7) Then press "150,000 *ENTER* 3.5 % -" to get the amount actually lent, or
    - $144,750.

(8) Next press "*PV*" to enter $144,750 as the loan.

(9) Finally, press "*i*" to recalculate the effective monthly yield of 1.142651,
    which when multiplied by 12 is 13.71%.

F.   Calculating the Effective Yield on Wraparound Mortgages

When existing first mortgages contain high prepayment penalties, as is common on large non-residential mortgages, or when contract interest rates are far below current market rates then it may not be desirable on the part of borrowers to pay off an existing mortgage. New funds may sometimes be derived through a second mortgage. When a second mortgage lender wants to be certain that unexpected default on a first mortgage loan will not occur, they may require that the total mortgage payments required for the first and second mortgages be paid directly to them. A legal note is set up for the full dollar amount of the existing as well as the new loan. This new note is technically a second mortgage that includes the first mortgage amount, and is referred to as a **wraparound mortgage**.

An interest rate is then applied to the wraparound mortgage and an appropriate term to maturity is used to derive the new payments. The interest rate and term are negotiable, but usually the interest rate is greater than the existing first mortgage rate, although less than the current first mortgage interest rates, effectively becoming a blend of the two. The term of the wraparound can be shorter than, the same or longer than the existing remaining first mortgage term, depending on what the borrower is attempting to accomplish. The easiest structure is to have a term on the wraparound that is the same as the remaining first mortgage term. Some examples will illustrate the yield calculations of various combinations.

Example 34:

A lender agrees to provide a second mortgage on a wraparound basis to a borrower with an existing first mortage balance of $80,500 and monthly payments of

$816.48 for the remaining term of 15 years. The first mortgage contract rate is 9.0%. Current second mortgage rates are 15.0%. The wraparound lender agrees to provide an additional $40,000 with a 15 year term. The total wraparound note is thus $120,500. What should the contract rate on the wraparound note be, and what will the corresponding wraparound payments be? (Assume no point charges.)

To derive the total payments on the wraparound note, simply calculate the payments required for a $40,000, 15.0% rate loan for 15 years and add these to the existing payments:

Total monthly payments = First mortgage payments + second mortgage payments

$$= \$816.48 + \$559.83$$

$$= \$1,376.31$$

The contract rate necessary can now be solved utilizing a mortgage constant for the note, where the mortgage constant is calculated as:

$$MC = \frac{\$1,376.31}{\$120,500}$$

$$= .0114217$$

Recalling that a mortgage constant is equal to the inverse of the present value of an annuity, then the mortgage constant can be converted to a present value of an annuity factor by taking the inverse, resulting in $1/.0114217 = 87.5529496$. Then we could solve for the effective yield, r, as:

$$87.5529496 = \left(\frac{1 - \frac{1}{(1 + r/12)^{180}}}{r/12} \right)$$

Alternatively, using tables from Chapter 6 for mortgage constants of 15 year terms, one could look up the closest contract rate and use this estimation procedure to narrow down the trial and error process. By using tables, one could see that the monthly mortgage constant at 11.0% for 15 years is .01137, which is just under the desired .0114217. At 11.25%, the mortgage constant is .01152. Therefore, the desired contract rate, r, will be just over 11.0%.

Try 11.09%:

$$= \left(\frac{1 - \frac{1}{(1 + .1109/12)^{180}}}{.1109/12} \right)$$

$$= 87.54614$$

Since this is very close, the calculated yield is just under 11.09%, which is precise enough for most lender applications. (The exact yield is 11.088%).

One may also use the present value of an annuity table to try and match the present value of an annuity factor for the known term to eliminate some of the guesswork. The closer the table factor to the desired answer, or the less accuracy required, the fewer additional trials are necessary. Example 34 was a little easier because the remaining mortgage term on the first loan and the new term on the second were identical. When these terms differ the process becomes a little more complex, as illustrated in Example 35.

Example 35:

A lender offers a wraparound note of $180,000 total with a 25 year amortization term and a call provision on the wraparound second mortgage (new money) in 15 years at 12.0%. The existing first mortgage balance is $130,000 with payments of $1,682.17 per month over the 10 remaining years based on an original rate of 9.5%. The lender also is charging 2 points on the entire wraparound note at closing. What is the effective rate on the wraparound mortgage if the borrower accepts this arrangement?

The call provision requires the wraparound mortgage balance ($180,000 - $130,000 = $50,000 "new money") to be paid off in 15 years, with a 12.0% contract rate and a 25 year amortization term. The payments on the $50,000 actually lent at 12.0% for 25 years are $526.61 monthly. Calculating the mortgage balance remaining on the $50,000 lent at the 12.0% contract rate of interest at the time of the loan is called in the 15th year amounts to $36,705.14. The mortgage payments on the entire note are based on $180,000 at 12.0%, for a 25 year term, which results in monthly payments on the wraparound mortgage of $1,895.80. Therefore, for 10 years the lender will net:

Net Payment = New Payments - Underlying First Mortgage Payment

$$= \$1,895.80 - \$1,682.17$$

$$= \$213.63$$

and for the 11th through the 15th years, the lender will receive the full $1,895.80, since the underlying first mortgage will have been paid off. At the end of the 15th year a mortgage balance of $36,705.14 remains to be paid. The amount of funds actually advanced by the lender is:

Net Money Lent =Wraparound Note - Points - First Mortgage Balance Remaining

$$= \$180,000 - (.02)(\$180,000) - \$130,000$$

$$= \$46,400$$

Therefore, the effective yield, IRR, can be found by solving for:

$\$46,400 = (\$PV$ of Annuity,$i=IRR$,10 yrs.)($\$213.63$) + ($\$PV$ of Single Sum, $i=IRR$,10 yrs.)(($\$PV$ Annuity,$i=IRR$,5 yrs.)($\$1,895.80$)) + ($\$PV$ of Single Sum,$i=IRR$,15 yrs.)($\$36,705.14$)

$$\$46,400 = \left(\frac{1 - \dfrac{1}{(1 + IRR)^{120}}}{IRR}\right)(\$213.63) + \left(\frac{1}{(1 + IRR)^{120}}\right)$$

$$\left(\frac{1 - \dfrac{1}{(1 + IRR)^{60}}}{IRR}\right)(\$1,895.80) + \left(\frac{1}{(1 + IRR)^{180}}\right)(\$36,705.14)$$

The years are again converted to months to match up with the monthly payment annuities. Again, solving for the *IRR* is a trial and error process, where the answer will be approximately 12.097%.

Note the benefit to the borrower of a 25 year amortization term on the entire note. This effectively lowers the present cash outflow requirement on the new $46,400 money to only $213.63 per month, or $2,563.56 per year, which is only 5.525% of the new dollar loan. The interest cost has been partially shifted into the future resulting in the required yield of 12.097%, but lowering current cash flow requirements.

Example C-35 (a repeat of Example 35):

To solve this problem on a trial and error basis, the easiest method is to write a short program on a programmable calculator. There will basically be three components to the program, where the first calculates the present value of the $213.63 annuity over the 10 years, at the *IRR*. The second part calculates the present value of the $1,895.80 annuity over 5 years at the *IRR*, and then discounts it to the present from the tenth year. Finally, the mortgage balance remaining of $36,705.14 is discounted to the present from year 15 at the *IRR*. Again using the HP-12C keystrokes, the program is:

(1) Clear all registers, including the program register via "*f PRGM*".

(2) Enter the program mode by keying "*f P/R*".

(3) Enter the program as:

    "*RCL 0 PMT*"
    "*10 g n*"
    "*RCL 2 g i*"
    "*PV*"
    "*STO 3 f FIN*"

"*RCL 1 PMT*"
"*5 g n*"
"*RCL 2 g i*"
"*PV*"
"*f FIN*"
"*CHS FV*"
"*10 g n*"
"*RCL 2 g i*"
"*PV*"
"*STO 4 f FIN*"
"*36,705.14 CHS FV*"
"*15 g n*"
"*RCL 2 g i*"
"*PV*"
"*RCL 3 +*"
"*RCL 4 +*"
"*f FIN*"
"*f P/R*"

(4) Next, hit "*f REG*" to clear the registers, and input the variables:

"*213.63 CHS STO 0*"
"*1,895.80 CHS STO 1*"

(5) Finally, input your first guess of the *IRR*, say 13.0%, into memory cell 2:

"*13 STO 2*"

(6) To run the program, hit "*R/S*", and the calculated present value should be $42,451.81. Since this is lower than the desired $46,400, we must lower the interest rate to raise the present value.

(7) Next try 12.0% by keying in "*12 STO 2*", then "*R/S*" to get an answer of $46,834.89. This number is too high, indicating a higher *IRR* is needed.

(8) Keying in "*12.094 STO 2*" then "*R/S*" results in an answer of $46,400.03, indicating the *IRR* is 12.094%.

G.   Refinancing Yield or Cost Calculations

For a lender, refinancing often means a reduction in yield on the mortgage balance outstanding for a currently held mortgage. Refinancing becomes more attractive to borrowers as current market rates decrease relative to existing mortgage contract rates. Deterrents to refinancing are large prepayment penalties, and lenders setting lower initial contract rates but charging more points at closing to arrive at the same expected yield,

thus lowering the risk of refinancing. Setting lower contract rates means that market
rates have to move that much lower in order to induce borrowers to desire refinancing.

For example, a lender could charge a 15.0% contract rate and 5.0 points on a 30
year loan resulting in a 15.829% *APR*, or a 15.75% contract rate and .5 points resulting
in an *APR* of 15.833%. Even though the *APR* is greater on the second combination, the
effective yield on the first loan would be greater over most prepayment year assumptions.
Further, market rates would have to slip by absolute levels of one half of a percent more
with the first choice in order to reach levels where refinancing might be attractive.

For the borrower, the refinancing decision is a choice between the present value
of the alternatives. One must be certain to include all relevant costs of refinancing,
including prepayment costs on the old loan and all closing costs on the new loan. The
time horizon is also critical. A borrower must forecast the expected time period before
the new loan would be paid off in order to properly calculate the present value of
alternatives.

Example 36:

Assume that a borrower takes out a loan from Gimme Savings and Loan of
$100,000 for 30 years with a fixed contract rate of 15.0% and 5 points to close, and a 3%
prepayment penalty. Then three years later market mortgage rates move to 13.5% for 30
year fixed rate loans with 2 points to close, 1.5 points of other closing costs and with a
3% prepayment penalty again. Is refinancing worthwhile if the borrower plans to keep
the new loan 30 years? 5 years?

The loan balance on the existing loan in 3 years is $99,348.35 and monthly
payments are $1,264.44. A payoff would require:

$$\$99,348.35 + \$99,348.35(.03) = \$102,328.80$$

To cover the payoff of $102,328.80, the borrower would also need to borrow the points
and closing costs (or provide them in cash with the same assumed opportunity cost).
Thus, the borrower needs:

$$\$102,328.80 + \$102,328.80(.02 + .015) = \$105,910.31$$

The monthly payments on the above amount at 13.5% for 30 years would be $1,213.11,
which is lower than the $1,264.44 on the original loan. At first glance, the refinancing
seems the best choice. But this comparison is based on continuing payments over 30
years.

If the borrower were planning on prepaying the new loan in 5 years, the
remaining loan balance would be $104,071.97 plus .03($104,071.97) for the prepayment
penalty:

$$\$104,071.97 + (\$104,071.97)(.03) = \$107,194.13$$

The present value decision calculation must assume an opportunity cost of money. In this case the current mortgage rates would be appropriate. Current *APR*s would be around 14.0%, including all closing costs. Effective yields would run 14.5% for assumed payoffs in 5 years. These rates indicate the opportunity cost range. Try 14.5% for the 5 year present value decision.

In the first case, the borrower must pay $1,264.44 for 5 more years, then $97,347.48, the loan balance at the end of the 8th year of the loan term, plus a 3% penalty for a total of $100,267.91. The present value of this alternative is:

Existing Loan:

$$\$PV = \left(\frac{1 - \dfrac{1}{(1 + .145/12)^{60}}}{.145/12} \right)(\$1,264.44) + \left(\frac{\$100,267.91}{(1 + .145/12)^{60}} \right)$$

$$= \$53,741.28 + \$48,773.69$$

$$= \$102,514.97$$

In the second case the present value alternatives will include payments of $1,213.11 for 5 years plus $107,194.13 in 5 years. The present value of this decision is:

New Loan:

$$\$PV = \left(\frac{1 - \dfrac{1}{(1 + .145/12)^{60}}}{.145/12} \right)(\$1,213.11) + \left(\frac{\$107,194.13}{(1 + .145/12)^{60}} \right)$$

$$= \$51,559.65 + \$52,142.83$$

$$= \$103,702.48$$

Since the present value of the new loan is higher than the alternative of keeping the current mortgage, the conclusion should be that, if the borrower thought there was a significant probability of selling or prepaying the new loan within 5 years, refinancing would not be worthwhile. Rates would have to drop below 13.5% (or prepayment penalties less than 2.3%) before refinancing was worthwhile.

To make the decision, the time assumption is critical. To determine how much time is necessary before refinancing is worthwhile, one would extend the number of months (n) in the above present value comparison until both present values are equal. That n which provides such a result would be the minimum expected duration before prepayment, at current rates, for refinancing to be worthwhile.

Another consideration not explicitly handled by the above present value comparison would be the tax effects of either decision. This can be easily incorporated by using after tax dollar outlays instead of before tax dollars and comparing present values again. Unfortunately, using after tax dollars makes the calculations more difficult because each year (and actually each month), the after tax outlay changes as the interest portion changes. In the above example, the decision would have been identical on an after-tax basis, and slightly stronger in favor of not refinancing for periods under 5 years.

H.   Pricing Mortgages for Purchase or Sale in the Secondary Market

The value of a mortgage after origination by a lender to a borrower in the "primary market" depends on market yields at the time. If a $100,000 mortgage is originated at 13.0%, and current rates, or yields, are still 13.0%, then the value of the mortgage is $100,000. As market yields go up, the investment or market value of mortgages with contract rates below the "new" market yields must go down in order to equal the higher yields. The reverse also holds where mortgage market values increase as required market yields decline. When an existing mortgage is sold, purchased or resold, these activities are part of the "secondary market." To buy or sell a mortgage with an existing contract rate and an expected mortgage payment pattern requires an investment value calculation based on current market yields. Often the primary mortgage lender will continue to service the mortgage (collect payments) for a servicing fee. To a buyer of one or several mortgages in a "package," the net payments after servicing charges are of particular relevance.

Pricing mortgages based on net payments at required market yields is again simply a present value calculation. In most cases an average expected mortgage life of 7, 9, or 12 years is assumed even though amortization terms run 30 years. Many mortgage loans are sold immediately after origination and so have a full 30 year amortization term left. Other mortgages may be sold a few years after origination, but this is less common. Examples to illustrate this pricing mechanism will be shown next.

Example 37:

What is the value of a 30 year term mortgage with a contract rate of 14.75%, a 12 year prepayment assumption and a servicing fee of .25% when required market net yields are 14.0%? (Assume no prepayment penalties.)

There are two ways this problem may be solved. One would be to pick a dollar amount, say $100,000 and proceed with the calculations of payments, mortgage balance remaining and then present value. Another approach would be to solve the problem for any size mortgage by using $1.00 as the mortgage value. Using an arbitrary amount of $100,000 to illustrate the concept, the calculations are:

Net Mortgage Payments   = $100,000 (MC, 14.5%, 30 yrs.)

= $100,000 (.01224556)

= $1,224.56

The remaining mortgage balance after 12 years is $93,772.89, solved by taking the present value of the remaining payments or by using a remaining mortgage balance factor from Chapter 6. The current market value of the mortgage at the required yield of 14.0% is thus:

$$PV = \left(\frac{1 - \frac{1}{(1 + .14/12)^{144}}}{.14/12} \right)(\$1,224.56) + \left(\frac{\$93,772.89}{(1 + .14/12)^{144}} \right)$$

$$= \$85,208.89 + \$17,647.61$$

$$= \$102,856.50$$

which means a premium of \$2,856.50 would be paid for this mortgage, or 2.857% for any similar yield mortgage of any amount (with the same assumptions) due to the decline in market yields.

Table 2-3 summarizes similar calculations for two different combinations of net contract rates, three prepayment assumptions, and various required market yields.

TABLE 2-3   Mortgage Pricing as a Percent of Loan Amount with 30 Year Amortization

			Net Contract Rate			
	12.0%			15.0%		
Required Market Yield	Prepayment Year			Prepayment Year		
	7	9	12	7	9	12
9.75%	1.11225	1.13196	1.15457	1.26360	1.31050	1.36483
12.25%	.98844	.98665	.98471	1.12791	1.14806	1.17002
12.50%	.97706	.97354	.96976	1.11541	1.13337	1.15283
15.00%	.87210	.85476	.83723	1.00000	1.00000	1.00000
15.25%	.86244	.84402	.82552	.98936	.98791	.98645
15.50%	.85292	.83347	.81405	.97886	.97603	.97317
17.75%	.77324	.74647	.72115	.89093	.87788	.86541

Interpreting this table indicates that a number less than 1.0 would be a discount from the mortgage face value, and a number greater than 1.0 would be a premium paid to the seller of the mortgage. Note how the shorter expected term before payoff reduces the impact on market values of mortgages. An expanded secondary mortgage market table has been pre-calculated in Chapter 6 as Table 8.

Example 38:

Use Table 2-3 above, or Table 8 from Chapter 6, to calculate the market value of a 30-year mortgage with an $80,000 stated balance, a 15.0% contract rate, net after servicing, when a 9 year prepayment is assumed and a 15.5% market yield is required.

To solve this problem, find the required yield factor of 15.50% and move along that same row until you are under the 15.0% contract rate and the 9 year prepayment column. The .97603 means that the current mortgage value will be 97.603% of the stated loan balance if a 15.5% market yield is required. Thus the calculated market value of the mortgage is:

$$\$80,000 \ (.97603) = \$78,082.40$$

Example C-39 (a new calculator example):

What is the market value of a mortgage with net monthly payments of $13,000, a mortgage balance of $1,250,800 and a remaining term of 24 years and 3 months (or 291 months) with required market yields at 12.75%? Assume full term repayment (i.e., no prepayment).

(1) After clearing all registers, enter "- 13,000 *PMT*" for the monthly payment.

(2) Enter "12.75 *g i*" for the monthly interest rate.

(3) Enter "291 *n*" for the term, then press "*PV*" to get $1,167,046.96, which is the current market value at a required yield of 12.75%. Note that the existing mortgage balance and the old contract rate are not needed when using a calculator to solve for the present value.

Example C-40 (a new calculator example):

What is the current market value of a mortgage with monthly payments of $2,500 and a remaining term of 240 months, if a current effective yield of 14.0% is required, and the loan is called in 120 months (10 years from now)?

Hopefully, you noticed that no solution is possible with the information provided. The one more piece of information needed is either the existing contract rate or the current mortgage balance remaining. If you find out that the contract rate is, say 12.5%, then you can calculate the mortgage balance as:

(1) Enter "- 2,500 *PMT*" for the monthly payment.

(2) Enter "12.5 *g i*" for the monthly interest rate.

(3) Enter "240 *n*" for the remaining term of the loan.

(4) Press "*PV*" to derive the current mortgage balance of $220,043.20.

If this mortgage balance were known instead, then the annual contract rate could have been similarly calculated. Next the mortgage balance remaining in 12 months must be calculated, after which the original problem can be solved:

(5) Again enter the monthly payment as "2,500 *CHS PMT*".

(6) Enter the monthly interest rate as "12.5 *g i*".

(7) Enter the period at which the loan will be called, or "120 *n*".

(8) Finally, press "*PV*" to derive the mortgage balance of $170,792.83.

(9) Next, enter this as the future value, as a negative, via "*CHS ENTER FV*".

(10) Enter the required interest rate by pressing "14.0 *g i*".

(11) Press "*PV*" to derive $203,473.23, which is the market value of the mortgage discounted at 14.0% with a prepayment assumed after 10 years.

Example C-41 (a new calculator example):

A mortgage with an amortization term of 300 months pays a net amount of $20,945.55 per month. The loan is due in 60 months and will have a payoff balance of $2,170,475. If someone is asking $2,305,000 for this mortgage in the secondary market, what would be the expected yield?

(1) Enter "20,945.55 *CHS PMT*" for the monthly net payment.

(2) Enter "2,170,475 *CHS FV*" as the mortgage balance in 60 months.

(3) Enter "2,305,000 *PV*" for the asking price.

(4) Enter "60 n" for the term of prepayment.

(5) Press "*i*" to get the answer of .83333, which when multiplied by 12 gives a current market yield of 10.0%

Further Problems and Solutions

Problems Using Formulas

1. What is the monthly mortgage constant for a 10%, 25 year amortization term mortgage?

2. Given the monthly mortgage constant in problem 1, what are the monthly mortgage payments and total payments for one year on a $75,000 mortgage?

3. What are the first month's interest and principal repaid on the $75,000 mortgage in problem 2?

4. What is the total interest cost in dollars if the mortgage in problem 2 is paid over the full 25 year term?

5. What are the monthly payments, and total payments made in any one year, on a 30 year amortization, 10.0% loan of $75,000?

6. What is the mortgage balance on the mortgage in problem 5 after 5 years?

7. If a lender makes a $20,000 loan with monthly payments of $170.41 for 20 years, what annual rate of interest is being charged?

8. A lender makes a 9.0%, $30,000 loan for 31 years, with monthly payments of $239.89. To bring the *APR* yield up to 9.5%, how much in points must be charged? (Assume no prepayment.)

9. A borrower arranges a wraparound mortgage with the terms based on $192,814 at 10.5%, payable for 10 years. The old mortgage was originally for $200,000 at 10.0% for 30 years, but has been paid down to $132,814 with 10 years to go. What is the effective yield on the new money, if paid over 10 years on a monthly basis?

Solutions to Problems Using Formulas

1. The monthly mortgage constant is calculated as:

$$MC = \cfrac{1}{\left(1 - \cfrac{\cfrac{1}{(1 + .10/12)^{300}}}{.10/12} \right)}$$

$$= .009087008$$

$$= .00909$$

2.   Monthly Payment $= .00909\ (\$75,000)$

$$= \$681.52$$

Total Annual Payment $= \$681.52\ (12)$

$$= \$8,178.24$$

3.   Monthly Interest Rate $= .10/12$

Interest in First Month $= .10/12\ (\$75,000)$

$$= \$625.00$$

Principal Reduction $=$ Total Payment - Interest

$$= \$681.52 - \$625.00$$

$$= \$56.52$$

4.   Payments for 25 years $= 25\ (\$8,178.24)$

$$= \$204,456.00$$

Total Interest Paid $=$ Total Payments - Original Loan

$$= \$204,456.00 - \$75,000.00$$

$$= \$129,456.00$$

5.   Mortgage Constant $= \dfrac{1}{\left(\dfrac{1 - \dfrac{1}{(1 + .10/12)^{360}}}{.10/12} \right)}$

$$= .0087757$$

Monthy Payment $= .0087757\ (\$75,000)$

$$= \$658.18$$

Note that by increasing the term from 25 to 30 years, the monthly payment decreases from \$681.54 to \$658.18. The annual payments on the new 30 year loan are \$7,898.16.

6. Solve for the mortgage balance using the remaining term for n in the numerator:

$$MBR \text{ end of year } 5 = \left(\frac{1 - \dfrac{1}{(1 + .008333)^{360-60}}}{1 - \dfrac{1}{(1 + .008333)^{360}}} \right)(\$75{,}000)$$

$$= \left(\frac{.917060}{.949590}\right)(\$75{,}000)$$

$$= .9657431 \, (\$75{,}000)$$

$$= \$72{,}430.73$$

7.   Monthly Mortgage Constant $= \dfrac{\$170.41}{\$20{,}000}$

$$= .0085205$$

$$\text{PV of an Annuity at } ?\% = \frac{1}{.0085205}$$

$$= 117.364005$$

and the PV of an Annuity for 20 years at the unknown rate of interest is:

$$117.364005 = \left(\frac{1 - \dfrac{1}{(1 + ?\%)^{240}}}{?\%} \right)$$

Using a trial-and-error process provides a solution of a monthly rate equal to .006875, which when multiplied by 12 gives an annual interest rate of 8.25%

8. There are several ways of solving for discount points. One approach is:

Dollar Value of Points $=$ Loan Amount $-$ (*PV* of Annuity @ desired yield) (Payment)

$$= \$30{,}000 - \left(\frac{1 - \dfrac{1}{(1 + .095/12)^{372}}}{.095/12} \right)(\$239.89)$$

$$= \$30{,}000 - (119.59382) \, (\$239.89)$$

$$= \$30{,}000 - 28{,}689.36$$

$$= \$1{,}310.64$$

$$\text{Percentage Points} \; = \frac{\$1{,}310.64}{\$30{,}000.00}$$

$$= .04369 \quad \text{or } 4.369 \text{ discount points}$$

9. The monthly payment on the full note is $2,601.74, with $1,755.14 needed for the first mortgage, leaving a net of $846.60 on the new money. The monthly loan constant for 10 years is derived by:

$$M\,C \; = \frac{\$846.60}{\$60{,}000.00}$$

$$= .0141100$$

Since the MC by definition is the inverse of the PV of an Annuity, then the PV of an Annuity for 10 years is calculated to be:

$$\text{PV of an Annuity} \; = \frac{1}{.01410987}$$

$$= 70.871722$$

and the rate of return is calculated as:

$$70.871722 \; = \left(\frac{1 - \dfrac{1}{(1 + ?\%)^{120}}}{?\%} \right)$$

Using a trial-and-error procedure yields a monthly interest rate of .0096568, which multiplied by 12 yields an annual rate of return of 11.5881%

Problems Using Tables from Chapter 6

1. What is the present value of $75,000 to be received in 15 years, with a required rate of return of 15.0% with monthly discounting?

2. What is the present value of $100,000 to be received in 5 years, with a required rate of return of 9.0% with monthly discounting?

3. What is the present value of $1,000 to be received in 30 years, with a required rate of return of 19.0% with monthly discounting?

4. What is the present value of a monthly annuity of $250 to be received at the end of each month for 5 years at a required yield of 10.5%?

5. What is the present value of a monthly payment of $2,850 to be received at the end of each month for 20 years at 13.5%?

6. What is the present value of a triple net lease payment of $1,000 monthly for 10 years along with the expected net resale price of $178,000 at the end of the lease term with a required yield of 12.0%? (Assume end of month payments and monthly compounding.)

7. What is the monthly mortgage payment required for 25 year term mortgages of $75,000 at 9.0%, 10.25%, 12.75%, and 15.25%?

8. What is the mortgage balance remaining at the end of the 15th year for a 30 year, 11.25% mortgage, paid monthly, with an initial value of $150,000?

9. What is the present value of a 30 year, 9.0% contract rate mortgage of $90,000 with an assumed prepayment in the 12th year, when discounted (monthly) at an annual rate of 12.0%?

10. What is the annual percentage rate, *APR*, with a 12.5% contract rate and point charges of 1.0, 2.0, and 4.0 for a 30 year mortgage?

Solutions to Problems Using Tables from Chapter 6

1.   Table 2 factor, 15.0%, 15 years = .10688

$$\$PV = .10688 \ (\$75,000)$$

$$= \$8,016$$

2.   Table 2 factor, 9.0%, 5 years = .63870

$$\$PV = .63870 \ (\$100,000)$$

$$= \$63,870.00$$

3.   Table 2 factor, 19.0%, 30 years = .00350

$$\$PV = .00350 \ (\ \$1,000)$$

$$= \$3.50$$

4.   Table 4 factor, 10.5%, 5 years = 46.52483

PV of an Annuity = 46.52483 ($250.00)

= $11,631.21

5.   Table 4 factor, 13.5%, 20 years = 82.82433

PV of an Annuity = 82.82433 ($2,850.00)

= $236,049.34

6.   This problem consists of two parts, an annuity and the future reversion value:

Table 4 factor, 12.0%, 10 years = 69.70052

Table 2 factor, 12.0%, 10 years = .30299

$P V$ = 69.70052 ($1,000) + .30299 ($178,000)

= $123,632.74

7.   Table 5 factor, 9.0%, 25 years = .00839

Mortgage Payment = .00839 ($75,000)

= $629.25

Table 5 factor, 10.25%, 25 years = .00926

Mortgage Payment = .00926 ($75,000)

= $694.50

Table 5 factor, 12.75%, 25 years = .01109

Mortgage Payment = .01109 ($75,000)

= $831.75

Table 5 factor, 15.25%, 25 years = .01300

Mortgage Payment = .01300 ($75,000)

= $975.00

8.   Table 6 factor, 11.25%, 30 years = .84286

$$MBR = .84286\ (\$150,000)$$

$$= \$126,429.00$$

9. There are two methods to solve this problem:

Method 1:

Calculate the payments and *MBR*:

Table 5 factor, 9.0%, 30 years = .00805

Mortgage Payments = .00805 ($90,000)

= $724.50

Table 6 factor, 9.0%, 12 years = .85923

$$MBR = .85923\ (\$90,000)$$

$$= \$77,330.70$$

Next, take the present value of the payments and *MBR* discounted at 12.0% (monthly) for 12 years.

Table 4 factor, 12.0%, 12 years = 76.13716

Table 2 factor, 12.0%, 12 years = .23863

$$\$PV = 76.13716\ (\$724.50) + .23863\ (\$77,330.70)$$

$$= \$55,161.37 + \$18,453.43$$

$$= \$73,614.80$$

Method 2:

Use Table 8 to calculate directly the present value of a mortgage assuming a given contract rate and required yield.

Table 8 factor, 12.0%, 12 years = .81765

$$\$PV = .81765\ (\$90,000)$$

$$= \$73,588.50$$

where the difference between the two methods is due to rounding.

10. These APRs can be looked up directly in Table 7:

APR, 12.5% contract rate, 1.0 point   = 12.64%

APR, 12.5% contract rate, 2.0 points = 12.78%

APR, 12.5% contract rate, 4.0 points = 13.07%

CHAPTER 3

MORTGAGE INSTRUMENTS

LEGAL ASPECTS OF THE MORTGAGE CONTRACT

A. Mortgage Definition

A mortgage can be defined as a pledge of property to secure the repayment of a debt. Technically, a mortgage is any form of instrument whereby title to real estate is conveyed or reserved as security for the payment of a debt, or whereby a lien is created against the property. A lien is a legal claim against the property that allows the lender holding the mortgage to force the sale of the pledged property and apply the proceeds of the sale to repayment of the debt if the debt is not repaid as agreed.

All mortgages are basically composed of two parts, the first being a promise to repay the debt, evidenced by a promissory note, and the second part being a pledge of the collateral. Mortgages without a pledge of collateral are called **non-recourse debt** and are rarely used for residential single family mortgage loans. The promissory note spells out the rights and interests of the lender and borrower as well as the financial terms of repayment. Since the promissory note is a personal promise to repay the debt, the borrower still has an obligation to repay the note even in the absence of any security in real estate.

The pledge of collateral can be a mortgage deed, a deed of trust, or a security deed, depending on the state in which the secured property is located. The type of instrument used varies by whether the property is located in a title theory or lien theory state. In the ten states that subscribe to title theory, the title is held by, or rests with, the mortgagee (lender). Title is then reconveyed to the borrower (mortgagor) upon repayment of the debt. Thirty-two states have adopted lien theory, whereby the mortgagor retains title to the property with the mortgagee holding a lien against the property. The remaining eight states plus the District of Columbia can be described as intermediate theory states in that they take a position somewhere between the lien and title theories. For those jurisdictions subscribing to the intermediate theory, title does not pass to the lender with the mortgage, but is only conveyed upon default. Table 3-1 lists the states with the nature of the mortgage and the customary security instrument each uses.

Table 3-1   STATE BY STATE COMPARISON OF MORTGAGE TYPE

State	Nature of Mortgage	Customary Security Instrument
ALABAMA	Title	Mortgage
ALASKA	Lien	Trust Deed
ARIZONA	Lien	Trust Deed
ARKANSAS	Intermediate	Mortgage
CALIFORNIA	Lien	Trust Deed
COLORADO	Lien	Trust Deed
CONNECTICUT	Intermediate	Mortgage
DELAWARE	Intermediate	Mortgage
DIST. OF COLUM.	Intermediate	Trust Deed
FLORIDA	Lien	Mortgage
GEORGIA	Title	Security Deed
HAWAII	Lien	Mortgage
IDAHO	Lien	Mortgage
ILLINOIS	Intermediate	Mortgage
INDIANA	Lien	Mortgage
IOWA	Lien	Mortgage
KANSAS	Lien	Mortgage
KENTUCKY	Lien	Mortgage
LOUISIANA	Lien	Mortgage
MAINE	Title	Mortgage
MARYLAND	Title	Trust Deed
MASSACHUSETTS	Intermediate	Mortgage
MICHIGAN	Lien	Mortgage
MINNESOTA	Lien	Mortgage
MISSISSIPPI	Title	Trust Deed
MISSOURI	Lien	Trust Deed
MONTANA	Lien	Trust Deed
NEBRASKA	Lien	Mortgage
NEVADA	Lien	Trust Deed
NEW HAMPSHIRE	Title	Mortgage
NEW JERSEY	Intermediate	Mortgage
NEW MEXICO	Lien	Mortgage
NEW YORK	Lien	Mortgage
NORTH CAROLINA	Intermediate	Trust Deed
NORTH DAKOTA	Lien	Mortgage
OHIO	Lien	Mortgage
OKLAHOMA	Lien	Mortgage
OREGON	Lien	Trust Deed

TABLE 3-1 (Continued)

PENNSYLVANIA	Title	Mortgage
RHODE ISLAND	Title	Mortgage
SOUTH CAROLINA	Lien	Mortgage
SOUTH DAKOTA	Lien	Mortgage
TENNESSEE	Title	Trust Deed
TEXAS	Lien	Trust Deed
UTAH	Lien	Trust Deed
VERMONT	Title	Mortgage
VIRGINIA	Intermediate	Trust Deed
WASHINGTON	Lien	Trust Deed
WEST VIRGINIA	Lien	Trust Deed
WISCONSIN	Lien	Mortgage
WYOMING	Lien	Mortgage

Source: Mortgage Bankers Association, A State Legislative Compilation.

The basic difference between these theories lies in the rights of the borrower and lender during the process of foreclosure. In all states, the lender must initiate the foreclosure process upon the borrower's default to recover the balance of the note owed. In a lien theory jurisdiction, the borrower would have the right to retain possession of the property until the foreclosure process is completed. In a title theory state, the right of control and possession of the property during the foreclosure process would belong to the lender, who is the title holder. In reality, many lenders are patient in exercising their eviction rights since it is usually in their best interest to attempt to work with the borrower to clear up any problem loans.

B.   Mortgage Default

When the borrower fails to fulfill the terms of the mortgage contract, a default is said to have occurred. The default can be caused for any number of reasons, as specified in the clauses in the mortgage, although failure to make the payments of principal and interest is the normal cause of a default. Defaults are relatively common, running 5% to 7% of all outstanding mortgages as of the first quarter of 1986, and do not necessarily lead to a foreclosure. The reason for this is simply that lenders are generally not interested in taking possession, or forcing the sale, of property they have made loans on.

For this reason, most lenders are willing to work with the borrowers on problem loans to avoid a foreclosure. This may take the avenue of restructuring the loan if necessary, or possibly providing counseling on financial affairs to assist the borrower in working out existing problems. The most important thing a borrower can do is to be open and honest with the lender if problems arise. Trying to hide information from the lender, or failing to let the lender know the circumstances behind a default, will almost certainly lead to a foreclosure.

C.   Foreclosure Process

Technically, a foreclosure refers to the elimination of the borrower's equity of redemption. An equity of redemption is the right of the borrower to clear up all problems by meeting any outstanding obligations, such as making up any missed payments, plus penalties. When the property is sold through foreclosure, a borrower's equity of redemption ceases, although it is possible for the borrower to stop the foreclosure up to the time of sale, called an **equitable right of redemption**. In a few states, there is a similar right that extends beyond the point of sale, called the **statutory right of redemption**. In those states, the borrower may get back title to the property within a specified time period by paying the foreclosure price plus any additional costs incurred at the foreclosure sale.

In the event the lender must resort to foreclosure, a specific procedure must be followed. In some states, a lawsuit must be filed whereby the lender asks the court for a judgment directing that the interests of the borrower in the property be cut off and the property be sold at a public auction to pay off the lender's claim. The same thing is accomplished in other states, but without going through the lawsuit. In either case, the property must be properly advertised and sold at a public auction. The borrower and lender hope that someone will bid more than the amount of the defaulted loan at the auction. However, the probability of this is not high, because if the property were substantially more valuable than the outstanding loan amount, the borrower would sell the property prior to having it foreclosed. So in most forclosure sales the lender will bid the amount of the outstanding loan, in some cases more or less, to get clear title to the property. Then the lender may sell the property, possibly taking a loss on the sale, or retain title to the property until any problems with the property have been eliminated, at which point the property will be sold. Table 3-2 lists the foreclosure remedies by state, plus the time period from posting the foreclosure through the sale date, and the equitable period of redemption.

TABLE 3-2   COMPARISON OF FORECLOSURE ASPECTS BY STATE

State	Predominant Method of Foreclosure	Months to Complete Initial Action	Equitable Period of Redemption
ALASKA	Power of Sale	3	None (A)
ARIZONA	Power of Sale	4	None (B)
ARKANSAS	Power of Sale	5	None (C)
CALIFORNIA	Power of Sale	5	None (A)
COLORADO	Power of Sale	2	2.5 mo. (D)
CONNECTICUT	Strict Foreclosure	6	None (E)
DELAWARE	Judicial	9	None
DIST. OF COLUM.	Power of Sale	2	None

TABLE 3-2 (Continued)

FLORIDA	Judicial	6	None
GEORGIA	Power of Sale	1	None
HAWAII	Judicial (F)	6	None (F)
IDAHO	Judicial (G)	6	6 mo. (G)
ILLINOIS	Judicial	6	6 mo. (H,I)
INDIANA	Judicial	7	3 mo. (J,K)
IOWA	Judicial	6	6 mo. (L)
KANSAS	Judicial	4	12 mo. (M)
KENTUCKY	Judicial	9	None (N)
LOUISIANA	Judicial	4	None
MAINE	Entry & Possession	1	12 mo.
MARYLAND	Power of Sale	2	None
MASSACHUSETTS	Power of Sale	9	None
MICHIGAN	Power of Sale	4	6 mo. (0)
MINNESOTA	Power of Sale	3	6 mo. (P)
MISSISSIPPI	Power of Sale	1	None
MISSOURI	Power of Sale	2	None (Q)
MONTANA	Power of Sale (R)	1	None (R)
NEBRASKA	Judicial	7	None (J,S)
NEVADA	Power of Sale	5	None (T)
NEW HAMPSHIRE	Power of Sale	2	None
NEW JERSEY	Judicial	6	None (U)
NEW MEXICO	Judicial	6	1 mo. (V)
NEW YORK	Judicial	8	None
NORTH CAROLINA	Power of Sale	1	None
NORTH DAKOTA	Judicial	3	6 mo. (L)
OHIO	Judicial	8	None
OKLAHOMA	Judicial	6	None (W)
OREGON	Power of Sale	9	None (X)
PENNSYLVANIA	Judicial	6	None
RHODE ISLAND	Power of Sale	1	None
SOUTH CAROLINA	Judicial	5	None (U)
SOUTH DAKOTA	Judicial	6	6 mo. (L,Y,Z)
TENNESSEE	Power of Sale	1	None (C)
TEXAS	Power of Sale	1	None
UTAH	Power of Sale	5	3 mo. (J,A1)
VERMONT	Strict Foreclosure	1	6 mo. (A2)
VIRGINIA	Power of Sale	2	None
WASHINGTON	Power of Sale	1 (A3)	None
WEST VIRGINIA	Power of Sale	2	None
WISCONSIN	Power of Sale (A1)	3	12 mo. (A1)
WYOMING	Power of Sale (A1)	3	3 mo. (A1)

TABLE 3-2 (Continued)

NOTES:

(A) Deed of Trust - however, if there is a judicial foreclosure, there is a 12 month redemption period.

(B) Judicial foreclosure under mortgage is also available. Time to complete would be 4 months followed by a 6 month redemption. However, if property was abandoned, the redemption can be reduced to 1 month if so stated in the Decree.

(C) Provided redemption rights have been expressly waived in the security instrument, if no waiver, redemption period is 12 months in Arkansas, 24 months in Tennessee.

(D) Redemption period is 5 months on security instruments executed before July 1, 1965.

(E) Redemption (law date) depends entirely on the equity in the property. If little or no equity exists, there is a 30 day law date prior to completion; otherwise, length is determined by the court.

(F) Foreclosure by Power of Sale or Entry and Possession also available under Deed of Trust.

(G) For properties over 20 acres, redemption is 12 months. Power of Sale Foreclosure also available under Trust Deed.

(H) Statute permits both Strict Foreclosure (where value of property does not exceed 90% of debt) and Foreclosure with Consent of the Mortgagor; in either case, the foreclosure sale is eliminated, the mortgagee waives deficiency judgment and the decree vests title directly in the mortgagee subject to a 3 month redemption period.

(I) Redemption is 6 months from sale if the judgment date is after January 1, 1982 (previously was 12 months from date of service).

(J) The redemption period precedes sale in Indiana, Nebraska (court stays sale on mortgagor's request), Oklahoma (without court appraisement), Wisconsin (if judicial foreclosure is used) and Utah (if foreclosure is by Power of Sale); in Nebraska can redeem only between day of sale and confirmation of sale.

(K) On security instruments executed before July 1, 1975, redemption period is 6 months before sale, time to complete is then 10 months with a 12 month transfer time.

(L) If security instrument specifically provides for 6 month redemption period and includes a waiver of deficiency judgment as of 1977; otherwise, redemption period is 12 months - for Iowa, if the property was abandoned, redemption can be reduced to 2 months.

(M) Provided no suit is instituted for deficiency - also, redemption period is reduced to 6 months in cases of abandoned property or on purchase money mortgages with less than 1/3 down.

(N) If foreclosure sale brings less than 2/3 of appraised value (court appraiser), there is a 12 month redemption period.

(O) Redemption period is 12 months on security instruments dated prior to January 1, 1965. Redemption may be reduced if the property was abandoned.

(P) If deed is executed after July 1, 1967, the redemption is 6 months provided the deficiency judgment was waived.

(Q) Within 10 days after sale, mortgagor may give notice of intention to redeem including security deposit for taxes, interest, etc. the redemption period is then 12 months.

(R) For estates over 15 acres, a mortgage is used and foreclosed judicially, 1 year redemption.

(S) Foreclosure by Power of Sale is available under a Deed of Trust effective 1965. Time of completion would then be 3 months; no redemption following sale.

(T) Judicial foreclosure is available under a mortgage with a 12 month redemption following the sale.

TABLE 3-2 (Continued)

(U) Provided no suit is instituted for deficiency; otherwise, redemption is 6 months.   In South Carolina, the redemption is one month if a deficiency judgment was obtained.
(V) Provided mortgage specifically calls for shorter redemption period - otherwise redemption period is 6 months.
(W) Provided sale is with court appraisement - otherwise, there is a 6 month redemption period preceding the sale.
(X) If security instrument was executed prior to May 26, 1959, judicial foreclosure is necessary with a 12 month redemption period following sale.
(Y) Foreclosure by Power of Sale with Service is also available for properties under 40 acres.
(Z) Redemption period can be extended to 24 months upon filing of affidavit to mortgagor including provision for accruing taxes, interest, etc.
(A1) Judicial foreclosure is also available. If used, the 6 month redemption period precedes the sale. In Utah, the 6 month redemption would follow the sale - in Wyoming, a 3 month redemption follows the sale plus 30 days for successive lien holders.
(A2) For mortgages executed after April 1, 1968, the redemption period is 6 months from date of judgment unless a shorter period is granted per the complaint - redemption is 12 months for mortgages executed before April 1, 1968.
(A3) Loan must be in default at least 120 days before day fixed for sale.

Source: Mortgage Bankers Association, <u>A State Legislative Compilation</u>.

In the event the proceeds from the sale are insufficient to cover the lender's costs, or if the lender sells the property at a loss, it is possible in some states to petition the courts for a deficiency judgment. This judgment would allow the lender to proceed against the borrower's other unsecured assets in the amount of the deficiency. It is also common to see the use of a **deed in lieu of foreclosure**. In this instance, the borrower would voluntarily deed the property over to the lender, thereby avoiding going through the foreclosure process, but foregoing any chance of recovering possible equity in the property.

D.   Mortgage Clauses

Despite the type of mortgage or mortgage instrument used, most mortgages contain clauses which will affect all parties involved. Technically, all of these clauses are negotiable between the borrower and lender, although in reality the lender will generally dictate the clauses that are to be included, and the borrower is then faced with a "take it or leave it" situation. However, various lenders do differ on how they handle these clauses and what they insist on including. Some of the more common mortgage clauses are:

1.   **Acceleration clause** - this allows the lender, in the event of default by the borrower, to call the full amount of the obligation immediately due and payable. Without such a clause, the lender would have to bring suit for each occurrence of default, such as each time a borrower missed a payment. This clause is also used to effect a "due-on-sale," in which the lender can call the entire loan amount due in the

event that the borrower sells the property. While this clause does not have to be exercised by the lender, it does give the lender the flexibility to foreclose or allow an assumption as necessary.

2. **Covenants** - can be any clause whereby the borrower agrees to do, or refrain from doing, some particular act. Typically mortgage covenants have the borrower agreeing to keep the property insured against hazard loss, to pay the property taxes as they become due, and to keep the property in good repair.

3. **Defeasance Clause** - voids the mortgage upon repayment of the entire debt. This is sometimes called a "mortgage release," and is the technical aspect of the mortgage that keeps the document from being an absolute conveyance.

4. **Escalator Clause** - would allow the lender to adjust the mortgage interest rate, thereby making it a varying rate loan. While this type of mortgage will be covered in depth, it is sufficient at this point to note that it is usually a clause added to the mortgage instrument that creates a particular type of mortgage.

5. **Estoppel Clause** - basically states that the lender will furnish a written statement to the borrower, called an **estoppel certificate**, upon the borrower's request, duly acknowledging the amount of the loan remaining to be paid. Also typically included are the specifics of the mortgage, such as interest rate, term, payments, etc.

6. **Prepayment Clause** - generally describes the rights of the borrower to pay off the loan before it is fully amortized. These clauses often give the borrower the right to prepay the loan, but assess a fee if this right is exercised. The prepayment penalty is normally a small percent of the outstanding loan balance, such as one percent, and may be waived at the option of the lender. Typically, if the property is being sold, no penalty will be assessed, but if the borrower is refinancing the property by securing a loan at a lower interest rate, lenders will generally impose the fee. The lack of significant prepayment penalites increases prepayment risk significantly for lenders, causing huge demand for refinancings when general mortgage rates decline.

7. **Subordination clause** - asserts a lower lien position for the immediate mortgage, for whatever reason. As an example, if a loan were made by a lender to acquire vacant land, then this loan would have a first lien position. But if the borrower then needed additional funds to construct a building, it may be necessary for the initial lender to relinquish this first lien position to provide the incentive to a subsequent lender to make the building loan. While the initial lender subordinates their position, it is probably to their advantage to do so, since the increased value of the property resulting from the construction of a building enhances their overall positon.

Different Types of Mortgages

A. Lien Position

Mortgages are generally classified by the order of their lien position. A first mortgage is one that has the highest lien position, i.e. a first lien. This simply means that in the event of foreclosure, a first mortgage would have the highest priority in terms of a claim against the property. The first lien, however, would still be inferior to any tax liens that might exist against the property. Any other mortgages then, whether they are a second mortgage or a third mortgage, would have a descending order of claim against the property in the event of foreclosure.

Second and third mortgages go by several different names, but their lien position would still be inferior to tax liens and a first mortgage. Financing provided by a seller is usually called a **Purchase Money Mortgage**, and again occupies a second lien position if a first mortgage exists. A special type of a second mortgage is called a **Wraparound Mortgage**, which is structured such that a new, second mortgage is created that includes, or "wraps around," an existing first mortgage. And if any liens exist against the property for work or materials that have been provided on the property, which are called **Mechanic's Liens**, they would typically occupy a lien position below the above-mentioned junior financing, based on time of recording.

B. Mortgage Categories

Mortgages can be categorized by whether they are some form of government-backed mortgage or whether they are conventional in nature. The primary government-backed mortgages are those insured by the **Federal Housing Administration** (FHA) or those guaranteed by the **Veterans Administration** (VA). The FHA comes under the jurisdiction of the Department of Housing and Urban Development, and was created to encourage homeownership through the availability of affordable housing finance. While the FHA has many financing programs, their basic feature is that the FHA *insures* financing provided by lenders to qualified borrowers. This financing is often at very competitive interest rates, with very low down payments required of the borrowers. The borrowers pay for this program through a monthly insurance premium, which in the most popular FHA programs in effect adds .5% interest onto the contract rate of the loan. Often times, however, the advantages of these programs outweigh the additional cost of the mortgage.

The VA also provides relatively inexpensive financing to qualified applicants, although their program differs from the FHA in that the VA is a *guarantee* program, rather than an insurance program. To qualify for a VA mortgage, one must be an honorably discharged U.S. veteran, or the spouse of a veteran who died in active service. A qualified borrower may finance up to 100% of the lower of the purchase price or appraised value of a property meeting VA standards. The interest rates on VA loans are often between .5% and 1% below conventional market interest rates, with any discount points charged to raise the lender's yield being paid by the seller.

If the VA approves an applicant for a mortgage, then the VA will guarantee the payment of the top portion of the loan, currently $27,500 or 60 percent of the loan, whichever is less, to the lender in the event of foreclosure. This guarantee greatly reduces the risk of loss to the lender, thus making the loan attractive even at rates slightly below alternative mortgage rates. Since these loans and the specifics such as interest rates and maximum amounts constantly change, it is recommended that an interested borrower contact any savings and loan, mutual savings bank or mortgage banker or broker for current loan information.

The term **conventional mortgage** refers to any mortgage that is not government-backed. These loans are made by the traditional sources of mortgage funds, such as savings and loans and mutual savings banks, at rates and terms that are dictated by market demands. While the lenders are free to set their rates and determine their individual underwriting standards, in reality most lenders use prescribed formulas and criteria that are set forth by secondary mortgage market agencies, such as the **Federal National Mortgage Association** (FNMA) or the **Federal Home Loan Mortgage Corporation** (FHLMC). This enables the lenders to sell these loans in the future through the secondary mortgage market agencies if desired or necessary.

Most conventional mortgages differ from the government-backed loans in terms of the amount of money that can be borrowed. Conventional lenders often lend in the 80% to 90% of loan-to-value range, where the government-backed loans often range from 95% to 100% of loan-to-value. The reason for this is, of course, related to the increased risk of the conventional loans, in that the borrower and property are the underlying collateral of the loan and not a governmental agency. But many lenders are now transferring some of this increased risk to others through the use of **Private Mortgage Insurance** (PMI). Private mortgage insurance can be required on conventional loans exceeding 80% loan-to-value.

PMI came about as a result of a number of factors, the primary ones being the bureaucracies involved in dealing with the governmental agencies, as well as the limits placed on the governmental loan programs. Conventional loans are able to circumvent these problem areas, although leaving the lenders with a greater degree of risk exposure, especially on high loan-to-value mortgages. So, in 1957 the Mortgage Guarantee Insurance Corporation (MGIC) was formed to provide private mortgage insurance to lenders. MGIC is still the largest private mortgage firm in existence, although it has since been joined by a host of others.

Most lenders today require PMI on conventional loans that exceed 80% loan-to-value. In addition, some lenders require the use of a **budget mortgage**, which has the borrower pay an amount equal to 1/12 of the annual hazard insurance and property taxes into an escrow account each month. This reduces the lenders risk exposure in these areas by ensuring that sufficient funds exist to pay for the taxes and insurance when these items come due.

The fee for private mortgage insurance is a premium, much as in an FHA mortgage. The typical charges to the borrower vary, but are usually a one-time premium paid at closing in the amount of 2.5% of the mortgage, or a 1.0% premium at closing with a .25% charge thereafter on the mortgage balance. These charges would provide coverage on the approximately top 20% of the mortgage balance in the event a deficiency arose after foreclosure. This would effectively cover the lender from all but the most severe cases of default and property value decline. It may be noted that as competition in the private mortgage insurance industry increases, and as this sector takes over the functions of the FHA through more efficient, less expensive coverage, rates will continue to vary. This makes comparison shopping among lenders even more important.

Mortgage Payment Alternatives

In this section we will discuss many of the alternatives in mortgage payment patterns available, ranging from fixed rate mortgages to variable term, variable balance and variable payment mortgages. One must not be fooled by brand names. There are only so many generically different mortgage types possible, and dozens of variations begin to evolve as several alternative features are simultaneously changed. To understand the differences, one must consider the risks and benefits to the lender and consumer of each feature. Other than the fixed rate mortgage, which will be discussed first, lenders may also provide the alternatives below, in response to interest rate changes:

1. Change the level of payment (variable or adjustable rate mortgage):

    a. frequency of change (monthly, quarterly, semi-annually, annually; two, three, four or five year intervals).
    b. amount of change (unlimited to some type of "capped" interest rate, or difference in payment cap).

2. Change the term (increase or decrease, usually to a maximum of 40 years).

3. Change the balance (increase or decrease):

    a. unlimited change in response to changes in interest rates,
    b. cap the payment but allow unlimited balance changes.

4. Various combinations of the above.

Other specialized instruments deal with particular problems or economic conditions. As an example, if there is high, uncertain inflation, a **Price Level Adjusted Mortgage** (PLAM) may be warranted. With high, certain inflation, a **Shared Appreciation Mortgage** (SAM) might be advantageous. If a borrower has relatively low current income, but anticipates a degree of growth in income, a **Graduated Payment Mortgage** (GPM) might be the best route to go. There are variations that can be used with the GPM, such as a **Supplemental Account GPM** or an **Interest Only GPM**. If the borrower is in a retirement situation and desires current income, then a **Reverse Annuity Mortgage** (RAM) might be the ticket. And finally, if the borrower desires a general line of credit from a lender, then an **Open Ended Home Equity Loan** (OEHEL) would probably be indicated. All of these loan types will be discussed in turn.

A. Fixed Rate Mortgages

The **Fixed Rate Mortgage** (FRM) is the industry standard that has been in existence for a number of years. While the popularity of the FRM waned during the most recent period of high interest rates, it still continues to be the predominant form of mortgage being used. The FRM, as the name implies, is identified by an interest rate that does not vary over the life of the loan. In other words, if a lender were to commit to an 11.5%, 30 year FRM, the payments to principal and interest would be calculated and would remain constant for the life of the loan.

But while the total monthly payment to principal and interest remains constant, the portion going to the respective parts would vary. The reason for this is simply that the portion of the payment going to interest is calculated based on the outstanding loan amount. Since this outstanding balance decreases over time, the amount of the payment going to interest must correspondingly decrease over time. However, a characteristic of the FRM is that the amount of the outstanding balance decreases very slowly in the early years of the loan, which means that the portion of the monthly payment that goes to principal reduction is relatively small in the early years.

Using the 11.5%, 30 year loan as an example, it is relatively easy to calculate the percent of the mortgage balance remaining, as was illustrated in Chapter 2. For this particular loan, 92.86% of the loan still remains to be paid after the twentieth year. It is only during the last 10 years of the loan that the majority of the outstanding principal is reduced.

The calculation of FRM payments was covered in Chapter 2, so we do not need to cover the specifics again at this time. But it is important to note that the very definition of the FRM is what has made this instrument popular in the past, and will continue to make it popular in the future. Many borrowers like the certainty of knowing what their monthly mortgage payments will be, at least in terms of the portion going to principal and interest. The disadvantage of this type of instrument is that the lender must bear the full burden of the uncertainty of future interest rate changes. To compensate for this uncertainty, lenders usually charge a premium for the FRM over an adjustable rate mortgage instrument that transfers some of this interest rate risk to the borrower. However, the demand for the FRM by these borrowers will continue to ensure its use.

A FRM may be offered for any term, although 25 and 30 year terms are most typical. It is certainly possible to request a 15 or 20 year term from a lender. The advantages of using a shorter term are primarily that the loan is paid off much quicker, contract rates are usually lower, and a substantially lower dollar amount of interest is paid to the lender over the life of the loan.

As an example, assume an $80,000.00, 11.5%, 30 year FRM. Using the techniques developed in Chapter 2, the monthly payment to principal and interest would be $792.23. Multiplying this payment by the 360 months of the term, a total payment of $285,202.80 would be made to the lender over the life of the loan. After subtracting out the original $80,000 principal, that leaves total payments to interest of $205,202.80.

If we use the same assumptions, but substitute a 20 year term for the initial 30 year term assumed, that would increase the monthly payments of principal and interest to $853.14, or an additional $60.91 per month. But since the loan is paid off after 20 years, a total amount of interest of only $124,753.60 is paid. So by paying an additional

$14,618.40 in monthly payments over the 20 year loan period, $80,449.20 in interest can be saved. After subtracting the additional payments of $14,618.40 and ignoring the time value of money, this results in a total dollar interest savings of $65,830.80!

But there may be disadvantages of using a shorter term FRM. One disadvantage would revolve around the opportunity cost of the additional amount of payment. This money may be put to a more profitable use elsewhere. As an example, if there is a 9.0% tax exempt instrument available, a person in a 35 percent tax bracket would be better off putting the additional mortgage payment in the tax exempt instrument, since she would effectively earn a before tax yield of 13.85%. In general, it would be beneficial to invest in the shorter term mortgage only if the after tax yield on the alternative instrument divided by one minus the marginal tax rate is less than the mortgage interest rate. This analysis assumes that it is possible to invest such a relatively small amount in the alternative instrument on a monthly basis.

Still another variation of a FRM involves the making of biweekly payments, and is called a **Biweekly Mortgage** (BWM). The advantages of a BWM are basically that it is a budgetary aid to the borrower and it also allows a much faster loan amortization in that by making a payment every two weeks, a total of 26 payments are made each year.

Example 42:

This concept can best be illustrated by continuing the above example, assuming an $80,000, 11.5%, 30 year loan with a monthly payment of $792.23. If this were set up as a BWM, what would the payments be and how long would it take to amortize this loan?

Dividing the payment of $792.23 by two provides a biweekly payment of $396.12. Keeping the loan amount and interest rate constant, the new amortization term can be calculated based on the 26 biweekly payments of $396.12:

$$\$80,000 = \$396.12 \left(\frac{1 - \dfrac{1}{(1 + .115/26)^n}}{.115/26} \right)$$

$$201.9590 = \left(\frac{1 - \dfrac{1}{(1 + .115/26)^n}}{.115/26} \right)$$

Solving for n provides a new amortization term of 507 compounding periods, which divided by 26 periods per year is approximately 19.5 years, assuming the 11.5% interest rate is compounded biweekly. Obviously, by paying off the loan in 19.5 years instead of 30 years will result in a substantial savings in interest paid by the borrower.

B.   Variable Rate Mortgages

A **Variable Rate Mortgage** (VRM) goes by several different titles, such as an Interest Variable Mortgage or an Adjustable Rate Mortgage. But regardless of the title used, the basic concept of a VRM is the same, that being an interest rate that does not remain constant over the life of the loan. The mechanisms used in the mortgage instrument to allow a change in the interest rate during the loan period will vary by instrument, as will the means of handling any increase in terms of change in payment or principal. But most VRMs could be considered variations of the standard generic format.

The use of VRMs became extremely popular during the early 1980s given the relatively high level of interest rates prevailing during that time. Lenders preferred to shift some of the uncertainty of interest rate changes to the borrowers. So by providing inducements to the borrowers for sharing in this interest rate risk, VRMs had a lower initial contract interest rate than corresponding FRMs, generally from a 1.5 to 2.0 percentage point spread. These lower initial interest rates, sometimes reduced even further and called *teaser rates*, helped induce borrowers into accepting the VRM instruments.

The primary method of determining what the subsequent interest rates of a VRM will be over the life of the loan is to tie the mortgage to some index. Typically, this index corresponds to some government agency financial series or specific financial instrument. Some common indexes are the Federal Home Loan Bank Board's index of average mortgage yields or cost of funds, or any of the Treasury Bill Yields. New "adjusted" contract rates typically run two or three hundred basis points over the one, three or five year Treasury Bill rate to which the mortgage is tied. An acceptable index would have to be one that cannot be manipulated by the financial institution making the loan, although it is possible to find indexes that might favor either the borrower's or the lender's preferences.

While today there are no regulations that limit the changes in the interest rates of VRMs, in the past the existence of regulations gave the borrowers a degree of protection. Prior to 1981, VRMs were restricted to maximum allowable interest rate adjustments, both in timing and magnitude. A limit of one or two adjustments annually, with a maximum of no more than .5% per adjustment, was fairly typical, with no more than a total adjustment of 5.0% over the life of the loan.

Most VRMs today are called **Adjustable Rate Mortgages** (ARMs), with the basic distinction between the two being that the VRMs generally contained the previously mentioned restrictions, while the ARMs do not have any restrictions as to amount or timing of rate adjustments. Despite the fact that those regulations no longer exist, market forces from consumer preferences serve to keep lenders in line concerning the number and amount of adjustments to ARM interest rates. So while changes as often as monthly are permissible, most lenders will attempt to keep change frequency to a minimum so as to remain competitive in the market.

Another form of VRM is the **Renegotiated Rate Mortgage** (RRM), also called a "rollover" mortgage, which was very popular during the 1980-81 period. The RRMs were set up to allow interest rate and payment adjustments every three or five years. Typically, the mortgage instruments had provisions to tie the new rates to some index, but also had maximum adjustments built in, such as no more than .5% or 1.0% change in interest per year, with a 2.5% or 3.0% interest rate cap on a five year RRM.

Given the fact that the RRM was tied to some index, the term "renegotiated rate" is somewhat of a misnomer. But a key feature of the RRM used in the United States, as opposed to those used in other countries, is that the lenders must roll over the RRMs if the borrower has not defaulted during the initial rate term. In addition, there is no prepayment penalty on the RRM mortgages, which means that if more attractive financing is available at the time of renegotiation, the borrower can simply refinance with a new loan.

Regardless of what specific type of VRM the lender is dealing with, be it a VRM, an ARM, or a RRM, the administrative costs involved in changing the interest rates, re-calculating the monthly payments or new balance remaining, and notifying the borrowers in advance is prohibitive to many lenders. When interest rates do change, borrowers are typically given several options as to how to incorporate that change in their mortgage. We now turn our attention to the specific mechanics of dealing with an interest rate adjustment.

Interest Variable Mortgage Mechanics

A.   Changing Payments

The most common means of dealing with a change in interest rates of a VRM is to adjust the monthly mortgage payment. This basically involves calculating the mortgage balance remaining at the time of adjustment, then simply recalculating the new payment based on the new rate and the remaining period of the loan. As an example, assume that an individual has borrowed $75,000 on a variable rate mortgage, with an initial interest rate of 11.0% on a 30 year, monthly amortization. Using the techniques covered in Chapter 1, that would provide an initial monthly payment to principal and interest of $714.24. Additionally assume that after the end of the first year, the index that this particular mortgage is tied to moves up .75%, which makes our new interest rate 11.75%.

To incorporate this change by changing the monthly payment, we first need to calculate the mortgage balance remaining after the first year. Again using the format addressed in Chapters 1 and 2, we get a remaining mortgage balance of:

$$\$75,000.00 \ (.99550) = \$74,662.50$$

The new monthly payments will thus be calculated on this new mortgage amount, the new interest rate of 11.75%, and the remaining term of 348 months. This provides a monthly payment to principal and interest of $765.55, or a 5.92% change in the monthly payment.

This change would be smaller if the lender would use the original 360 month amortization period to calculate the new payment, even though 12 months of the mortgage have already been paid. This is an acceptable alternative, although the resulting lower payment would not be sufficient to completely amortize the loan at the new rate. This would cause a balloon payment to be due at the end of the original loan term if a corresponding decrease in interest rates and payment does not occur during the life of the loan.

B.   Constant Payments with Variable Terms

Still another alternative in dealing with an increase (or decrease) in interest rates would be to keep the monthly payment constant, and simply adjust the term of the loan. As in the above example, again assume that interest rates go from 11.0% to 11.75% during the first year, and further assume that the borrower wishes to keep the monthly payment constant at $714.24. To accomplish this by adjusting the term, the tables would be used in reverse. By this we mean that you would begin with the monthly payment of $714.24 and the new mortgage interest rate of 11.75%. The mortgage constant would be calculated by dividing the mortgage payment of $714.24 by the new mortgage balance remaining of $74,662.50, to get .00957. The corresponding term to provide the same payment with an 11.75% annual contract rate is not listed in the table. In fact, with this large of an increase, it is impossible to set up a loan that will fully amortize the $74,662.50 remaining at a payment of $714.24 at 11.75% interest. While the above format is technically correct, this example does illustrate the insensitivity of payment changes based on increasing the term above the 30 year level. Thus, while this technique is an alternative, it is one that is not commonly used.

C.   Variable Balance Mortgages

A variation of the VRM concerns the adjustment of the amount of the mortgage remaining to be paid given a change in interest rates. The use of a **Variable Balance Mortgage** (VBM) has the primary advantage of keeping the monthly payments constant as well as keeping the initial amortization term constant. In some areas this type of loan is known as a "stretch" mortgage and is popular with borrowers. Lenders, however are concerned about the VBM secondary market appeal if resale is necessary. If interest rates were to increase, then the amount of the fixed payment going to interest would increase, causing a slower rate of amortization of the outstanding balance. If the increase in rates were large enough, this might even result in a "negative amortization," meaning that the borrower is in effect borrowing more money each month to pay the interest owed due to the higher interest rate.

In the case of a negative amortization, a balloon payment would be required at the end of the initial loan term. In the case of a decrease in interest rates over the life of the loan, the loan balance would be retired ahead of the amortization schedule. In reality, any increases and decreases in interest rates over the life of a loan may average out to zero, meaning that in a VBM the payments would remain constant, and the loan would amortize itself over a period roughly equal to the original amortization period, although the portions of the payment going to principal and interest might fluctuate over the life of the loan. The major disadvantage of this type of mortgage instrument stems from the uncertainty of the interest rates. If rates were to increase over the loan period, causing a balloon payment to be due at the end of the original amortization period, it might be necessary for the borrower to sell or refinance the house to meet this balloon payment.

Example 43:

Assume a $120,000 mortgage at 12.5% interest with a 30 year term. This would require monthly payments over the life of the loan of $1,280.71. At the end of the first month, assume that the index to which the interest rate is tied moves up, requiring a new interest rate of 12.75%. How would the balance be affected?

To solve this problem, first we must calculate the mortgage balance remaining after one month :

$$\text{Interest portion of payment} = (.125/12)\,(\$120,000)$$

$$= (.010417)\,(\$120,000)$$

$$= \$1,250.00$$

and the principal portion of the payment would be:

$$\text{Total payment - interest} = \text{principal repaid}$$

$$\$1,280.71 - \$1,250.00 = \$30.71$$

The mortgage balance remaining after one month would thus be:

$$\$120,000.00 - \$30.71 = \$119,969.29$$

In the second month, since the interest rate has increased to 12.75%, the new monthly payment would be calculated as:

$$\text{(new interest rate)} \; (MBR) \; = \text{interest due}$$

$$(.1275/12)\,(\$119,969.29) \; = \$1,274.67$$

Since the object of a VBM is to hold the monthly payments constant, the principal reduction portion of the payment will now be calculated as:

$$\text{Total payment - new interest portion} = \text{principal repaid}$$

$$\$1,280.71 - \$1,274.67 = \$6.04$$

and the mortgage balance remaining after the end of the second month would be:

$$\$119,969.29 - \$6.04 \; = \$119,963.25$$

It should be apparent at this point that a VBM could require extensive calculation if mortgage rates are even the least bit volatile. But with the greatly increased use of computers by lending institutions, the calculation aspect is not a prohibitive problem.

The VBM concept has become increasingly popular during the 1980s, since it allows the lenders to pass on some of the interest rate risk to the borrowers while limiting the budgetary impact on the borrower. There are several different variations of the VBM, where the most common form includes the above example, with the monthly payments remaining constant. Additional variations of the VBM are discussed next.

(1)   Split Rate Mortgage

In this variation of a VBM, the **Split Rate Mortgage** (SRM) consists of payments that remain constant over a given time period, such as three or five years. At the end of that period, the payment would be adjusted to incorporate the amortization of the outstanding remaining balance at the time of renegotiation. In that manner, if interest rates had gone up over the initial period, causing a negative amortization situation, the payment adjustment for the next period of time would preclude a large balloon payment being due at the end of the loan term.

(2)   Capped Payment VRM

The **Capped Payment VRM** (CPVRM) has been around for some time, but has sometimes taken the name of the Wachovia Plan given the pioneering work in this technique by that bank. In a CPVRM, the interest rate is varied with an index at certain intervals (such as monthly, quarterly, annually, etc.). The mortgage payment would be adjusted up or down with each interest rate change. However, the mortgage note would limit the amount the payment could increase over each period or over the life of the loan. In that respect, the upper limit the mortgage payments could reach is *capped*, thus prohibiting extremely high payment movements.

Example 44:

Assume a borrower gives a $150,000 VRM mortgage at 12.0% interest and a 30 year amortization under a capped payment plan. The initial monthly payments would be $1,542.92. Using semi-annual adjustments, assume that the index to which the contract rate is tied requires an interest increase to 13.5% after 6 months. What are the new payments under a CPVRM?

Without a cap on the increase in payments, the new monthly payment would be $1,717.26 based on a balance remaining of $149,735.96 at the end of the 6th month, and a remaining term of 354 months. But if the payments were capped at say a 5% increase for each adjustment period, then the maximum new payment after the first 6 months would be $1,620.07.

The question is then how do you treat the amount of the new payment above the permissible maximum payment? The answer involves determining how much of the new amount owed is tacked on to the outstanding mortgage amount. Since the interest due during the first month of the second payment period is based on 13.5%, the interest portion of the payment would be:

$$\text{Interest Due} = (.135/12)\ (\$149{,}735.96)$$

$$= (.01125)\ (\$149{,}735.96)$$

$$= \$1{,}684.53$$

It is obvious that the interest due in the seventh month exceeds the capped payment of $1,620.07. This would thus leave a deficit of:

$$\$1{,}684.53 - \$1{,}620.07 = \$64.46$$

that would be added onto the remaining balance. Similar additions in each of the succeeding months would be made as necessary, including interest owed on the increased balance as well.

The advantages of this plan are obvious, in that potential increases in monthly payments are limited to a range that the borrowers could still afford. The disadvantage, of course, is that a balloon payment may be necessary at the end of the loan term if overall rates have increased over the life of the loan.

(3)   Price Level Adjusted Mortgages

The **Price Level Adjusted Mortgage** (PLAM) is based on a contract rate that does not change over the term of the loan. The mortgage balance, however, does change based on an index traditionally tied to some inflationary measure, such as the Consumer Price Index (CPI). This type of loan, very common in the South American countries with their relatively high rates of inflation, transfers all of the inflationary consequences from the lender to the borrower.

Example 45:

Assume that a borrower agrees to a 5.0% *real rate* of interest, 30 year amortization PLAM mortgage for $100,000, with annual adjustments. If the inflation rate during the first year is 12.0%, what will the payments be in the second year of the PLAM?

The initial rate is relatively low given the fact that the 5.0% will be the true yield to the lender, which is a historically high real rate of return. The initial monthly payments would be $536.82.

The mortgage balance remaining after the first year is $98,524.63. If the inflation rate, as measured by the index the PLAM is tied to, is exactly zero, then the amount owed would remain at $98,524.63 and the payment would not change. However, assuming that the inflation rate over the year was 12%, this would mean that the new mortgage balance would be ($98,524.63) (1.12) = $110,347.59 at the start of the second year. The new mortgage payment for this amount, at the 5.0% contract interest rate and a 29 year term, would be $601.24.

Obviously, in a PLAM the lender is guaranteed against inflationary induced losses since the increases are all passed to the borrower. The real rate of return to the lender will be equal to the contract rate. While this type of mortgage has been heavily touted, it has not been widely used in the United States given the fact that inflationary rates have not been high enough to warrant it.

(4)   Graduated Payment Mortgages

The **Graduated Payment Mortgages** (GPM) plans were developed to facilitate homeownership among young, upwardly mobile borrowers. The concept behind the GPM is that payments are initially set low to enable the borrower to afford the monthly payment. The payments gradually increase over time as the borrower is better able to afford the higher payments. This is accomplished by having a negative amortization in the early years, i.e. the initial payments are lower than the interest owed on the loan. Eventually the payments will level out at an amount that will not only cover the interest on the loan, but that will also amortize the additional amounts "borrowed" in the early years of the loan.

By definition, any mortgage payment plan that incorporates an increasing mortgage payment after beginning with a payment below a corresponding FRM is considered a GPM. There are a number of variations of the GPM, with most plans differing by how the payments are increased and at what intervals. Most plans, however, have the payment increases specified in advance and usually incorporate the changes in the early years of the loan, giving the payments a chance to level out and then amortize the total amount borrowed. Several types of GPMs are detailed next.

(a) Federal Housing Administration Plans

The Federal Housing Administration was one of the major innovators in the GPM, and had endorsed five major plans where FHA insurance was available. The five plans differ by how fast the plans increase and over what period of time. The plans are:

Plan I   Five years of increasing payments at 2.5% each year, then level payments for the remaining life,

Plan II   Five years of increasing payments at 5.0% each year, then level payments for the remaining life,

Plan III   Five years of increasing payments at 7.5% each year, then level payments for the remaining life,

Plan IV   Ten years of increasing payments at 2.0% each year, then level payments for the remaining life,

Plan V   Ten years of increasing payments at 3.0% each year, then level payments for the remaining life.

A characteristic of each of these plans is that the payments in the early years of the GPM are less than the interest due in the given month, meaning a negative amortization exists. Therefore, the mortgage balance remaining actually increases in the early years. Eventually, the payments level off at an amount sufficient to completely amortize the original amount borrowed plus the additional interest added to the mortgage principal.

Example 46:

Assume that a GPM structured along Plan I is established for $100,000 at a contract interest rate of 13.0% and a 30-year term. What are the monthly payments?

The monthly payment to principal and interest under a normal FRM would be $1,106.20. The first year payment under the Plan I GPM would be $1,015.60 as taken from a set of tables that were calculated using a trial and error procedure. [1]

In the first month of the GPM, the interest owed is (.13/12) ($100,000) = $1,083.33. Since the monthly payment in the first month is only $1,015.60, there is a shortfall in interest paid of $67.73. This amount would be the negative amortization, and is added to the original balance so that at the end of the first month the total mortgage balance remaining is $100,067.73. This process would be repeated each month until the payments eventually became large enough to begin paying not only the total interest owed in the given month, but will amortize the outstanding principal as well.

The advantage of this type of mortgage is obvious, where it might enable a borrower to afford a given mortgage by making the initial payments lower than they would be under a comparable FRM. As can be seen from the above example, the payments under a FRM would be $1,106.20, where the payment under the GPM is initially set at $1,015.60, for an initial savings of $90.60 per month. The disadvantage should also be as obvious, where the borrower would actually owe more than was originally borrowed in the early years of the loan. And, if the price of the home does not increase as rapidly as the deficit payments, the owner could conceivably be faced with having less equity in his home at time of sale than when he bought it.

One variation of a GPM that has recently been advanced is an **Adjustable Rate GPM** (ARGPM). This format would simply combine the elements of the ARM and the GPM, both of which have been discussed in depth.

(5)   Supplemental Account GPM Plans

As a means of providing for the handling of the negative amortization portion of a GPM, lenders have developed **Supplemental Account GPM** (SAGPM) plans. In these instruments a sum of money is pledged in a supplemental account that will exactly cover the planned negative portion of the payments. These plans go by a number of different names, such as **Pledged Account Loans** (PAL), **Flexible Loan Insurance Program** (FLIP), as well as **Equalizer** and **Action** mortgages.

---

[1]See *The Buyer's, Seller's and Broker's Guide to Creative Home Finance*, Miller, N.G. & Goebel, P.G., Prentice-Hall, Inc., Englewood Cliffs, New Jersey, (1983).

All of these plans have one basic thing in common, in that they avoid a negative amortization through the use of a supplemental account. Under a SAGPM, part of the borrower's down-payment is placed in an interest-bearing savings account that is pledged to be used to supplement the monthly mortgage payments. Each month in the initial years of the loan, the lender collects the payment from the borrower that is insufficient to cover the total amount due, but takes out the shortfall in principal and interest due from the pledged saving account. This in effect makes the borrower's payment to the lender "whole," such that there is no negative amortization. The monthly payments made by the borrower increase over time, while the pledged account is eventually reduced to zero as the borrower finally gets the payment level to a sufficient amount to cover the principal and interest due.

Example 47:

Assume a borrower is purchasing a $150,000 home, giving a $110,000 mortgage at 13.0% with a 30-year amortization. The monthly payments necessary to amortize this loan would be $1,216.82. Also assume that the borrower has an additional $10,000 to put into the purchase, and would prefer a lower monthly payment in the initial years. Under this set of assumptions, the borrower could put the $10,000 into an escrow account yielding say 5.5% annually, what would the monthly payments be for three years?

Using the $10,000 escrow account to subsidize the monthly payments for the first three years, the subsidized payment amount is calculated as:

$$\$10,000 = \left(\frac{1 - \frac{1}{(1 + .055/12)^{36}}}{.055/12} \right) (\$PMT)$$

$$\$10,000 = (33.117075)\,(\$PMT)$$

$$\$PMT = \$301.96$$

Thus, for the first three years, the borrower would pay $1,216.82 - $301.96 = $914.86 to the lender. The difference of $301.96 would be taken from the pledged account such that the total payment received by the lender would be the full $1,216.82 owed.

There are several points that are evident from this type of arrangement. The first pertains to the tax aspect of the payment. Under current tax law, the interest portion of the mortgage payment is deductible. So while the borrower is only paying $914.86 directly to the lender in the first three years, he is still able to deduct the full amount of the interest portion of the total payment since the pledged account portion of the payment are part of the borrower's funds. Also, any type of payment could be structured under this arrangement. If, for example, the borrower desired to make even smaller payments in the first year, then increase the payments in the second and third years, this could be incorporated through some additional calculations of the amounts needed to be taken from the pledged account.

(6)   Early Year Interest-Only GPM

One of the simplest variations of a GPM involves an interest-only payment format in the early years. This variation would keep the outstanding mortgage balance constant, i.e. there would be no negative amortization, while lowering the initial monthly payments.

Example 48:

To illustrate the interest-only GPM assumes a $75,000 mortgage at 9.0% interest with a 30 year term. Additionally assume that the first three years would be set up as interest-only payments. What are the monthly payments?

The interest due each month for the first three years would be:

$$\text{Interest Payments} = (.09/12) \ (\$75,000)$$

$$= \$562.50$$

The payments due under a full term amortizing loan would be $603.47, meaning that the borrower would save $603.47 - $562.50 = $40.97 per month for the first three years. However, since the full $75,000 would still be owed after the end of the third year, the borrower would then have to make a payment of $617.34 to completely pay off the original loan in the remaining 27 years. This type of loan could also be used with a plan where the interest rate in the third year could be adjusted if market conditions have changed, making the loan an interest-only GPM with a renegotiable rate feature.

Recent Mortgage Innovations

A.   Growing Equity Mortgages

One of the most popular forms of a FRM is currently the **Growing Equity Mortgage** (GEM). This instrument involves payments that increase over time, similar in concept to a GPM, but the major distinction of a GEM is that the entire increase in payments goes toward principal reduction. The effect of this type of loan is that the loan balance is paid off prior to the original amortization period. The annual increases in payments are agreed to in advance and specified in the mortgage instrument, with the typical increase ranging from 2% to 5% per year.

Example 49:

To illustrate a GEM, assume a $200,000 growing equity loan with an interest rate of 14.0% and a 30 year amortization. Additionally assume that the monthly payments will increase by 3.5% per year for years 2 through 10. What are the payments, and how long will it take to amortize the loan?

The initial payment would be calculated as in a traditional FRM, where the payment to principal and interest would be $2,369.74 per month. Calculating the monthly payments for the second year of the loan would involve multiplying the original payment of $2,369.74 by 1.035, which yields a new payment of $2,452.68. The monthly payments for each additional year would be calculated in a similar fashion, where the payments would level off in the tenth year at $3,229.71. Payments would continue at this amount until the loan was completely paid off.

Again, the increase in monthly payments over the first ten years goes to reducing the principal balance outstanding. Additionally, since the amount of principal is reduced faster in the early years than the normal amortization schedule allows for, the portion of the monthly payments going to principal reduction also increases. The net effect of the increased payments and the decreased principal upon which the amount of interest owed is calculated is a decrease in the term of the complete payoff of the loan. Without illustrating the calculations, in this example the loan would be completely paid off in just under 14 years, instead of the 30 year amortization originally established.

It should be readily apparent that the advantage of this type of plan is that the loan is paid off much sooner than the original amortization period calls for, meaning a substantial savings in interest paid. If the loan in the above example were paid off over the 30 year amortization period, a total interest amount of $653,106.40 would be paid. Using a GEM of the above configuration, the total interest amount paid would be $277,244.32. This savings of $375,862.08 obviously deserves consideration if one intends owning a house for the full 13.75 years of this plan's payoff.

B.   Shared Appreciation Mortgages

With the rapid increase in property value and hence the increased return to investors in the early 1980s, many lenders became discontent with the seemingly small return they were making by earning only interest on a loan. As a result, they created an instrument that allowed them to participate with the investors in the increase in value of an investment. This instrument, called a **Shared Appreciation Mortgage** (SAM), enjoyed a relatively brief popularity with residential mortgage loans, which has since waned slightly given a slowing in the rate of property appreciation.

The percentage of participation by the lender is agreed upon in advance during the underwriting period. For federally chartered lenders, the SAM loan can allow as much as 40% of the net appreciation to go to the lender, with a settlement due in up to 10 years from the date of origination. The settlement can occur sooner if the property is sold, at which time an accounting would be made and the net proceeds would be divided accordingly. In exchange for receiving a portion of the increase in the value of the property, the lender normally charges the borrower a below-market rate of interest. At the time of scheduled settlement, if the property is not sold then an appraisal is undertaken and the borrower must still pay the lender their portion of the "net appreciated value."

This net appreciated value is calculated by subtracting from the market value, which is either the selling price or the appraised value, (1) the original cost of the property, (2) the cost of any capital improvements made by the borrower to the property, and (3) the direct selling expenses of the property, including an appraisal, commissions, title insurance, inspection fees, legal fees, etc.

The concept of the SAMs have been more widely accepted in commercial than in residential finance. While a commercial arrangement can incorporate a SAM, the usual format is to structure a joint venture between a lender and borrower where the lender would share in any increase in value of the property and cash flow during the ownership period, in exchange for charging a lower rate of interest on the initial loan. Also, many residential borrowers have been reluctant to agree to a SAM. The reason for this stems basically from the amount of control given up to the lender by the borrower in something as personal as what you do with your house. The lender now has an even greater interest in how you maintain or modify your home, being particularly sensitive to actions that could negatively affect value. And while there is a limited degree of protection afforded by the structuring of legal documents detailing the rights of each party, all problems and conflicts can obviously not be foreseen.

One reason why the SAMs are not as popular today as they were in periods of rapid price appreciation deals with the risk/return tradeoff to the lender. To compensate for this increased risk, the lender must realize a return that is higher than he would earn on a straight interest only or amortizing loan. If property values do not increase at a fast enough rate, which is often the case in periods of general price stability, the lenders will not be adequately compensated for their increased risk from the use of the SAM. Thus, the SAM loan will usually only be popular to the lender when relatively high rates of property appreciation are expected.

SAM plans have several variations, going by the names **Shared Equity Participation** (SEP) and **Equity Participation Mortgage** (EPM). In addition, a variation of the SAM involving a third party arrangement has become popular since 1982. The arrangement, termed a **Partnership Mortgage**, basically pairs a cash-short home buyer with an investor that wants to put money in housing equity. The third-party investor thus provides all or part of the down payment in exchange for a share of the appreciation of the value of the house. The monthly payments are also split between the buyer and the investor, with the exact arrangement dictated by local custom. These loan types have been pushed not by the lenders, but by real estate brokerage firms who have used the technique as a means of increasing home sales.

C.   Reverse Annuity Mortgages

The **Reverse Annuity Mortgage** (RAM) has been in existence for a number of years, although it is used relatively infrequently. The reason for this stems from the fact that it is more of a retirement annuity than a traditional mortgage. A RAM allows the homeowner to draw down the equity in his home, usually to facilitate a retirement plan. As such, it is typically used by elderly homeowners with significant equities built up in their homes.

The effect of a RAM is to provide the homeowner with a stream of payments from the lender, which is exactly opposite of the traditional mortgage where the homeowner makes payments to the lender. There are two predominant types of RAMs, explained as follows:

(1) The first type involves equal, or annuity, payments made directly from the lender to the borrower. Each payment would increase the balance of the debt owed to the lender, along with compounded interest on the balance. The payments are determined in advance based on the current rate of interest and the length of time over which the "reverse annuity" is needed. The length of time can either be a fixed term or for the life of the borrower.

Example 50:

Assume that the homeowner has an equity in his house of $200,000.00, which is needed to provide living expenses for retirement. If the lender must earn a return of 11.0% interest on any funds advanced, and the homeowner has a life expectancy of 12 years, then a RAM can be constructed. What would the RAM payments to the homeowner be?

Using the techniques covered in Chapters 1 and 2, the amount of monthly payment that would provide a future value of $200,000 at 11.0% interest over 12 years is $673.78. In other words, if the lender pays the homeowner $673.78 each month for 12 years, then a debt of $200,000.00 would be created by the end of that term, assuming an interest rate of 11.0%. At the end of the 12 years, or sooner if the homeowner dies, that debt must be repaid by refinancing or selling the house.

Current regulations do protect the elderly homeowner in that the lender must negotiate the loan at the end of the term with the beneficiary or estate if the homeowner should die prior to the end of the term. In the event of the borrower's death, the proceeds of the estate would be used to pay the lender any funds advanced up to the time of death. To avoid the possibility of a forced sale, many homeowners will purchase a term life insurance policy whose proceeds will be used to pay off the mortgage balance in the event of death of the homeowner.

(2) The second form of RAM involves a lump-sum payment from the lender to the borrower. This is structured as a fixed debt interest-only loan that is then used to purchase either a straight-life annuity or a straight plus variable life annuity combination. The net effect of this form of RAM is to borrow under an interest-only mortgage and use the proceeds to buy a retirement annuity from a life insurance company. In a straight annuity, the annuity payment must be sufficient to cover the interest payments on the mortgage loan. The difference above the interest payment would be paid to the borrower. The annuity plans available from the life insurance companies resemble the plans mentioned in (1) above, where they can be a fixed term or for life. In the fixed term plan, the same disadvantage exists where the property may need to be refinanced or sold at the end of the initial annuity period.

D.   Open Ended Home Equity Loans

In most states, it is possible to borrow against the equity in one's home. There are several ways to go about this, such as taking out a second mortgage for a specific purpose, like a home improvement loan. But it may be desirable to access this equity on an as-needed basis for purposes other than improving the loan collateral, such as financing a child's education or purchasing a new recreational vehicle. In this case, an **Open Ended Home Equity Loan** (OEHEL) would be an excellent vehicle to accomplish such a purpose.

This type of loan is exactly as the name implies, basically being an open line of credit that is secured by the borrower's property. The specifics of the loan can be handled in a number of ways, although one common means is for the lender to agree to provide money on a draw basis to the borrower. A maximum amount of money able to be drawn is set in advance, normally amounting to the difference between any existing liens and 80% of the appraised value. A nominal fee is then normally assessed on the unused portion of the balance, with the borrower paying a fixed or variable rate of interest on the outstanding money actually borrowed.

Example 51:

Assume that the borrower has a property with a current appraised value of $200,000, against which they owe $70,000 on an existing first mortgage. Setting up an OEHEL at the 80% of value figure would amount to a line of credit in the amount of $200,000(.80) - $70,000 = $90,000 being available. Further assume that the borrower needs $30,000 of this available credit immediately, upon which they agree to pay the lender 12.0% annual interest, amortized over a 10 year period on a monthly basis. What are the payments to repay this amount, and what other charges are necessary?

Again using the techniques developed in Chapters 1 and 2, the borrower would pay the lender $430.41 per month in principal and interest each month over the 10 year period to repay the $30,000 actually borrowed. In addition, the borrower would also pay the lender a fee of say 1% of the outstanding credit line per year for the right to keep this credit available. This would amount to an additional ($90,000 - $30,000) (.01) = $600 per year, which could be paid on a monthly or annual basis. Often such loans are adjusted monthly and tied to "prime rates" or "T-Bill rates," such as "prime plus 2.0%."

The advantage of this type of loan is that it allows borrowers to tap their property equity on an as-needed basis, using their property as collateral. While the borrower must pay for this right, it often provides a source of financing that is less expensive than other sources of consumer credit, such as credit cards or unsecured personal loans. A number of major realty and security firms, such as Merrill Lynch and Sears, are entering into the open end home equity loan business.

There are a number of other specific types of mortgage instruments available to borrowers, most of which will be covered in Chapter 4 under Seller Financing and Non-Traditional Mortgages.

CHAPTER 4

SELLER AND NON-TRADITIONAL FINANCING

Seller Financing

With the dramatic increase in interest rates during the late 1970s and early 1980s, many sellers were faced with difficulties in selling their homes. One solution was to offer financial assistance to potential buyers, hence the term "seller financing." During peak interest rate periods such as 1981, the National Association of Realtors estimated that over one half of all existing property sales involved seller financing. While this percentage has dropped with the easing of interest rates and increased home affordability, sellers are no longer forced into providing financing to induce a sale, although there are other reasons which will be discussed in this chapter as to why seller financing will continue.

A. The Tax Angle

One must keep in mind the trade-off between price and terms in all real estate transactions. The more attractive the terms offered, such as with a below-market interest rate charged, the higher the price typically will be. Traditionally, this trade-off has provided a significant tax advantage to sellers. Interest income, such as the interest on the seller provided mortgage, is taxed as ordinary income, where until December of 1986 tax rates extended to the 50% level, falling to 38.5% in 1984, and 28% in 1988. Capital gains received before the end of 1986, such as those received from price appreciation, were taxed at 40% of the ordinary income tax rate, and also could be deferred when homeowners purchased another home at equal or higher price levels within 24 months of the sale of their last home. Under the 1986 tax law, the tax deferral as well as the $125,000 one time exclusion of principal home capital gains have been preserved. Unfortunately, the advantage of the portion treated as capital gains has been removed with the increase in the capital gains rate to that of ordinary income rates. So, while under the old tax laws it was advantageous to lower the interest rate to the lowest legal level while increasing the price to take the maximum benefit of the decrease in tax rates upon monies received, the only advantages which now remain are that of tax treatment, and the possibility of a sale which may not have otherwise occurred.

B.   How Much Financing to Provide?

The more financing provided by a seller, the greater is the postponement benefit of deferred tax liabilities. Under the installment method, the portion of each payment received of principal which would have been profit if paid at the time of sale will be taxed as it is received. This postponement of gains taxation has a present value benefit, but it also has an opportunity cost in that the funds are unavailable for alternative investments. This is why seller financing should be viewed as an investment. Installment sales will be discussed later in this chapter.

To minimize the risk inherent in seller financing, the seller should finance the minimum possible proportion of the selling price. Providing more than the minimum assistance only makes sense if the interest rate provides a market return relative to the risk, or if it creates a sufficiently higher price and faster sale to be worth the risk.

One typical example of seller financing involves what is termed an "80/10/10" arrangement. In this agreement, the buyer gets a new loan in the amount of 80% of the value of the property. The buyer then puts up 10% of the selling price as an equity downpayment, with the seller carrying back the remaining 10% in the form of seller financing. The seller financing is usually short term, in the range of two to four years, at an interest rate slightly below the going market rate. The lien position of the seller financing is secondary to the 80% first mortgage. While the amortization period on the seller financing may be for a longer term to aid in lower payments, or perhaps even be an interest only arrangement, the normal situation in this type of loan is to have a balloon feature. This means that at the end of a stated period of time, such as two years, the entire remaining balance of the seller financed loan becomes due and payable.

The balloon feature of seller financing is one of the primary disadvantages. Many buyers will purchase property in the anticipation that interest rates will drop in the future, or that the value of the property will go up substantially in the near term. Under these assumptions, it is thought that any second liens, including seller financing, can be refinanced when the balances come due. Unfortunately, if these assumptions have not come true, the property may have to be sold or lost at foreclosure if the seller financing cannot be repaid or refinanced at the time of the balloon payment.

Another consideration is the fact that some banks will refuse to lend on a first mortgage if the buyer has not put up enough personal equity. When a lender sees that seller financing is involved in the purchase of property, this often triggers a more strict underwriting of the loan, and possibly a decreased loan to value ratio on the first mortgage.

One facet of seller financing that is often overlooked is the paying of closing costs on the transaction. When seller financing is provided, this obviously reduces the amount of cash received by the seller at the time of closing. Yet the costs of closing the transaction, represented by discount points, assurance of quality of title and brokerage fees, among others, are generally due immediately. So, if the seller does not receive enough funds at the time of closing to cover these costs, additional equity must be put up by the seller. In light of this, it is realistic for the seller to require enough money to be paid by the buyer to one of the parties, i.e. the broker involved in the transaction, if any, to defer their fees until the money from the seller financing is received.

After a seller has "carried paper" as part of their property sale, the next concern is collecting this financed portion when it is due. An alternative to waiting to receive their money is for the seller to sell the second lien "paper" created upon the sale of their property to a third party. There are several ways to accomplish this, such as advertising the loan for sale in the local market. In most cases, selling a second mortgage involves taking a rather substantial discount, sometimes as much as one half of the loan amount, to facilitate a sale. The reason for this is that the loan is considered riskier than a first mortgage, and as such requires a higher rate of return as compensation for the additional risk. Since the contract interest rate of the second lien is often slightly less than the going market rate of mortgage loans, the only way to increase the yield to the purchaser of this loan is to discount it.

Example 52:

Assume you have sold your property and carried back a second mortgage in the amount of $20,000, amortized monthly over 5 years at a contract annual interest rate of 12.0%. You now wish to sell this loan, and find an advertisement in the local paper where an investor offers to purchase second liens at a yield of 25%. What is your second mortgage worth?

The payments to amortize this loan, using the techniques established in Chapters 1 and 2, are $444.89 per month. To find out how much the investor would be willing to pay, the known relationship must be established:

$$\$PV = \$PMT \ (PVa,60 \text{ months},.25/12\%)$$

$$= \$444.89 \left(\frac{1 - \dfrac{1}{(1 + .25/12)^{60}}}{.25/12} \right)$$

$$= \$444.89 \ (34.070014)$$

$$= \$15,157.41$$

Yet another alternative to the loan discounting and sale process is to go through the secondary mortgage market where both first and second lien mortgages are bought and sold. The Federal National Mortgage Association (FNMA), nicknamed "Fannie Mae," has a program that buys mortgages from the initial lenders. To qualify for this program, the loans must be structured and documented in a fashion acceptable to FNMA. This is often not possible without the help of mortgage brokers dealing in this aspect of the mortgage markets, meaning that an additional cost will be incurred by the seller. But this cost may be justifiable, especially if the seller has raised the price of the property as a result of having attractive financing available on the property. In dealing with the secondary mortgage market, the seller must recognize that mortgages are sold at *current market yields*. This means that if interest rates have gone up since the mortgage loan was originated, or if the loan was originated at a below market yield, then the loan will be sold at a discount. In most cases, however, the amount of discount is not as deep as if the loan were being sold to brokers not involved in the Fannie Mae program.

Example 53:

Assume a sales price of $150,000, with an 80% loan-to-value first mortgage of $120,000 made by a conventional lender at 12.0% interest with a 30 year amortization; a $15,000 second mortgage carried back by the seller with a 10 year amortization with a balloon due after 4 years, at 11.0% interest; and the remaining $15,000 paid by the buyer in cash at closing. Further assume that the seller wished to "cash out" of this transaction by selling the second mortgage through Fannie Mae. To qualify for this program, the seller would have to pay a servicing fee to a qualified lender to collect the monthly payments and pass the principal and interest on to the ultimate purchaser of the loan. Assume this will cost the seller .5% of the outstanding balance of the note, resulting in a net contract interest rate of 10.5% to the seller. Finally, assume that the current market yield to Fannie Mae will be 13.0%, which means that for the seller to sell the second mortgage, it will have to be sold at a discount to increase the yield. What is the amount of discount the seller must take to cash out of the second mortgage?

The total principal and interest mortgage payment would be $1,440.97 per month, consisting of $1,234.34 per month on the first mortgage and $206.63 per month to the seller on the second mortgage. The procedure used to calculate the amount of discount, as discussed in Chapters 1 and 2, basically requires solving the relationship:

Discount = 1 - *PV*a(13.0%, 4 yrs) x *MC*(10.5%, 10 yrs) - *PV*s(13.0%, 4 yrs) x *MBR*(10.5%, 4 yrs)

where *PV*a and *PV*s are present values of an annuity and a single sum, respectively; *MC* is the mortgage constant for the net contract interest rate; and *MBR* is the mortgage balance remaining for the designated net contract interest rate and term. Working through this equation provides:

$$\text{Discount} = 1 - \left(\frac{1 - \dfrac{1}{(1 + .13/12)^{48}}}{.13/12} \right) \left(\frac{1}{1 - \dfrac{1}{\dfrac{(1 + .105/12)^{120}}{.105/12}}} \right)$$

$$- \left(\frac{1}{(1 + .13/12)^{48}} \right) \left(\frac{\left(1 - \dfrac{1}{(1 + .105/12)^{72}} \right)}{\left(1 - \dfrac{1}{(1 + .105/12)^{120}} \right)} \right)$$

$$= 1 - (37.275189)(.013493) - (.596185)(.718543)$$

$$= 1 - .502954 - .428385$$

$$= .068661$$

And the dollar value of the discount is $15,000 (.068661) = $1,029.92, which indicates that the seller would only realize $13,970.08 of the $15,000 second mortgage. When this amount is added to the $15,000 downpayment received from the buyer and the $120,000 first mortgage proceeds, the seller would net $148,970.08 on the sale of the $150,000 property, less any transaction costs.

C.   Seller Financing Using Assumable Loans

To this point, the discussion of seller financing has dealt with a straightforward second lien combined with a new mortgage acquired by the buyer from a new lender. An alternative to this is to have the seller provide financing in conjunction with the assumption by the buyer of an existing loan. This was common in the late 1970s and early 1980s, since many loans originated in the late 1960s and early 1970s were relatively low interest rate loans with no due-on-sale or escalation clauses. The combination of a low interest rate assumable loan and seller financing proved to be a strong selling feature to many buyers. Obviously, since there is an advantage to having low monthly payments, many sellers received a premium for their properties in exchange for providing this attractive combination. But this alternative will become increasingly more difficult to find in the future, for two reasons. The first is that since the mid-1970s many lenders have been structuring new loans such that if they are assumable, then the lender has the option of adjusting the future interest rate, which lessens the desirability of assuming the loan. The second reason is that a federal law passed in 1982 allows banks and thrift institutions to enforce due-on-sale provisions of loans that are not specifically written to be assumable.

Due-on-sale provisions give the lender the right to accelerate the loan, i.e. require immediate payment of the mortgage balance by the owner upon the sale of the property. These due-on-sale provisions are worded in a number of ways, some of which simply call the loan due and payable in the event of sale, others that call the loan due even if the property is leased out. Some loans even contain a "due on encumbrance," which means that the property owner is barred from placing a second lien on the property. Obviously, in this type of instrument it would be impossible for the seller to transfer the property with an assumption and seller financing. It should be mentioned that most FHA and VA loans are fully assumable, which means that most future transactions including an assumption of existing financing and seller financing will revolve around these loan types.

Buydowns

With the existence of high interest rates in the early 1980s, "buydown" mortgage arrangements came into existence. This technique basically involves the payment of points to the lender to increase the effective yield on the mortgage, at a given contract rate. Buydowns can be used on any type of instrument, with the points being paid by the buyer, seller, or builder. The paying of points to raise the yield to the lender is not new. Many lenders have charged and continue to charge anywhere from 1 to 5 points as a matter of course in setting their loan terms. This stems from the fact that the contract rate is usually rather inflexible, moving in either one-quarter or one-half percentage point increments. By charging points, lenders can "fine-tune" their yields to achieve an exact return.

The use of points in buydowns by sellers and builders became popular in recent years when relatively high contract interest rates charged by lenders slowed down the pace of home sales. When rates, and consequently monthly payments, rise, many borrowers are pushed out of the mortgage market due to the affordability problem. And in theory when interest rates rise the price of housing will normally fall. But one alternative available to sellers and builders to lowering their prices to facilitate the sale of their property has been to use part of the sale proceeds to pay all or part of the increased financing costs for the buyer. As one would expect, the cost of this buydown arrangement is often passed, at least in part, by the seller to the borrower in the form of a higher selling price. But as long as the net effect to the buyer is to reduce monthly payments, especially in the early years, then this arrangement will still be attractive to many purchasers.

Example 54:

Assume a buyer is faced with paying 15.0% interest on an 80 percent loan-to-value mortgage for the purchase of a $200,000 home. This means that the monthly payment, assuming a 30 year monthly amortizing loan, to principal and interest on the resulting $160,000.00 mortgage would be $2,023.11. Further assume that the buyers are only able to afford approximately $1,700.00 per month at their current level of income, and that they expect the current 15.0% rates to fall within a few years. What would the payments be for the borrower under a "3-2-1" buydown plan, and what would this cost?

One way to overcome this affordability problem is to have the interest rate bought down for the first few years of the loan. The 3-2-1 buydown is fairly typical, which means that the interest rate is bought down 3 interest percentage points in the first year, 2.0% in the second year, and 1.0% in the third year of the loan, with the rate again leveling off at 15.0% in years 4 through 30. If this plan were used, that would make the monthly payments to principal and interest in the first year $1,645.78, which would be within the affordability range of the buyer. The monthly payments in the second year of the loan would be $1,769.92, while the payments to principal and interest in the third year would be $1,895.79.

The cost of this buydown plan is calculated by adding together the present values of each of the payment differences between the actual and the reduced payments for the three years. The calculations in this example would be:

<u>Payment Difference</u>   <u>12 months</u>

Year 1: $2,023.11 - $1,645.78 = $377.33 x 11.0793 x 1.000 = $4,180.55
Year 2: $2,023.11 - $1,769.92 = $253.19 x 11.0793 x .8615 = $2,416.65
Year 3: $2,023.11 - $1,895.79 = $127.32 x 11.0793 x .7422 = <u>$1,046.96</u>

Total Present Value of Buydown $7,644.16

In these calculations, the present values of the monthly differences must be discounted back to the beginning of each year at the 15.0% assumed cost of capital. The resulting present values in years two and three must also then be discounted back to the present by using a present value of a single sum factor, again assuming a 15.0% rate of discount.

The total value of the buydown, $7,644.16, would be paid at the closing of the escrow by either the buyer, seller or builder. As far as the lender is concerned, they are still getting the full amount of their payments for the first three years, but part of it is in the form of a lump sum payment. The buyer is obviously reducing her monthly payment in the early years of the loan, thus facilitating the purchase. Plus, if the interest rates go down in the future as the buyer assumes, she would be able to refinance at a lower rate. And the seller is able to sell the property, even though the buyer may not have been able to afford the payments on the property without the buydown.

An alternative to a 3-2-1 buydown is to have the interest rate bought down over the full life of the loan. This type of arrangement is often used in conjunction with pre-committed financing secured by builders. But as in the previous example, any buyer or seller could also use this type of buydown.

Example 55:

Assume a situation where a builder is developing a subdivision of single-family homes, and as part of the marketing of the subdivision wishes to secure long-term, fixed rate financing on the properties. One method is to approach a lender to receive a "commitment" from the lender for this financing. The builder pays a fee for the commitment, but obviously benefits by having fixed rate financing to offer as an inducement to help market the homes. The lender receives the commitment fee, but must also guarantee the interest rates on the fixed rate loans to qualified buyers, which might not be utilized for a number of months. While the lender will charge higher fees for having to incur this interest rate risk as it goes further into the future (or hedge the commitment in the mortgage futures market), this is nonetheless a fairly common arrangement that benefits both parties.

In addition to the commitment fee, the builder may want to buy down the interest rate on the committed loans to provide even more of a marketing tool. Assume that current market interest rates are 12.5%, with 2 points to close, for 30 year term fixed rate loans. A builder of 20 homes in the $150,000 to $200,000 price range arranges for pre-committed financing of 80% loan-to-value mortgages on each of the homes. To make the homes more appealing, the builder offers the financing at a below market rate of 11.0% interest for the full 30-year term of the mortgage. What would the payments under this buydown be, and what would the cost be?

For the lender to receive the market rate of 12.5% interest, plus the 2 points closing costs on each loan, the amount of points or commitment fees to charge the builder must be determined. Assuming an average price of $175,000, the average loan would be $140,000. The relationship that will provide the amount of points to be charged by the lender on the average loan begins with the monthly difference in payments, which is:

$$\text{Payment Difference} = \$PMT(12.5\%, 30\text{yrs}) - \$PMT (11.0\%, 30\text{yrs})$$

$$= \$1,494.16 - \$1,333.25$$

$$= \$160.91$$

The buyers of the houses with the "subsidized" loans would thus save $160.91 per month on their mortgage payments, which makes the homes more affordable for the buyers. But the lender must collect this additional $160.91 per month from the builder to achieve the required 12.5% interest rate.

To calculate the number of points the lender will charge to raise the yield from the 11.0% stated rate to the 12.5% contract rate, the present value of this difference in payments must be determined. But one further assumption must be made to allow the calculation. It is very common in mortgage finance to assume that the mortgage will not be paid off over the full life of the loan, but instead will be prepaid. The typical assumption is that the average loan will be prepaid within 12 years. So, incorporating a 12 year average life assumption with the previous facts, the calculation required to provide the amount of money the lender must charge is:

$$\$\text{Discount} = (\$160.91)\ PVa(12.5\%, 144\ \text{mo})$$

$$= (\$160.91)\ (74.41266)$$

$$= \$11,973.74$$

Dividing this amount by the $140,000 average loan amount provides approximately 8.5 points to be charged. Further, if the builder wanted to pay all of the points at closing so that the buyer could move in with only the downpayment, then the builder would pay the 8.5 points for the buydown plus the 2 points for closing, for a total of 10.5 points, or approximately $14,700.00 per house.

Obviously, no builder that wishes to stay in business will be able to absorb this type of cost out of profits otherwise realized. So it is expected that most, if not all, of the additional financing fees will be passed on to the buyer in the form of a higher price.

Does this mean that it is a bad deal for the buyer, builder, or lender? Not necessarily, since all parties gain in the transaction.

The lender receives the going rate of interest, 12.5%, for the funds that they have committed, part of which is collected in a lump sum at closing. The seller is able to market the homes using advertising that calls attention to the fact that their homes have below-market financing in place, with the builder paying all points to close. And finally, the buyer receives property with fast, favorable financing, although they probably paid for this financing via a higher purchase price. And even though the lender has assumed that the average loan will be prepaid in 12 years in calculating the amount of points to charge, the individual buyers receive a 30 year mortgage at the 11.0% interest rate.

Buydowns can be a very beneficial method of negotiating a purchase or sale of property, since they are an additional component of the financial trade-off between price and terms. As would be expected, any number of combinations of buydowns can be created, based on the amount of, time period of, and party paying for the buydown. In addition, there may be tax advantages to the seller of paying the points if the tax law continues to allow sellers to deduct this charge in the year of closing while buyers must amortize loan points over the full term of the loan, or until the year the loan is called, if earlier. So it is expected that buydowns will continue to be used in the future, even if interest rates decrease.

Wraparound Mortgages

During periods of low interest rates in the 1960s and 1970s, lenders usually did not put escalation or due-on-sale clauses in the loan notes. This allows the assumption of these loans at the existing interest rate. The amount of the mortgage balance remaining on the existing low interest rate mortgage may not be enough to completely satisfy the capital requirements of the buyer of the property, however the relatively low interest rate is worth preserving. An obvious method of preserving this existing mortgage is to have the buyer assume the first lien, and then give a second mortgage either to the seller or to another lender. Another alternative is to use a "wraparound" mortgage.

A **wraparound mortgage** is a second mortgage that includes, or "wraps around," the existing first mortgage. A wraparound, sometimes referred to as a "blended" mortgage, keeps the first mortgage intact while advancing additional funds equal to the difference between the wraparound mortgage amount and the remaining first mortgage balance. Payments on the wraparound are sufficient to cover principal and interest portions to both the first mortgage and the amount of the additional funds advanced under the wraparound mortgage. The wrapraround lender, whether it be a seller or traditional mortgage source, "services" the wraparound by collecting the total payment and passing the principal and interest portion for the existing first mortgage on to that lender.

Example 56:

To illustrate the use of a wraparound mortgage, assume that you had purchased a house 15 years ago for $50,000. At that time, you had financed the purchase with a $40,000, 9.0%, 30 year FRM. The monthly payments for principal and interest to service this loan are $321.85. The house has increased in value over the years to its present worth of $150,000. The mortgage balance remaining on the first mortgage is $31,732.

A buyer for the house has been found at the $150,000 amount, and while he has $20,000 to offer as a downpayment, he cannot afford a new mortgage at the assumed current mortgage rates of 14.0%. So, to facilitate the sale of the property, you offer a wraparound mortgage in the amount of $130,000, the difference between the $150,000 purchase price and his $20,000 equity. Since you are planning on keeping the low interest rate first mortgage intact, you are actually lending $130,000 minus the $31,732 remaining first mortgage balance, or $98,268. You agree to an interest rate for the new wraparound mortgage of 11.0% with a term corresponding to that remaining on the underlying first mortgage, or 15 years. What are the payments to the buyer on the wraparound, and what is the yield to the seller by providing this financing?

The buyer's payments on the wrapround mortgage would be calculated based on the $130,000 mortgage amount, since that is what he is borrowing. This would make his monthly payment to principal and interest $1,477.58, which is less than the payment would be at the market rate of 14.0%, even with a 30 year amortization. It is obvious then that the buyer benefits by this mortgage arrangement, both with a lower monthly payment as well as a much shorter amortization period. But how do you as the seller fare in this transaction?

First, you would collect the $1,477.58 payment each month on the wraparound mortgage. After collecting the $1,477.58, you in turn make your original payment of $321.85 on the underlying first mortgage, leaving $1,155.73 as principal and interest debt service for the $98,268 actually loaned on the wraparound mortgage. The annual yield to you would be calculated using the methodology developed in Chapter 2:

$$\$PMT = \$PV \ (MC,11.0\%,15 \text{ yrs.})$$

But since the payment going to service the amount actually loaned of $98,268 is known to be $1,155.73, then the same relationship would hold, except now we must solve for the rate of interest, or yield, that equates the known elements:

$$\frac{\$PV}{\$PMT} = PVa(i\%,15 \text{ yrs.})$$

$$\frac{\$98,268}{\$1,155.73} = \left(\frac{1 - \dfrac{1}{(1 + i/12)^{180}}}{i/12} \right)$$

$$85.02678 = \left(\frac{1 - \dfrac{1}{(1 + i/12)^{180}}}{i/12} \right)$$

Solving for i provides a yield of approximately 11.62%. The interest rate earned is greater than the contract rate on the wraparound mortgage of 11.0% due to the fact that you are earning 11.0% on the new funds advanced, as well as 11.0% minus 9.0% or 2.0% on the remaining first mortgage amount. And since the property serves as collateral on the loan, should the buyer default you would be able to foreclose and possibly reclaim the property.

Use of a wraparound mortgage in this example would appear to benefit almost everyone, the one possible exception being the original first mortgage lender. They may not be overwhelmed that the 9.0% first mortgage remains on the books when hopefully it would be paid off, allowing them to re-lend the money at the 14.0% current rate. But if the first mortgage instrument does not contain a due-on-sale or escalation upon assumption clause, then they can do nothing to prohibit the use of the wraparound. It should be mentioned that some sellers have sold property using a wraparound type arrangement where the first mortgage does prohibit an assumption but the seller does not notify the original lender of the sale. In those cases, which in many areas may be illegal, a variation of this technique is used, called an installment sale, or "contract for deed," to which we now turn our attention.

Installment Sales and Land Contracts

Typically, when seller financing is involved in a purchase transaction, title passes from seller to buyer. It may be beneficial for the seller to provide financing not just to facilitate the sale of the property, but to provide a tax advantage as well. Thus, installment sales have become popular since they allow the seller to defer recognition of profits from the sale until the money is actually received.

Tax laws are continually changing, but a treatment common in the 1980s was to allow sellers to automatically qualify for an **installment sale method** upon sale of real property. This applies regardless of how much is received by the seller in cash at the close of escrow. Under this method, the profit from the sale of the property is calculated as the difference between the sales price, minus all selling costs and capital improvements, and the original purchase price. The percentage profits of the total selling price is calculated and applied to the principal portion of the mortgage payments received by the seller in determining taxable income in each year that the payments are received. In addition, the Internal Revenue Service (IRS) may treat part of the payments as interest on the amount carried as installment payments, if an interest rate for this carried amount is not specified in the sales contract. In this case, the interest rate will be imputed by the IRS at the prevailing federal rates.

The greatest advantage to the seller of using an installment sale is that profits are not taxed until they are received, rather than at the time of sale. Installment sales are generally more common on commercial rather than residential transactions, due primarily to the deferral feature allowed on owner occupied principal residential sales. The tax law has been such that sellers can defer all taxes on capital gains from the sale of their personal residences if they purchase another home of equal or greater value within 24 months of the first sale. In addition, if the seller is 55 years of age or older, they may take a once-in-a-lifetime exclusion of $125,000.00 of all profits on the sale of personal residences, with certain restrictions.

But with the constantly changing tax law climate, these influences on the use of seller financing may shift the orientation of installment sales. The best strategy for a buyer or seller of real estate to follow is to get competent advice from an accountant or tax attorney prior to entering any real estate transaction that could be considered out of the ordinary, and then follow that advice.

As discussed in the previous sections, some sellers have low interest rate loans that exist on their properties which they would prefer to be able to keep intact to aid the sale of the property. But if the mortgage instrument prohibits an assumption of this lien, it might be necessary for the seller to keep the title in their name while at the same time providing financing for the buyer. Or the seller might own the property free and clear, but want to sell it with the use of seller financing while retaining title. These are primary examples of a **land contract**, also called a **contract sale** or **contract for deed**.

The example of a wraparound deed in the previous section illustrates the mechanics of a land contract with existing financing. When no existing financing is present the payments would be calculated just as in a first mortgage, be it a FRM or any other variation. The basic feature of a land contract is that the seller provides financing for the buyer, whether there is an existing first mortgage or not, while title to the property remains with the seller. After all of the payments have been made to the seller, the title is then transferred to the buyer. As one would expect, there are advantages and disadvantages in this arrangement for both parties.

The seller retains title, making it easier to foreclose on the note in the event of default. But retaining title also means that the seller is legally responsible for all taxes and assessments on the property, as well as any other liens that might be created. The obvious advantage to this transaction for the buyer is that they receive financing that might not be available to them elsewhere, often at very favorable interest rates. Because they do not receive title to the property at the time of closing, there is an added risk. Sellers have been known to transfer property under a land contract to one purchaser, only to turn around and re-sell the property to one or more additional purchasers! This is possible if the buyer does not record their interest in the property. Although the first purchaser may have legal recourse against the seller in such a situation, that may not help them retain possession of the property.

Buyers can protect themselves from this type of occurrence simply by getting a title abstract or title insurance policy at the time of purchase to make sure the seller has good title, and then recording their interest in the property at the time of the transaction. Remember, all interests in land are recordable, and should in fact be recorded to be enforceable. The moral is that if a seller asks that you not record your interest, possibly for the reason of their attempt to hide the "illegal" sale of the property from a first lien holder that had a due-on-sale clause in the mortgage, make sure you get legal advice on how to proceed prior to consummating the transaction.

Lease with Purchase Option or Purchase Contract

In some instances, it is not possible for the seller and buyer to come to an agreement on the purchase of the property. This may be due to several factors beyond disagreement concerning price, such as the buyer not having sold their old home or the buyer not being able to qualify for a loan to purchase the property or the seller not being in a position to transfer title until some point in the future. One solution to this dilemma is to structure a **lease purchase** arrangement.

Typically, when a lease purchase is set up, the prospective buyer takes possession of the property in exchange for the payment of rent. Title rests with the seller, but a contract is drawn that specifies the conditions of the "future" purchase. These conditions will include not only the amount of the purchase price, but also the amount of the escrow, the terms on which escrow may be forfeited, the date of closing, whether the rent payments are applied to the purchase price, as well as the normal contractual items relating to documents and closing costs.

Example 57:

To illustrate, assume you are attempting to sell your home in a relatively slow market, and are able to move without taking your home equity along. After having listed the property for nine months with several different real estate agents, you finally place a sign in the front yard and attract a prospective purchaser through an open house. Several problems exist in completing the sale transaction, one being that the buyer lives out of state and will be moving his family to your town in six months, although he needs a place to live right away. In addition the buyer wants to purchase the property subject to getting a VA mortgage at the low prevailing interest rates. What is the most attractive alternative in structuring this transaction?

Given these circumstances and the uncertainty of whether the buyer will qualify for the new loan, the logical solution is to lease the property to the buyer while structuring a contract for the ultimate purchase. But there is obvious risk to the seller in this transaction. If the buyer is not approved for the new loan, then the seller has given up possession of the house and will have to begin marketing it again, while at the same time incurring the transaction costs of having moved their belongings to another residence. So it is reasonable for the seller to require a relatively high escrow amount that will be forfeited in the event the buyer does not go through with the purchase for any reason other than not being approved for the loan. The seller would also expect to receive rent payments sufficient to cover their out of pocket property expenses and an amount sufficient to compensate them for the added risk of moving out of the property only to have the buyer ultimately fail to exercise the purchase "option." While the rental payments are agreed upon by both parties subject to the above considerations, local market conditions will also dictate to an extent the amount of rent that the seller will be able to charge.

Thus, you negotiate an agreement with the purchaser such that you agree to sell the house for $83,000, with the purchaser to apply for a VA loan in the amount of $78,000 and the remaining $5,000 to be paid in cash at closing. The buyer must apply for the loan within 7 days of the execution of the contract, and must be approved within 10 weeks of application for the contract to remain valid. Closing on the purchase will occur within 2 weeks of loan approval, making the closing date 3 months after execution of the sales contract. At the same time the purchase contract is executed, a residential lease document is prepared whereby the purchaser takes possession of the property within

2 weeks of execution of the contract. Rent is to be 1.0% of the sales price per month, or $830, payable in advance of each month.

The amount of escrow is set at $3,000, which is several times higher than the normal rate on a transaction of this size in this particular area. The reason of the higher escrow amount is to partially compensate for the lack of security deposit on the lease, but more importantly to assuage the risk the seller bears by giving up possession of the home prior to the closing of the sale. If the term of the lease were longer than 3 months, the purchase price might be raised to further compensate for the risk to the seller, or the amount of escrow might also be raised or made non-refundable for any reason.

While the example above is relatively straightforward, some lease purchase transactions can be quite complex. It goes without saying that if you are involved in a transaction that is for a long period of time or has any other twists or turns, an attorney should be involved in preparing the documents.

A recent variation of the lease purchase arrangement has been in existence since 1981. Termed the **Homeowners Easy Land Lease Program** (HELP), it is a product of the Assurance Financial Corporation based in Irvine, California. The concept of HELP is very simple; the homeowner purchases the house but leases the land on which the house is located. This reduces the amount of money the buyer needs to purchase the house since the land is not included in the purchase price. The buyer can therefore qualify more easily for the loan because the needed loan amount is less.

The program is set up so that the land is leased to the buyer at a fixed rate of 8.0% of the land value per year, with payments made monthly. The land value is adjusted annually and is tied to movements in the Consumer Price Index (CPI). But the amount of the lease rate remains fixed at 8.0% per year. Obviously the lease payment will rise over time as the CPI increases, but unless a period of rampant inflation again ravages the economy, this should present little problem to the typical homebuyer. In terms of the loan qualification process, the lender would take the lease payment in consideration along with the borrower's other fixed payment obligations. But this should again provide the borrower with an advantage given the reduced loan amount and resulting lower monthly payments of not having to purchase the land.

The lease is set up with a 55 year life, allowing the buyer to remain on the lot even after the mortgage on the house has been paid off. Further, the buyer has the option of buying out the lease at any time in the future, should interest rates fall or the buyer's income rise enough to allow the purchase. However, the lease must be paid in full if the property is sold prior to the expiration of the lease.

Although HELP has been around since 1981, it has not enjoyed overwhelming acceptance. However, it has gained approval by FNMA of purchasing mortgages of houses with leased lots, so HELP should become more popular in the future.

Land leases on residential homes are very common in some areas of the country, principally in Hawaii. In Hawaii a property is known as either a "leased fee," where the land is leased, or "fee" estate where the land comes with the building. To the extent such land leases have been "inexpensive," often as low as $100 per month on a $200,000 house, they have forced up home prices by allowing more of a buyer's income to be put towards the building portion of the home price. With many of these long term land leases now being renegotiated, land leases are being increased several times over. The problem with separate land ownership is the monopoly power it creates over the owner of the house, unless the land lease includes a purchase option at a predetermined price or formula to derive the price. The lack of such a repurchase option is now driving many Hawaiian leased fee homeowners into the courts. The Hawaiian experience should make new homeowners cautious of setting up even long term land lease arrangements.

Convertible ARM

One of the "innovative" mortgage instruments that has received attention since the mid-1980s has been the **Convertible ARM** (CARM). Traditionally, a "convertible" mortgage refers to an arrangement whereby a lender takes a progressively greater equity interest in the mortgaged real estate in lieu of cash amortization payments by the borrower. In a sense, this type of mortgage is a joint venture between the lender and borrower. Recently, however, a new definition for a convertible mortgage has surfaced in reference to an ARM.

In a CARM, the mortgage begins as a normal ARM, with interest adjustments every 6 or 12 months. But after a specified period, typically three years or more, the borrower can choose to convert the unpaid principal balance into a FRM at the then current FRM interest rates. For instance, assume that current FRM interest rates are running around 12.0% on a 30 year amortized loan, while ARM interest rates are only 10.0% with annual adjustments. Further assume that after three years, the ARM has increased to 13.0%, due to increases in the index to which the ARM is tied, while the FRM rates have remained steady at 12.0%.

Under the CARM, you would be able to convert your ARM to a FRM, thus reducing your interest rate and locking in at the prevailing FRM rate for the remainder of the mortgage term. As one would expect, there is a price for this convertibility. It may be a higher fee at closing, although typically it is a slightly higher initial interest rate on the ARM.   In addition, the lender will normally charge a refinancing fee of say 1.0% of the outstanding balance at the time of conversion.

The cost of financing with a CARM can be much less expensive in the long run if rates do increase substantially. In the event interest rates in general remain stable or even decrease, it is to the borrower's advantage to keep the ARM and forego the cost of conversion, assuming their corresponding ARM index has remained stable. But if rates rise, converting to the FRM under the convertible arrangement would cost less than simply refinancing. As previously discussed, refinancing any type of mortgage will normally cost a minimum of three points in fees, title policies, appraisals and other associated closing costs.

One of the greatest advantages of using the CARM is the flexibility that the borrower obtains in controlling the type of instrument to use, even after the initial financing decision is made. CARMs have been extremely popular since the mid-1980s, again due in large part to FNMA's decision in late 1984 to purchase convertible adjustables as a standard loan product.

Money-Back Mortgages

There continue to be a number of "promotional" mortgage types advanced by sellers and builders that come into vogue from time to time. Normally they are simply variations of the mortgage types covered previously. We will close this chapter with one such promotional mortgage instrument that has gained fairly widespread use, although it is recognized that it might fade away as fast as it materialized.

The mortgage is popularly referred to as a **money-back mortgage**, which supposedly allows homebuyers to get in on owning a home while still putting something away for the future. The mechanics of this mortgage are very simple; buyers are presented with a zero-coupon municipal or Treasury bond at closing that is equal to the price of the house. When the bond matures in 30 years, the owner can receive the full purchase price back by cashing in the bond.

Since the bond is not attached to the house, the buyer can do anything they wish with it. The longer the bond is held the more it is worth. But it could be cashed in at anytime, say in 15 years to help pay for a child's college education. Since the bond pays off only when it is sold, it does not provide a yearly income. It is tax free until sold. Capital gains taxes are paid only on the initial face value of the bond, and not on the compounded interest as earned by the bond over its life.

To illustrate the concept, assume that you purchase a home for $100,000, getting a FRM from a lender for $80,000. At closing the seller presents you with a zero-coupon municipal bond with a face value of $100,000, maturing in 30 years. The cost of this bond to the seller will vary with the prevailing rates of interest on these instruments, but will normally be approximately 3.0% to 4.0% of the face value. In this example, assume the seller paid $4,000 for the bond presented to you at closing.

The seller has probably advanced the logic that you are in effect getting the house for "free," since you have been presented an instrument that will give you the full purchase price back when the loan matures. But as we now know, there is no such thing as "free" in mortgage finance! While it is true that you have received something of value in addition to the property you have purchased, the price of the house was no doubt raised to cover the cost of the bond, either all or in part.

If you as the buyer recognize that you are probably paying for the bond, which is actually an annuity, is this a bad deal for you? Not necessarily, since it is included in the cost of the house and therefore financed in part and paid for over the life of the loan. The real trick if dealing with a seller offering this type of "promotion" is to get the purchase price of the property discounted back to its true worth, and then also get the bond thrown in as part of the deal. This would be akin to having your cake and eating it too!

CHAPTER 5

LOTUS TEMPLATES

Introduction

This chapter is written for Lotus 1-2-3 (1-2-3) users. Beginners, with very little knowledge of spreadsheets, should benefit by being able to immediately analyze more difficult mortgage math problems. Advanced users of Lotus should be able to see some fairly efficient ways of setting up a template for mortgage problems or unique types of mortgages. The actual templates are provided, rather than machine compiled versions, so that users will be able to modify them and develop their own variations. In order to conserve disk space, a macro is used to generate the initial spreadsheets, which may then be saved under any name the user wishes. The process is discussed below.

A.   Disclaimer

Many software products contain errors. When calculating mortgage payments, errors can result from improper use, improper assumptions, or where the use attempted is an exception to the typical case. While attempts have been made to minimize errors in these templates, we do not warrant that they are error free, nor do we wish anyone to rely on them without first testing the results for confirmation with known correct answers.

B.   Before Starting

The 5 1/4" disk provided is a double density, double sided disk set up for an MS-DOS based computer. If you need another type of disk, or a 3 1/2" disk, please see the instructions noted with the disk.

(1) For hard disk users only

Copy this disk to your hard disk, as follows:

a) type: **cd\123**   (this will change your hard disk to the lotus directory),

b) insert the disk in drive A and type: **COPY A:*.*   C:\123**
(this should copy all of the files from the disk to your 1-2-3 directory, assuming your hard drive is drive C).

111

(2) For disk drive only units

You will need to insert the disk in the A: drive each time you use a file. You will have to preface all file names with "A:." It is suggested that you make at least one or more backup copies of the disk before starting, and then work with a disk that is only partially full, so that you may save changes under another file name. If you have only one drive, then you will have to pull up the files (using the retrieve command as shown below), one at a time, and save them on a new disk.

Template Description

AUTO123.wk1 is the master MACRO file which briefly describes the contents of the disk, *and generates each template you need*. The screen will appear basically as illustrated in Table 5-1.

TABLE 5-1   AUTO123.wk1 File Screen

Enter a number and press 'Return' or 'Enter' ...

File	Function
1 PHAPR	Calculates APR, loan balance and effective yield with prepayment at a given month.
2 PHPOINTS	Calculates points required to change APR.
3 PHAMORT	Calculates mortgage payment schedule.
4 PHARM	Calculates ARM payments with interest rate change.
5 PHVBM	Calculates variable balance mortgage with rate change.
6 PHWRAP	Calculates payments and effective yield with a wraparound second mortgage.
7 PHGEM	Calculates payments with a growing equity mortgage.
8 PHREFIN	Calculates benefits from refinancing.
9 PHBUYRENT	Calculates value of buying versus renting.
10 PHQUAL	Calculates affordable home based on various criteria.
11 PHPROFOR	Calculates simple cash flow pro forma and lender ratios for 10 years.
12 PHPV-FV	Calculates present or future value of a single sum or an annuity.
13 PHPVTAB	Calculates present value and future value tables for single sum or annuities for up to 40 years.
14 HELP	Instructions for using these templates.
15 QUIT	Returns to Lotus 1-2-3 READY mode.

For all of the above templates, macros have been set up which will print out the summary of results. These macros will only work with a dot matrix printer which can compress print. Laser printers require the user to use the print commands in a more typical Lotus fashion, with a pre-defined range. Most of the templates are set up with the manual calculation key set "on", which means that you must hit the **F9** key each time you want a recalculation. By requiring the **F9** key, you may make several changes at one time, with less time required between the changes. Each recalculation takes from a few seconds to a few minutes, depending on the speed of your computer, and the spreadsheet you are using.

A.   Beginning from AUTO123.wk1

This master template generates the template that you select, in a two step fashion. First, it calls up the template file of interest which is only partially formed on the disk enclosed. Then it uses a *macro*, based on your answers, to generate the full template. The first time you use this process, the template selected will run slower, since it is generating the full file. In order to speed up the process, save the new template, under any file name of your choice, and use that file for all similar calculations in the future. If the retrieved file does not work for the new problem, then start back at AUTO123.wk1 again, and generate a new file.

B.   Using the Menu Driven Files

Each of the files selected has the following commands at the top of the spreadsheet. These commands can be selected by using the arrow keys and pointing to the desired command:

INPUT/SOLVE: This is used when new inputs are desired. When the enter key is hit twice, the template will be formed and all answers will be recalculated.

PRINT: This command will print the output desired.

SAVE: This command is used to name and save a file. This should always be used when a file may be needed again. Any name can be used, as long as it is eight characters or less. The next time this type of file is needed, using an old file will calculate much faster than when developed using the auto menu version, which creates the spreadsheet from scratch each time.

NEW-FILE: This will allow the user to choose another file for development. If it does not work, or shows an error, then it is because the AUTO123.wk1 file was not saved in the 1-2-3 general directory, but another subdirectory. In this case go back to /, **F**, **R** (backslash, file retrieve) commands and select the desired file in the normal lotus fashion.

READY-MODE: This will start back at the input mode again for any given spreadsheet. One may also use the simultaneous **ALT** and **S** keys to get back to the ready input mode, *if* the "type **ALT S**" message appears.

C.   Speeding up the Computer and Trouble Shooting

On many older computers, such as the IBM XT or PC or similar clones, without math coprocessor chips, these templates may take as long as ten minutes to run the first time starting from the macro driven menus listed previously. On newer computer models the macro driven approach may take up to two or three minutes. The reason that the files run so slow is that a macro command is telling the computer how to set up the template file from scratch each time. This means that all of the calculation formulas are being copied to the appropriate rows and cells, and then the specific inputs are being used to recalculate the desired output. *This process of building the file from scratch is only necessary once.* In all future runs using that file, the user may take a faster route. First, save the file using the **SAVE** command, at the top of the file, under a name which is easy to remember. Next time that same type of file is desired, use the lotus file retrieve commands to pull the file back. This is /, **F, R**, and then the file name under which it was saved.   Now, there will be no macro at the top of the file, and the user must use regular 1-2-3 commands, such as the **F9** to recalculate and the **Print, Range, Align, Go** commands to print out the results. But the recalculation will be much faster.

Another approach, which retains the macro driven commands, is to go into the **READY-MODE**. This can be done anytime by entering **R** for **READY-MODE** when this command is shown at the top of the file. Once this command is entered, one must use ordinary 1-2-3 commands in order to input and recalculate a spreadsheet file. However, once the recalculation is finished, the user can return to the macro commands in order to simplify printing and saving. This is done by pressing **ALT** and **S** simultaneously, *if* the "type **ALT S**" message is showing.

Some typical problems may include:

(1) The user hits **ALT** and **S** simultaneously but no menu appears:

Be sure to start from AUTO123 so that the macro commands are available. If one starts from a prior saved file, then the AUTO123 will not work. To start over hit /, **F, R**, then select **AUTO123**, and then any given file. One may then use the commands at the top to retrieve a previously saved file. Next use the **ALT** and **S** keys to return the macro commands to the top of the screen. *Do not hit ALT S if in the input/solve mode*, but instead hit the return key to leave that mode.

(2) The user hits **New-File** but the AUTO123 file list does not appear.

If this occurs, then the AUTO123 file was not saved in the general 1-2-3 directory, or the user is running the file in another subdirectory of 1-2-3, and the macro command is searching for AUTO1-2-3 but cannot find it. The user should re-copy the disk files into the 1-2-3 directory, and be sure not to use any sub-directories for saving files. If sub-directories are desired, then one must use regular 1-2-3 commands on saved files, or change the default directory on the macro command which saves the files and retrieves them as desired.

(3)   The print range results in an overflow which does not fit on one page.

If this occurs, then there are two options. The easiest is to use external commands located on the printer to compress the print, before printing. The other approach is to use the manual which comes with your printer to find out what type of string command to use to compress the print using Lotus 1-2-3 commands located in Print, under Set Up.

Starting with the Basics: Mortgage Payments, APR and Points

A. Using the PHAMORT.wk1 File

First load Lotus 123, then retrieve the file, using commands **/**, **F**, **R**, then either **A:PHAMORT.wk1** or **C:\123\PHAMORT.wk1** depending on where the file is, and whether you have a hard drive. If you are already in 1-2-3, you can start from the AUTO123.wk1 file and select **A:PHAMORT.wk1**, as described previously. You may later wish to use previously generated templates which have been saved if similar to those desired. After the file is loaded, notice that the cells for the inputs are in bold, or are of a different color if you have a color monitor. These are the only places where you have to type any information into the spreadsheet.

This template calculates the mortgage payments and provides an annual and a monthly summary of the results. Loans may start in any month, and as a result may end up with a partial year in the final year of the schedule. The inputs are:

(1) loan amount in cell D9 (enter without commas or $ sign),

(2) annual contract rate of interest in D10 (enter as decimal, ex., .10 for 10.0%),

(3) term of the loan in years in cell D11,

(4) month of origination, 1 through 12, in cell F10,

(5) year of loan origination in cell F11,

(6) use the **F9** key to recalculate, or hit the return key twice to recalculate inputs.

Table 5-2 contains a sample of the approximate image which the user should see when using this file, along with some of the annual summary of output. With a loan for $60,000 at 10.0% interest, amortized over 30 years the monthly payments are $526.54. The balance is shown at the end of each year, but could as easily be shown at the end of each month. Use the arrow keys to explore the lower part of the spreadsheet, or the page down key to move more quickly. To move to the end of a row or column, hit the end key then the arrow in the direction you want to move.

After reviewing the output, several other options are then available. If the output is acceptable, then the file can be saved or printed, simply by keying in **ALT S**

TABLE 5-2   PHAMORT Input and Output Summary

File Name: PHAMORT
AMORTIZATION TABLE FOR UP TO 30 YEARS
Inputs are shown in bold below.

File Input

LOAN AMORTIZATION SCHEDULE
~~~~~~~~~~~~~~~~~~~~~~~~~~~~~~

Loan Amount:	**$60,000.00**		
Annual Interest Rate:	**10.0%**	Month =	**9**
Term of Loan (years):	**30**	Year =	**89**
Monthly Payments:	$526.54		
Origination Date:	Sep-89		

File Output

ANNUAL TABLE

	Year	Mortgage Payment	Interest	Repaid Principal	Ending Balance
	====	======	=======	=======	========
1	1989	2,106.17	1,998.67	107.51	59,892.49
2	1990	6,318.52	5,973.73	344.78	59,547.71
3	1991	6,318.52	5,937.63	380.89	59,166.82
4	1992	6,318.52	5,897.74	420.77	58,746.05
5	1993	6,318.52	5,853.68	464.83	58,281.22
6	1994	6,318.52	5,805.01	513.51	57,767.71
7	1995	6,318.52	5,751.24	567.28	57,200.43
:	:	:	:	:	:
30	2018	6,318.52	714.06	5,604.46	4,058.67
31	2019	4,212.34	153.67	4,058.67	0.00

to get the macro menu, and moving the pointer to the desired option with the arrow or space keys, then hitting the return key. This same sequence can be used if the example needs to be redone, by selecting **INPUT/SOLVE**, or if a different spreadsheet is desired, by selecting **NEW-FILE**.

B. Using the PHAPR.wk1 File

This file calculates not only the Annual Percentage Rate (APR), but also the effective yield on a mortgage. Recall that the APR is based on the assumption of no early prepayment, and the effective yield is based on the expected period until prepayment. When a mortgage loan involves points, the earlier the loan is prepaid the greater will be the effective yield, although the APR by definition does not change. After selecting the **PHAPR** file from the main menu, the inputs are as follows:

(1) original loan dollar amount in cell D6 (without commas or $ sign),

(2) annual interest rate in cell D7 (enter as decimal),

(3) original term in months in cell D8,

(4) closing points in cell D9, where 1.0 point equals 1% of the loan (enter as number, ex., 2.5 for 2.5 points),

(5) month of expected prepayment in cell D10,

(6) prepayment penalty, if any, in cell D11 (enter as decimal, ex., .01 for 1.0%),

(7) use the **F9** key to recalculate, or hit the return key twice to recalculate.

The options available after running the program are similar to those discussed above. Some results from the use of this template are provided in Table 5-3.

TABLE 5-3   Selected PHAPR.wk1 Output

Contract Rate	Term in months	Points	Prepayment Month	APR	Effective Yield
9.50%	360	5.0	84	10.10%	10.54%
9.75%	360	3.0	84	10.11%	10.37%
9.75%	360	3.0	60	10.11%	10.54%
10.00%	360	1.0	84	10.12%	10.20%

C. Using the PHPOINTS.wk1 File

This file is used when one wants to know how many points to charge in order to bring a given contract rate up to a desired APR. Here one of the outputs is the number of points to charge, and one of the inputs is the desired APR. Inputs are as follows:

(1) original loan dollar amount in cell D8 (without commas or $ sign),

(2) annual interest rate in cell D9 (enter as decimal, ex., .09 as 9.5%),

(3) original term in months in cell D10,

(4) desired APR in cell D11 (enter as decimal),

(5) month of expected prepayment in cell D12,

(6) prepayment penalty, if any, in cell D13 (enter as decimal, ex., .01 for 1.0%),

(7) use the **F9** key to recalculate, or hit the return key twice to recalculate inputs.

The template input and output look similar to that shown in Table 5-4. Notice that in this case the contract rate was entered as 9.75% and the desired APR was entered as 10.11%, but the points were calculated. The results are the same as the one used in the PHAPR file, but this file requires no trial and error to achieve a given target APR. Trial and error would be necessary if the effective yield desired for a given prepayment term were the target. Results may vary slightly from the other PHAPR file results because of rounding.

TABLE 5-4   PHPOINTS.wk1 Input and Output Summary

File Name: PHPOINTS
CALCULATION OF APR OR DISCOUNT POINTS TO CHARGE
Inputs are shown in bold below.

File Input

LOAN AMORTIZATION SCHEDULE
~~~~~~~~~~~~~~~~~~~~~~~~~~~~~~~~

Original Loan Dollar Amount:	**$100,000**
Annual Interest Rate:	**9.75%**
Original Term (months):	**360** (Up to 360 months)
Desired APR:	**10.11%** (Enter .1011)
Month Prepayment Occurs:	**60** (Up to the full term)
Prepayment Penalty as percent of Balance:	**0.00** (Occurs in prepayment month)

File Output

The mortgage payment is	$859.15
Balance at the end of the 60th month:	$96,410.99
The annual percentage rate is:	10.11%
The percentage points charge will be:	3.00%
The points charge in dollars is:	$2,998.34
The effective yield	10.54%

Mortgage Variations

A. Using the PHARM.wk1 Adjustable Rate Mortgage File

This file is similar to PHAMORT where mortgage payments are calculated, except that the interest rate may vary for the second through eleventh years of the loan. The mortgage payments are adjustable based on the interest rate applied. The user must input all of the information normally required for a loan, as well as annual forecasts of mortgage rates (as a proxy for the index and margin which a lender may actually use). Other critical inputs include the annual cap and life cap, for the maximum amount that the interest may vary for a given year or for the life of the loan.

The applied interest rate in any given year is based on the lower of 1) the market rate, 2) the original rate plus the life cap, or 3) the prior year rate plus the annual cap. If the actual market rate exceeds the applied rate, then this interest rate risk is absorbed by the lender, and the cap interest rate constraints protect the borrower. However, if the applied rate equals the market rate, then the interest rate risk is being fully absorbed by the borrower.   The lower the life and annual caps are set, the more sensitive is the lender's position to interest rate risk, and the higher the initial mortgage rate is likely to be set. Inputs are as follows:

(1) Loan dollar amount in cell D8 (without commas or $ sign),

(2) Initial contract rate in cell D9, entered as a decimal,

(3) Loan term in years in cell D10,

(4) Points up front in cell D11,

(5) Annual cap rate limit in cell D12, entered as a decimal,

(6) Total life cap rate limit in cell D13, with the margin over the index in D14,

(7) Month to start the loan in cell F9, and year to start the loan in cell F10,

(8) Interest rate forecasts are input starting in C17, for years 2 through 11. The last year's rate is assumed to hold for the remainder of the loan life.

Output is provided in both annual and monthly summary form.

Experiment with the annual and life caps and examine the effect on the applied rate.   An example of the file format for input is shown in Table 5-5. The output is similar to the output for fixed rate amortization schedules.

TABLE 5-5   PHARM.wk1 Input Summary

File Name: PHARM
AMORTIZATION TABLE FOR UP TO 30 YEARS FOR ADJUSTABLE RATE LOAN
Inputs are shown in bold below.

LOAN AMORTIZATION SCHEDULE
~~~~~~~~~~~~~~~~~~~~~~~~~~~~~~~

Loan Amount:	**$60,000.00**		
Initial Contract Rate:	**10.0%**	Month =	**9**
Term of Loan (years):	**30**	Year =	**89**
Annual Rate Cap:	**0.50%**		
Total Life Cap:	**6.00%**		
Initial Monthly Pymts:	$526.54		
Origination Date:	Sep-89		

Enter your forecast of mortgage rates below, ignoring caps for 11 yrs.

Rate Applied

Year 1 =	**10.00%**	
Year 2 =	**10.50%**	10.50%
Year 3 =	**11.00%**	11.00%
Year 4 =	**12.00%**	11.50%
Year 5 =	**12.00%**	12.00%
Year 6 =	**16.00%**	12.50%
Year 7 =	**14.00%**	13.00%
Year 8 =	**13.00%**	13.00%
Year 9 =	**14.00%**	13.50%
Year 10 =	**16.00%**	14.00%
Year 11 on	**13.00%**	13.00%

B. Using the PHVBM.wk1 Variable Balance Loan File

This file requires exactly the same inputs as the PHARM adjustable rate mortgage file. The difference is that with a variable balance mortgage part or all of the change in interest rates may not be reflected through changes in payment, depending on annual and life caps. When the interest rate due, based on the market rate, is greater than that allowed by the capped payment, the excess is accrued and added to the balance of the loan. In some cases, where the mortgage payment does not even provide the interest due, the balance of the loan will increase (negative amortization). On the other hand, when the market rate of interest drops, the mortgage loan may be paid off faster than before, because less interest is required from the payment of a given size.

This particular file allows payments to drop if and when interest rates drop below the initial rate. However, if you want to constrain the minimum loan payments to the initial rate, you will need to enter these in the applied rate cells which are affected. Do not forget to retain the original file so that you do not lose the automatic calculations built into the applied rate column, which are lost when you input a number directly.

A pure variable rate loan has annual and life caps of zero, so that payments remain constant, but all interest rate changes result in the loan being paid down faster or slower. The larger the caps, the more like an adjustable rate loan this becomes. When payments are capped, and interest rates are rising, the possibility of a balloon payment exists since there may still be a loan balance at the end of the loan term. A sample of the input screen and some output are shown in Table 5-6.

TABLE 5-6   PHVBM.wk1 Input and Output Summary

File Name: PHVBM
AMORTIZATION TABLE FOR VARIABLE BALANCE LOAN
Inputs are shown in bold below. Maximum 30 year loan with adjustable rates.
Payment at less than the market rate results in balance increases.

File Input

LOAN AMORTIZATION SCHEDULE
~~~~~~~~~~~~~~~~~~~~~~~~~~~~~~~~~~

Loan Amount:	**$150,000.00**	Loan Start Date:	
Initial Contract Rate:	**10.00%**	Month =	**1**
Term of Loan (years):	**30**	Year =	**91**
Annual Rate Cap:	**0.50%**		
Total Life Cap:	**2.00%**		
Margin over Index:	**2.75%**	End of Term =	
Initial Monthly Payments:	$1,316.36	Balloon Payment =	
Origination Date:	Jan-91		
Effective Yield:	12.44%		

Enter your forecast of index rates below, ignoring caps for 11 yrs.

C. Using the PHGEM.wk1 Growing Equity Mortgage File

This file allows a borrower to accelerate the rate of principal repayment by increasing the size of the monthly mortgage payments. All of the increase in payments is assumed to apply to the principal repayment, while the interest rate is held constant. The result is that the loan can be based on an original amortization schedule of up to 30 years, but with the growing payments it can be repaid much more quickly.

TABLE 5-6   PHVBM.wk1 Input and Output Summary (continued)

Year	Forecast Index	Applied Rate	Actual Rate Due
===	======	======	========
1991	**8.50%**	10.00%	10.00%
1992	**8.75%**	10.50%	11.50%
1993	**9.00%**	11.00%	11.75%
1994	**9.50%**	11.50%	12.25%
1995	**10.50%**	12.00%	13.25%
1996	**12.00%**	12.00%	14.75%
1997	**14.00%**	12.00%	16.75%
1998	**13.00%**	12.00%	15.75%
1999	**12.00%**	12.00%	14.75%
2000	**10.00%**	12.00%	12.75%
2001 and on	**8.50%**	11.25%	11.25%

File Output

#	Year	Mortgage Payment	Interest Paid	Interest Accrued	Principal Repaid	Mortgage Balance
=	====	=========	==========	==========	=======	==========
1	1991	$15,796.29	$14,962.47	$14,962.47	$833.82	$149,166.18
2	1992	16,456.14	15,697.14	17,192.10	(735.96)	149,902.14
3	1993	17,295.35	16,505.81	17,631.21	(335.86)	150,238.00
4	1994	18,100.81	17,293.92	18,421.78	(320.97)	150,558.96
5	1995	18,915.37	18,126.07	20,014.21	(1,098.84)	151,657.80
6	1996	19,167.56	18,382.46	22,595.11	(3,427.55)	155,085.35
7	1997	19,733.96	18,970.09	26,479.08	(6,745.12)	161,830.47
8	1998	20,751.16	19,691.94	25,845.67	(5,094.51)	166,924.98
9	1999	21,592.18	20,204.63	24,834.85	(3,242.67)	170,167.65
10	2000	22,231.38	20,389.63	21,663.98	567.40	169,600.25
11	2001	21,354.49	18,959.01	18,959.01	2,395.48	167,204.77
12	2002	21,354.49	18,675.18	18,675.18	2,679.31	164,525.46
13	2003	21,354.49	18,357.72	18,357.72	2,996.77	161,528.68
:	:	:	:	:	:	:
30	2020	21,354.49	1,246.30	1,246.30	20,108.19	0.00

The inputs for the **GEM** mortgage are:

(1) loan dollar amount in cell D11 (enter without commas or $ sign),

(2) annual contract rate of interest in cell D12 (enter as decimal),

(3) initial amortization term in years in cell D13,

(4) first 5 year growth rate in cell D14,

(5) second 5 year growth rate in cell D15,

(6) month to start the loan in cell F19,

(7) year to start the loan in cell F20.

The loan payments do not grow after the 10th year in this file, and are assumed to hold steady. In cell D20, the last payment date is calculated and shown. For example, an initial 30 year, 10.0% loan which has payment growth of 5% for each of the first 10 years, and which started in January of 1989, would be paid off in October of the year 2000.

The advantage of this type of loan is that the borrower may build in a scheduled early prepayment of the loan without prepayment penalties, and with the early years being more affordable. Such a loan requires that the borrower has either an increasing income, or enough discipline, or that initial payments are low enough that increases in the payments are not a significant risk. For the borrower, many thousands of dollars of interest are saved. For the lender, the loan to value ratio is decreased more quickly.

Custom loans could be built to suit the plans of a specific borrower. For example, a borrower could request a loan which is amortized exactly a month before they are going to retire, or going to receive social security. A loan started in January of 1991 would terminate in November of 2004, if the growth rate was set at 3.5% for the first ten years on a 10.0% interest rate loan, originally based on a 30 year amortization. Both annual and monthly tables are available. A sample of the input screen as well as selected output are shown in Table 5-7.

TABLE 5-7 PHGEM.wk1 Input and Output Summary

File Name: PHGEM
AMORTIZATION TABLE FOR GROWING EQUITY LOANS
Only one growth rate on payments is permitted for each year in the first five year set and the second five year set.
Inputs are shown in bold below.

File Input

LOAN AMORTIZATION SCHEDULE (For 10 year to 30 year loans)
~~~~~~

Loan Amount:	**$60,000.00**		
Mortgage Rate:	**10.0%**	Month =	**9**
Initial Amortization Term:	**30 years**	Year =	**89**
First 5 year growth rate:	**5.00% per year**		
Second 5 year growth rate:	**5.00% per year** assumed constant from 11 years on.		

TABLE 5-7   PHGEM.wk1 Input and Output Summary (continued)

Initial Monthly Payments: $526.54
Origination Date: Sep-1989
Last Payment Date: Jun-2001

File Output

ANNUAL TABLE

	Year	Mortgage Payment	Interest Paid	Repaid Principal	Ending Balance
		========	========	========	=========
1	1989	2,106.17	1,499.33	80.29	59,919.71
2	1990	6,423.82	5,972.41	451.42	59,441.08
3	1991	6,745.02	5,910.18	834.83	58,606.24
:	:	:	:	:	:
13	2001	5,823.19	163.45	5,659.74	0.00

D.   Using the PHWRAP.wk1 Wraparound Mortgage File

This file determines the payments and yield for a second mortgage loan, which is combined with a first mortgage. Usually the second mortgage lender will service the first mortgage, and sometimes issue a *note* for the combined amount. The inputs are similar to those in any other mortgage, except that the borrower also needs to know the balance on the first mortgage, as well as the remaining term in months. The yield on the combined mortgage note is calculated, so that it could be used as the rate for the entire note. Sample input and output are provided in Table 5-8.

Templates to Aid User Decision Making

A. Using the PHREFIN.wk1 File for Refinancing Analysis

This file lets a borrower examine the costs and benefits of refinancing, on a before tax basis. After tax analysis is much more complex, but seldom would the decision be any different. A comparison between the old contract rate and new market rates are insufficient for a decision on refinancing. One must also consider prepayment penalties, new closing costs, prepayment penalties on the new loan along with loan balances, and how long the new loan is likely to be held. Once all of this is known, the present value benefits of refinancing can be calculated.

In this template, the present value benefits of refinancing are calculated using the contract rate, the APR, and the effective yield on the new money. The effective yield on the new money is the most conservative number to use. When the net present value

TABLE 5-8   PHWRAP.wk1 Input and Output Summary

File Name: PHWRAP
DESCRIPTION: AMORTIZATION TABLE FOR A WRAP SECOND MORTGAGE
Inputs are shown in bold below.
Maximum 30 year loan with variable second mortgage.

File Input

LOAN AMORTIZATION SCHEDULE
~~~~~~~~~~~~~~~~~~~~~~~~~~~~~~~

	FIRST MORTGAGE	SECOND MORTGAGE
	=================	====================
Remaining Loan Amount:	$60,000.00	$20,000.00
Annual Interest Rate:	10.0%	12.0%
Remaining Term of Loan (months):	4	4
Monthly Payments:	$15,313.80	$5,125.62
Points on second mortgage:		3.0%
Mortgage Start Date:		Month = 1
		Year = 9 1

File Output

Combined Mortgage Payment:	$20,439.42
Effective Yield for full term payoff:	14.17%

	|--------------FIRST MORTGAGE--------------|		
PAYMENT NUMBER	MORTGAGE PAYMENT	INTEREST PAID	PRINCIPAL REPAID	ENDING BALANCE
=========	==========	=========	===========	=========
1	$15,313.80	$500.00	$14,813.80	$45,186.20
2	15,313.80	376.55	14,937.24	30,248.96
3	15,313.80	252.07	15,061.72	15,187.24
4	15,313.80	126.56	15,187.24	0.00

	|-------------SECOND MORTGAGE-------------|		
PAYMENT NUMBER	MORTGAGE PAYMENT	INTEREST PAID	PRINCIPAL REPAID	ENDING BALANCE
=========	==========	=========	===========	=========
1	$5,125.62	$200.00	$4,925.62	$15,074.38
2	5,125.62	150.74	4,974.88	10,099.50
3	5,125.62	101.00	5,024.63	5,074.87
4	5,125.62	50.75	5,074.87	0.00

benefits are positive over the projected holding period, then refinancing might be worthwhile. The exception is when the borrower feels that interest rates might decline further in the future. This opportunity cost, which is forgone when one refinances, means that rates must drop further than the minimum (as determined by a net present value that is just positive). There is no hard and fast rule of thumb on whether or not refinancing is worthwhile, but clearly when the net present value exceeds several thousand dollars, it is worth considering. Since no one can accurately forecast interest rates over a long period of time, refinancing in order to save thousands of dollars should never be regretted, even if rates do decline further.

Inputs required include:

(1) remaining loan dollar amount in cell D10,

(2) annual interest rate on the old loan in cell D11,

(3) remaining term in months in cell D12,

(4) prepayment penalty on the old loan in cell D13,

(5) current mortgage rates in cell D17,

(6) closing points for new loan in cell D18,

(7) amortization term for new loan in cell D19,

(8) projected prepayment term for new loan in cell D20,

(9) prepayment penalty on a new loan in cell D21.

The results of the program include the old and new mortgage payment (using the current loan balance along with closing costs and the old loan prepayment penalty), the net cash monthly savings in payments, the net present value of the savings for the period of the expected term until prepayment, and future loan balances. Sample input and output are shown in Table 5-9.

B. Using the PHQUAL.wk1 Buyer Qualification File

Input for the variables used in this file are entered in cells H37 through H40 and H42 through H46. Output is simply the application of four simple criteria. This file is not intended for actual lender or borrower use in lending decisions, but is intended to give the user an idea of how such criteria might be applied. Some of the input and output are shown in Table 5-10.

TABLE 5-9   PHREFIN.wk1 Input and Output Summary

File Name: PHREFIN
CALCULATING THE COSTS AND BENEFITS OF REFINANCING BEFORE TAX
Inputs are shown in bold below.

File Input

OLD LOAN ASSUMPTIONS
~~~~~~~~~~~~~~~~~~~~~~~~~~~~

Remaining loan dollar amount:	**$100,000** (Enter without $ or ,)
Annual rate on existing loan:	**10.00%** (Enter in decimal form)
Remaining term in months:	**300** (Up to 360 months)
Prepayment Penalty as % of Balance:	**1.00%** (Enter 1.0% as .01)

NEW LOAN RATES AND INFORMATION
~~~~~~

Current Mortgage Annual Rate:	**8.50%** (Enter in decimal form)
Closing Points:	**2.5** (Enter 2.5% as 2.5)
Amortization Term for New Loan:	**300** (Months)
Projected Prepayment Month:	**85** (Up to original term)
Prepayment Penalty as % of Balance:	**1.00%** (Enter 1.0% as .01)

File Output

The existing mortgage payment is:	$908.70
The new mortgage payment would be:	$805.23
Monthly (before tax) cash savings:	$103.47

Net Present Value of Savings Before Tax for 85 months:

$5,017.67	At a discount rate of	9.096040% Effective Yield
$5,099.75	At a discount rate of	8.804857% APR
$5,187.02	At the contract rate of	8.500000%

Old Loan Balance at the end of the 85 month:	$90,732.95
With Prepayment Penalty:	$91,640.28
New Loan Balance at the end of the 85 month:	$88,755.11
With Prepayment Penalty:	$89,642.66

On the new loan:

The effective yield (IRR) is:	9.10%
The annual percentage rate (APR) is:	8.80%

TABLE 5-10   PHQUAL.wk1 Input and Output Summary

File Name: PHQUAL

This program uses standard buyer qualification criteria to determine whether a buyer can qualify for a given home loan.   These criteria may change from time to time, and the user may want to modify the factors used. In addition to the buyer criteria, a property must meet appraisal and other standards as determined by the lender.

General Criteria Include (where only the first is explicitly considered here):

1. Level of household income relative to the payments and housing expenses, such as property taxes, property insurance, and utilities.
2. Stability and type of income.
3. Financial condition: assets and liabilities, net worth.
4. Credit record and history of willingness to pay.
5. Other expenses or situations that affect ability to pay, such as alimony, number of dependents, outstanding loans, past criminal behavior, and so on.

Ratios used in the analysis below:

Loan to appraised value (or price if lower) ratio:	90%+	to 80%
	=======	=======

CRITERIA #1

Mortgage payment to household gross income ratio max:	25.00%	28.00%

CRITERIA #2

Mortgage payment + prop taxes and insurance to income max:	28.00%	30.00%

CRITERIA #3

Long-term debt (10 months+) and mortgage payment to income:	33.33%	36.00%

CRITERIA #4

All housing expenses, mortgage payments, child support, and short-term and long-term debt to income ratio max:	45.00%	50.00%

File Input

INPUT VARIABLES:

Dollar amount of loan requested:	**$145,000**
Contract rate of interest (in decimal form):	**10.00%**
Loan to value ratio assumed (in decimal form):	**80.00%**
Term of the loan in years:	**30**
Annual household total gross income:	**$58,700**
Estimated property taxes per year:	**$1,950**
Estimated insurance payment per year:	**$800**
Other long-term debt payments per month:	**$250**
Child support, short-term debt, alimony per month:	**$150**

TABLE 5-10   PHQUAL.wk1 Input and Output Summary (continued)

File Output

Monthly mortgage payments: $1,272.48

	STANDARD	ACTUAL	RESULT
Criteria #1 applied:	28.00%	26.01%	OK
Criteria #2 applied:	30.00%	30.70%	Problem
Criteria #3 applied:	36.00%	31.12%	OK
Criteria #4 applied:	50.00%	38.88%	OK

If 3 out of 4 criteria are met, lenders may relax the problem criteria and approve the loan, especially if the loan to value ratio is low enough, and income growth looks promising.

C.   Using the PHBUYRENT.wk1 File

The inputs for this file go into B12 through B19, and the key output is in cell B20. In the example provided here, the $126,086 is the "break even purchase price" for a renter who now pays $750 a month in rent, on an after tax first year basis. Most buyers would consider spending much more than this, if they expect significant future appreciation in local prices, or if they expect rents to escalate sharply in the future.

An example of the input and result is shown in Table 5-11.

TABLE 5-11   PHBUYRENT.wk1 Input and Output Summary

File Name: PHBUYRENT

This file estimates the home price which a renter could pay that will cost the same after tax per year as the rental payments. This program does not consider the appreciation or investment aspects of home ownership which would further increase the minimum rational price, nor are the lender criteria considered (See PHQUAL). Only first year equity buildup is considered.

Inputs are shown in bold below.

File Input

Current Market Rent:	**$1,200**
Acceptable Loan to Value Ratio:	**80.0%**
Federal Income Tax Rate:	**30.0%**
Mortgage Rates (decimal form):	**10.0%**
Term in Months:	**360**

TABLE 5-11   PHBUYRENT.wk1 Input and Results (continued)

File Input (continued)

Annual Property Insurance Costs:	**$750**
Other Maintenance and Repair Costs:	**$1,200**
Annual Property Tax Costs:	**$2,200**

File Output

Minimum Break Even Home Price = $180,908

Financial Templates

A. Using the PHPV-FV.wk1 and PHPVTAB.wk1 Time Value Files

These files calculate present and future values for both single sums and annuities. PHPV-FV performs a single calculation based on the number of periods and interest rate appropriate. PHPVTAB sets up tables for each present value and future value calculation for up to 40 years, with monthly compounding.

Examples of these files are shown in Tables 5-12 and 5-13, respectively.

TABLE 5-12   PHPV-FV.wk1 Input and Output Summary

File Name: PHPV-FV
THIS PROGRAM CALCULATES THE PRESENT OR FUTURE VALUE OF SINGLE SUMS OR ANNUITIES.
Compounding is assumed to be per period.
Inputs required are shown in bold below.

PRESENT VALUE OF A SINGLE SUM

Input the dollar amount to be received in the future:	**$25,000.00**
Input the number of periods until received:	**36**
Input the number of periods per year:	**12**
Input the discount rate per year:	**24.00%**
The resulting present value is:	$12,255.58

TABLE 5-12   PHPV/FV.wk1 Input and Output Summary (continued)

PRESENT VALUE OF AN ANNUITY

==

Input the dollar annuity to be received each period:	**$10,000.00**
Input the number of periods received:	**36**
Input the number of periods per year:	**12**
Input the discount rate per year:	**24.00%**
The resulting present value is:	$254,888.42

FUTURE VALUE OF A SINGLE SUM

==

Input the dollar amount to be invested now:	**$12,255.58**
Input the number of periods compounded:	**36**
Input the number of periods per year:	**12**
Input the compound rate per year:	**24.00%**
The resulting future value is:	$25,000.00

FUTURE VALUE OF AN ANNUITY

==

Input the dollar anuity per period to be invested:	**$10,000.00**
Input the number of periods compounded:	**36**
Input the number of periods per year:	**12**
Input the compound rate per year:	**24.00%**
The resulting future value is:	$519,943.67

SINKING FUND FACTOR

==

(The amount one must invest per period to equal $1 in the future.)	
Input the amount you wish to accumulate in the future:	**$519,943.67**
Input the number of periods compounded:	**36**
Input the number of periods per year:	**12**
Input the compound rate per year:	**24.00%**
The resulting sinking fund factor per dollar per period is:	$0.019233
The amount which must be deposited per period is:	$10,000.00

TABLE 5-13   PHPVTAB.wk1 Input and Output Summary

File Name: PHPVTAB
THIS FILE CALCULATES PRESENT AND FUTURE VALUE TABLES.
Inputs are shown in bold below.

TABLE 5-13   PHPVTAB.wk1 Input and Output Summary   (continued)

File Input

Annual compound or discount rate: (enter as decimal)	**12.00%**
Periods/Year: annual=1, monthly=12, daily=365:	**12**
Enter the dollar value of X below for table desired:	**$10.00**

File Output

Year	Future Value of a single $x	Present Value of a single $x	Future Value of $x / period	Present Value of $x / period
1	11.2683	8.8745	126.8250	112.5508
2	12.6973	7.8757	269.7346	212.4339
3	14.3077	6.9892	430.7688	301.0751
:	:	:	:	:
40	1,186.4773	0.0843	117,647.7251	991.5717

Investment Analysis

A. Using the PHPROFOR.wk1 Proforma File

This file calculates the before and after tax cash flows for a residential investment property for up to 10 years, along with a resale analysis and significant ratios. Inputs include income for up to five unit types, expenses, tax rates, equity and loan information. Output includes a proforma statement in cells I3 through S37 for a 10 year cash flow, with the after tax cash flow shown in I37 through S37. Key ratios include:

(1) Debt Coverage Ratio for each year in cells I40 - S40:

The minimum debt coverage ratio depends on the riskiness of the rental income. For residential real estate loans on existing property many lenders would like a minimum of 1.2 or 1.25 in the first year of ownership. A debt coverage ratio of 1.25 means that there should be 25% of the net operating income left over after paying debt service.

(2) Breakeven Point for each year in cells I41- S41:

The breakeven point is the percentage of total occupancy, at the given rent levels, required to break exactly even. Breakeven means that there would be no cash flow left over after paying for operating expenses and debt service. At the breakeven point, the debt coverage ratio is 1.0. A breakeven point above 100% is theoretically impossible to achieve. A breakeven point of 85% would mean that there could be up to 15% vacancy and still break exactly even. The lower the breakeven point the better, but generally one wants to see breakeven low enough that if the property had vacancy similar to local market vacancy, there would not be a problem.

(3) Operating Expense Ratio for each year in cells I42-S42:

The operating expense ratio is the percentage of income required for operating expenses. There is no good or bad number here, because some properties require more expenses paid by the owner than others, and comparisons must consider these differences. The use of this ratio lies in being sure that adequate allowances have been built into the proforma for expected expenses. Newer residential properties typically have operating expense ratios of about 40%. Older properties may run up to 60%.

(4) Cash on Cash Returns for each year in cells I43 - S43:

Cash on cash refers to the before tax cash flow (each year) on the initial cash equity. Initial cash equity includes the down payment, plus closing costs, plus any required cash reserves. The higher this number the better. Cash flow, however, is but one source of real estate returns, and one must consider equity buildup from principal repayment and appreciation potential as well. There may also be some value from tax shelter in the earlier years of the investment.

(5) Return on Asset (or Capitalization Rate) in cells I44 - S44:

The return on asset is the net operating income divided by the initial purchase price (or estimate of market value). This number is known as a capitalization (or "cap") rate in appraisal. A higher cap rate is typical of older or run down property or property with low appreciation potential (or real depreciation possibilities), or property that is riskier for some reason. Low cap rates are typical of newer properties in good condition, with strong appreciation potential. Typical market cap rates on residential property vary considerably by geographical location.

(6) After Tax Cash Flow on Equity in cells I45 - S45:

The after tax cash flow on equity is calculated by adjusting the before tax cash flow for taxes due or saved. The proforma file does not consider other external factors or regulations which may affect the ability of an investor to shelter income from taxes.

(7) Resale Analysis After Tax is shown in cells A46-B55, where the net after tax proceeds from resale are shown in cell B54:

The price is based on the net operating income in the 10th year divided by the resale cap rate input into the file. The taxes due are based on the net increase in price after transactions costs, like brokerage, plus the sum of all depreciation taken. There is a place to input the capital gains tax rate, which may change over time. In the event other tax laws change, the spreadsheet may require other modifications.

Selected input and three years of output are provided as illustration of the program in Table 5-14.

TABLE 5-14   PHPROFOR.wk1 Input and Output Summary

File Name: PHPROFOR
This program performs a simple cash flow proforma with some ratios and lender criteria for a 10 year holding period.
All assumption inputs in bold must be filled in.

File Input

INITIAL ASSUMPTIONS		ANNUAL RENTAL ASSUMPTIONS		
		Quantity and Average Monthly		
Purchase Price =	$600,000	Rent for Each Type Unit Below:		
Deprec Term Years =	27.5	Define:	Rent	# units
Depreciation Method =	SL	A	$250.00	5
Land Value as % of Price =	20.0%	B	$350.00	10
Mortgage Value =	$450,000	C	$450.00	10
Term of loan years =	25	D	$0.00	0
Points to close =	2.0%	E	$0.00	0
Interest Rate =	11.0%			
Prepayment Penalty =	1.0%			
Investor Tax Rate =	28.0%			
Growth Rate in Rents =	4.0%			
Vacancy Rate =	5.0%			
Cap Rate for Resale =	10.0%			
Selling Costs =	7.0%			
Capital Gains Tax Rate =	100.0%			

(As a percentage of ordinary tax rate)

ANNUAL OPERATING EXPENSES

Management % of Gross Rent =	1.0%
Other Annual Income =	$3,600.00
Other Income Growth Rate =	3.0%
Property Taxes =	$6,500.00
Prop Tax Growth Rate =	2.0%
Property Insurance =	$2,400.00
Property Insurance Growth Rate =	1.0%
Maintenance and Repairs =	$6,000.00
Maint. and Repair Growth Rate =	3.0%

TABLE 5-14   PHPROFORMA.wk1 Input and Output Summary (continued)

Other Expenses	=	**$10,750**
Other Exp growth Rate	=	**4.0%**
Resident Manager Salary	=	**$6,000**
Free Unit Value Resident Mgr.	=	**$6,000**

Annual Expense Growth Rate assumed to be same as Rent Growth Rate

File Output

SUMMARY CALCULATIONS BELOW (Do Not Input)
~~~~~~~~~~~~~~~~~~~~~~~~~~~~~~~~~~

Total Equity	=	$159,000
Loan to Value Ratio	=	75.0%
Land at 20%	=	$120,000
Gross Rent First Year	=	$111,000
Debt Coverage Ratio	=	143.24%
After Tax Internal Rate of Return	=	21.86%
Resale Price	=	$1,026,036
less Trans. Cost	=	(71,823)
less unamor points	=	(8,400)
less mortgage penalty	=	(3,805)
Net Selling Price	=	$942,008
less Mortgage Balance	=	(380,526)
less Taxes on Sale	=	(144,635)
Net Sales Proceeds	=	$416,847

PROJECTED INCOME STATEMENT
~~~~~~~~~~~~~~~~~~~~~~~~~~~~~~~~

	Year 1	Year 2	Year 3
	========	========	========
Gross Rent	$111,000	$115,440	$120,058
less Vacancy	(5,550)	(5,772)	(6,003)
plus Other Income	3,600	3,708	3,819
Effective Gross Income	$109,050	$113,376	$117,874

TABLE 5-14   PHPROFORMA.wk1 Input and Output Summary
            (continued)

	Year 1	Year 2	Year 3
	========	========	========
Operating Expenses			
Management	1,110	1,154	1,201
Resident Manager & Unit	12,000	12,480	12,979
Property Taxes	6,500	6,630	6,763
Property Insurance	2,400	2,424	2,448
Main. & Repairs	6,000	6,180	6,365
Other Expenses	10,750	11,180	11,627
Subtotal Operating Expense	$(38,760)	$(40,048)	$(41,383)
Net Operating Income	$70,290	$73,328	$76,491
less Debt Service	(49,070)	(49,070)	(49,070)
Equals Cash Flow Before Tax	$21,220	$24,258	$27,421
Net Operating Income	$70,290	$73,328	$76,491
less Depreciation	(17,455)	(17,455)	(17,455)
less Interest	(44,808)	(44,362)	(43,869)
less Amort of Points	(360)	(360)	(360)
Equals Taxable Income (TI)	$7,667	$11,151	$14,807
Tax Savings or Taxes Due			
equals TI x Tax Rate	(2,147)	(3,122)	(4,146)
After Tax Cash Flow	$19,073	$21,135	$23,275
	========	=======	========
Debt Coverage Ratio	143.3%	149.4%	155.9%
Break Even Point	79.1%	77.2%	75.3%
Expense Ratio	35.5%	35.3%	35.1%
Cash on Cash Equity	14.1%	16.2%	18.3%
Return On Asset	11.7%	12.2%	12.7%
After Tax CF/Cash Equity	12.7%	14.1%	15.5%

CHAPTER 6

FINANCIAL TABLES

TABLE	RANGE
1 Future Value of a Single Sum	1-35 years; 9.0 - 16.75%
2 Present Value of a Single Sum	1-35 years; 9.0 - 16.75%
3 Future Value of One Per Period (Annuity)	1-35 years; 9.0 - 16.75%
4 Present Value of One Per Period (Annuity)	1-35 years; 9.0 - 16.75%
5 Monthly Mortgage Constants	1-35 years; 9.0 - 16.75%
6 Remaining Mortgage Balance Percentage	5-40 years; 9.0 - 13.0%
7 Annual Percentage Rate (APR)	20, 25, 30 years; 7.0 - 16.75% .5 - 12.0 points charged
8 Mortgage Pricing as a Percent of Loan Amount	30 year; 9.0 - 16.75% 9, 12, 30 year prepayment

Table 1

Future Value Of A Single Sum
(With Monthly Discounting)

Years	Annual Percentage Interest Rate							
	9.00	9.25	9.50	9.75	10.00	10.25	10.50	10.75
1	1.0938	1.0965	1.0992	1.1020	1.1047	1.1075	1.1102	1.1130
2	1.1964	1.2024	1.2083	1.2144	1.2204	1.2265	1.2326	1.2387
3	1.3086	1.3184	1.3283	1.3382	1.3482	1.3582	1.3684	1.3786
4	1.4314	1.4457	1.4601	1.4747	1.4894	1.5042	1.5192	1.5343
5	1.5657	1.5852	1.6050	1.6250	1.6453	1.6658	1.6866	1.7076
6	1.7126	1.7382	1.7643	1.7908	1.8176	1.8448	1.8725	1.9005
7	1.8732	1.9060	1.9394	1.9734	2.0079	2.0431	2.0788	2.1152
8	2.0489	2.0900	2.1319	2.1746	2.2182	2.2626	2.3079	2.3541
9	2.2411	2.2917	2.3435	2.3964	2.4504	2.5057	2.5623	2.6200
10	2.4514	2.5129	2.5761	2.6407	2.7070	2.7750	2.8446	2.9160
11	2.6813	2.7555	2.8317	2.9100	2.9905	3.0732	3.1581	3.2454
12	2.9328	3.0215	3.1128	3.2068	3.3036	3.4034	3.5062	3.6120
13	3.2080	3.3131	3.4217	3.5338	3.6496	3.7691	3.8925	4.0200
14	3.5089	3.6329	3.7613	3.8942	4.0317	4.1741	4.3215	4.4741
15	3.8380	3.9836	4.1346	4.2913	4.4539	4.6227	4.7978	4.9795
16	4.1981	4.3681	4.5449	4.7289	4.9203	5.1194	5.3265	5.5419
17	4.5919	4.7897	4.9960	5.2112	5.4355	5.6695	5.9135	6.1679
18	5.0226	5.2520	5.4919	5.7426	6.0047	6.2787	6.5652	6.8646
19	5.4938	5.7590	6.0369	6.3282	6.6335	6.9534	7.2887	7.6401
20	6.0092	6.3149	6.6361	6.9735	7.3281	7.7006	8.0919	8.5031
21	6.5729	6.9244	7.2947	7.6847	8.0954	8.5280	8.9837	9.4636
22	7.1894	7.5928	8.0187	8.4683	8.9431	9.4444	9.9737	10.5325
23	7.8638	8.3257	8.8145	9.3319	9.8796	10.4593	11.0728	11.7223
24	8.6015	9.1293	9.6893	10.2835	10.9141	11.5832	12.2931	13.0464
25	9.4084	10.0105	10.6509	11.3322	12.0569	12.8278	13.6479	14.5201
26	10.2910	10.9767	11.7080	12.4879	13.3195	14.2063	15.1519	16.1603
27	11.2564	12.0363	12.8700	13.7613	14.7142	15.7328	16.8217	17.9857
28	12.3123	13.1980	14.1473	15.1647	16.2550	17.4234	18.6755	20.0173
29	13.4673	14.4720	15.5514	16.7111	17.9571	19.2956	20.7336	22.2784
30	14.7306	15.8689	17.0949	18.4153	19.8374	21.3690	23.0185	24.7950
31	16.1124	17.4006	18.7915	20.2932	21.9146	23.6652	25.5552	27.5957
32	17.6239	19.0802	20.6565	22.3627	24.2094	26.2082	28.3715	30.7129
33	19.2771	20.9219	22.7066	24.6432	26.7444	29.0244	31.4981	34.1822
34	21.0854	22.9413	24.9602	27.1562	29.5449	32.1432	34.9693	38.0433
35	23.0634	25.1557	27.4374	29.9255	32.6387	35.5971	38.8231	42.3406

Table 1

Future Value Of A Single Sum
(With Monthly Discounting)

Years	Annual Percentage Interest Rate							
	11.00	11.25	11.50	11.75	12.00	12.25	12.50	12.75
1	1.1157	1.1185	1.1213	1.1240	1.1268	1.1296	1.1324	1.1352
2	1.2448	1.2510	1.2572	1.2635	1.2697	1.2760	1.2824	1.2887
3	1.3889	1.3992	1.4097	1.4202	1.4308	1.4414	1.4522	1.4630
4	1.5496	1.5650	1.5806	1.5963	1.6122	1.6283	1.6445	1.6608
5	1.7289	1.7505	1.7723	1.7943	1.8167	1.8393	1.8622	1.8854
6	1.9290	1.9579	1.9872	2.0169	2.0471	2.0777	2.1088	2.1403
7	2.1522	2.1898	2.2281	2.2671	2.3067	2.3470	2.3880	2.4298
8	2.4013	2.4493	2.4983	2.5483	2.5993	2.6513	2.7043	2.7583
9	2.6791	2.7395	2.8013	2.8644	2.9289	2.9949	3.0623	3.1313
10	2.9891	3.0641	3.1409	3.2197	3.3004	3.3831	3.4678	3.5547
11	3.3351	3.4272	3.5218	3.6191	3.7190	3.8216	3.9270	4.0354
12	3.7210	3.8332	3.9489	4.0680	4.1906	4.3169	4.4471	4.5811
13	4.1516	4.2874	4.4277	4.5725	4.7221	4.8765	5.0359	5.2005
14	4.6320	4.7954	4.9646	5.1397	5.3210	5.5086	5.7027	5.9037
15	5.1680	5.3636	5.5666	5.7772	5.9958	6.2226	6.4579	6.7020
16	5.7660	5.9991	6.2416	6.4938	6.7562	7.0291	7.3130	7.6083
17	6.4333	6.7099	6.9985	7.2993	7.6131	7.9402	8.2814	8.6371
18	7.1777	7.5050	7.8471	8.2047	8.5786	8.9694	9.3780	9.8050
19	8.0083	8.3942	8.7986	9.2225	9.6666	10.1320	10.6197	11.1309
20	8.9350	9.3888	9.8656	10.3664	10.8926	11.4453	12.0260	12.6360
21	9.9690	10.5013	11.0618	11.6522	12.2740	12.9288	13.6184	14.3446
22	11.1226	11.7455	12.4032	13.0976	13.8307	14.6046	15.4217	16.2843
23	12.4097	13.1372	13.9072	14.7222	15.5847	16.4976	17.4638	18.4863
24	13.8457	14.6938	15.5936	16.5483	17.5613	18.6360	19.7763	20.9861
25	15.4479	16.4348	17.4844	18.6009	19.7885	21.0515	22.3950	23.8238
26	17.2355	18.3820	19.6046	20.9082	22.2981	23.7802	25.3604	27.0453
27	19.2300	20.5601	21.9818	23.5016	25.1261	26.8625	28.7185	30.7024
28	21.4552	22.9961	24.6473	26.4167	28.3127	30.3444	32.5213	34.8540
29	23.9380	25.7208	27.6361	29.6934	31.9035	34.2775	36.8277	39.5670
30	26.7081	28.7684	30.9872	33.3766	35.9496	38.7205	41.7043	44.9173
31	29.7987	32.1771	34.7447	37.5166	40.5090	43.7393	47.2266	50.9910
32	33.2470	35.9896	38.9578	42.1701	45.6465	49.4087	53.4801	57.8861
33	37.0943	40.2539	43.6818	47.4008	51.4356	55.8129	60.5618	65.7135
34	41.3868	45.0234	48.9786	53.2804	57.9589	63.0473	68.5811	74.5994
35	46.1761	50.3580	54.9177	59.8892	65.3096	71.2193	77.6623	84.6868

Table 1

Future Value Of A Single Sum
(With Monthly Discounting)

Years	Annual Percentage Interest Rate							
	13.00	13.25	13.50	13.75	14.00	14.25	14.50	14.75
1	1.1380	1.1409	1.1437	1.1465	1.1493	1.1522	1.1550	1.1579
2	1.2951	1.3015	1.3080	1.3145	1.3210	1.3275	1.3341	1.3407
3	1.4739	1.4849	1.4959	1.5071	1.5183	1.5296	1.5409	1.5524
4	1.6773	1.6940	1.7108	1.7278	1.7450	1.7623	1.7798	1.7975
5	1.9089	1.9326	1.9566	1.9810	2.0056	2.0305	2.0558	2.0813
6	2.1723	2.2048	2.2378	2.2712	2.3051	2.3396	2.3745	2.4099
7	2.4722	2.5154	2.5593	2.6039	2.6494	2.6956	2.7426	2.7905
8	2.8134	2.8697	2.9270	2.9854	3.0450	3.1058	3.1678	3.2310
9	3.2018	3.2738	3.3475	3.4228	3.4998	3.5785	3.6590	3.7412
10	3.6437	3.7350	3.8285	3.9243	4.0225	4.1231	4.2262	4.3319
11	4.1467	4.2610	4.3785	4.4992	4.6232	4.7506	4.8814	5.0159
12	4.7191	4.8612	5.0076	5.1584	5.3136	5.4735	5.6382	5.8078
13	5.3704	5.5459	5.7271	5.9141	6.1072	6.3065	6.5124	6.7249
14	6.1117	6.3270	6.5499	6.7805	7.0192	7.2663	7.5220	7.7867
15	6.9554	7.2182	7.4909	7.7739	8.0675	8.3721	8.6882	9.0161
16	7.9154	8.2349	8.5672	8.9128	9.2723	9.6462	10.0352	10.4397
17	9.0080	9.3948	9.7981	10.2186	10.6571	11.1143	11.5910	12.0880
18	10.2514	10.7180	11.2058	11.7157	12.2486	12.8057	13.3880	13.9966
19	11.6664	12.2277	12.8158	13.4321	14.0779	14.7545	15.4636	16.2066
20	13.2768	13.9500	14.6571	15.3999	16.1803	17.0000	17.8610	18.7654
21	15.1094	15.9148	16.7630	17.6561	18.5967	19.5871	20.6301	21.7283
22	17.1950	18.1564	19.1714	20.2428	21.3739	22.5680	23.8285	25.1591
23	19.5685	20.7138	21.9258	23.2085	24.5660	26.0025	27.5227	29.1315
24	22.2696	23.6313	25.0760	26.6087	28.2347	29.9597	31.7897	33.7311
25	25.3435	26.9598	28.6788	30.5070	32.4513	34.5191	36.7182	39.0570
26	28.8417	30.7571	32.7992	34.9764	37.2977	39.7724	42.4109	45.2237
27	32.8228	35.0892	37.5116	40.1006	42.8678	45.8252	48.9861	52.3642
28	37.3534	40.0315	42.9010	45.9756	49.2697	52.7992	56.5806	60.6321
29	42.5094	45.6700	49.0648	52.7112	56.6278	60.8344	65.3526	70.2054
30	48.3771	52.1026	56.1142	60.4337	65.0847	70.0925	75.4846	81.2902
31	55.0547	59.4413	64.1763	69.2875	74.8045	80.7596	87.1874	94.1253
32	62.6540	67.8136	73.3968	79.4385	85.9760	93.0500	100.7045	108.9868
33	71.3023	77.3651	83.9421	91.0766	98.8158	107.2109	116.3173	126.1950
34	81.1444	88.2620	96.0024	104.4198	113.5732	123.5269	134.3505	146.1201
35	92.3449	100.6938	109.7955	119.7178	130.5344	142.3258	155.1796	169.1913

Table 1

Future Value Of A Single Sum
(With Monthly Discounting)

			Annual Percentage Interest Rate					
Years	15.00	15.25	15.50	15.75	16.00	16.25	16.50	16.75
1	1.1608	1.1636	1.1665	1.1694	1.1723	1.1752	1.1781	1.1810
2	1.3474	1.3540	1.3607	1.3675	1.3742	1.3810	1.3878	1.3947
3	1.5639	1.5756	1.5873	1.5991	1.6110	1.6229	1.6350	1.6471
4	1.8154	1.8334	1.8516	1.8699	1.8885	1.9072	1.9261	1.9452
5	2.1072	2.1334	2.1598	2.1867	2.2138	2.2413	2.2691	2.2972
6	2.4459	2.4824	2.5195	2.5570	2.5952	2.6339	2.6731	2.7130
7	2.8391	2.8886	2.9390	2.9902	3.0423	3.0952	3.1491	3.2040
8	3.2955	3.3613	3.4283	3.4966	3.5663	3.6374	3.7099	3.7838
9	3.8253	3.9112	3.9991	4.0889	4.1807	4.2746	4.3705	4.4686
10	4.4402	4.5512	4.6649	4.7815	4.9009	5.0233	5.1488	5.2773
11	5.1540	5.2959	5.4417	5.5914	5.7452	5.9033	6.0656	6.2324
12	5.9825	6.1624	6.3477	6.5385	6.7350	6.9373	7.1457	7.3603
13	6.9442	7.1707	7.4046	7.6460	7.8952	8.1525	8.4181	8.6923
14	8.0606	8.3440	8.6374	8.9411	9.2553	9.5805	9.9171	10.2655
15	9.3563	9.7093	10.0756	10.4555	10.8497	11.2587	11.6830	12.1233
16	10.8604	11.2980	11.7531	12.2265	12.7188	13.2309	13.7634	14.3173
17	12.6063	13.1466	13.7100	14.2974	14.9099	15.5485	16.2143	16.9084
18	14.6328	15.2977	15.9927	16.7192	17.4785	18.2720	19.1015	19.9684
19	16.9851	17.8008	18.6555	19.5511	20.4895	21.4727	22.5029	23.5822
20	19.7155	20.7134	21.7617	22.8627	24.0192	25.2340	26.5099	27.8501
21	22.8848	24.1026	25.3850	26.7352	28.1570	29.6541	31.2305	32.8903
22	26.5637	28.0464	29.6116	31.2637	33.0077	34.8485	36.7916	38.8426
23	30.8339	32.6355	34.5419	36.5592	38.6939	40.9528	43.3430	45.8723
24	35.7906	37.9754	40.2931	42.7517	45.3598	48.1263	51.0611	54.1741
25	41.5441	44.1891	47.0019	49.9931	53.1739	56.5565	60.1534	63.9783
26	48.2225	51.4195	54.8277	58.4610	62.3342	66.4632	70.8648	75.5569
27	55.9745	59.8329	63.9565	68.3632	73.0726	78.1053	83.4836	89.2309
28	64.9727	69.6230	74.6052	79.9427	85.6609	91.7868	98.3493	105.3796
29	75.4173	81.0150	87.0269	93.4836	100.4177	107.8647	115.8622	124.4509
30	87.5410	94.2710	101.5169	109.3180	117.7168	126.7589	136.4936	146.9736
31	101.6136	109.6960	118.4194	127.8345	137.9960	148.9628	160.7987	173.5723
32	117.9485	127.6449	138.1362	149.4873	161.7686	175.0561	189.4319	204.9849
33	136.9092	148.5306	161.1358	174.8078	189.6366	205.7200	223.1636	242.0823
34	158.9180	172.8337	187.9648	204.4171	222.3055	241.7552	262.9020	285.8936
35	184.4648	201.1135	219.2609	239.0416	260.6022	284.1025	309.7164	337.6337

Table 2

Present Value Of A Single Sum
(With Monthly Discounting)

Years	9.00	9.25	9.50	9.75	10.00	10.25	10.50	10.75
				Annual Percentage Discount Rate				
1	0.91424	0.91197	0.90971	0.90746	0.90521	0.90297	0.90074	0.89851
2	0.83583	0.83169	0.82758	0.82348	0.81941	0.81536	0.81132	0.80731
3	0.76415	0.75848	0.75286	0.74728	0.74174	0.73624	0.73079	0.72538
4	0.69861	0.69172	0.68489	0.67812	0.67143	0.66481	0.65825	0.65176
5	0.63870	0.63083	0.62305	0.61537	0.60779	0.60030	0.59291	0.58561
6	0.58392	0.57530	0.56680	0.55842	0.55018	0.54205	0.53405	0.52617
7	0.53385	0.52465	0.51562	0.50675	0.49803	0.48946	0.48104	0.47277
8	0.48806	0.47847	0.46907	0.45985	0.45082	0.44197	0.43329	0.42479
9	0.44620	0.43635	0.42672	0.41730	0.40809	0.39908	0.39028	0.38167
10	0.40794	0.39794	0.38819	0.37868	0.36941	0.36036	0.35154	0.34294
11	0.37295	0.36291	0.35314	0.34364	0.33439	0.32540	0.31664	0.30813
12	0.34097	0.33096	0.32126	0.31184	0.30270	0.29382	0.28521	0.27686
13	0.31172	0.30183	0.29225	0.28298	0.27400	0.26531	0.25690	0.24876
14	0.28499	0.27526	0.26587	0.25679	0.24803	0.23957	0.23140	0.22351
15	0.26055	0.25103	0.24186	0.23303	0.22452	0.21633	0.20843	0.20083
16	0.23820	0.22893	0.22002	0.21146	0.20324	0.19534	0.18774	0.18044
17	0.21778	0.20878	0.20016	0.19190	0.18397	0.17638	0.16910	0.16213
18	0.19910	0.19040	0.18209	0.17414	0.16654	0.15927	0.15232	0.14567
19	0.18202	0.17364	0.16565	0.15802	0.15075	0.14381	0.13720	0.13089
20	0.16641	0.15836	0.15069	0.14340	0.13646	0.12986	0.12358	0.11760
21	0.15214	0.14442	0.13709	0.13013	0.12353	0.11726	0.11131	0.10567
22	0.13909	0.13170	0.12471	0.11809	0.11182	0.10588	0.10026	0.09494
23	0.12716	0.12011	0.11345	0.10716	0.10122	0.09561	0.09031	0.08531
24	0.11626	0.10954	0.10321	0.09724	0.09162	0.08633	0.08135	0.07665
25	0.10629	0.09990	0.09389	0.08824	0.08294	0.07796	0.07327	0.06887
26	0.09717	0.09110	0.08541	0.08008	0.07508	0.07039	0.06600	0.06188
27	0.08884	0.08308	0.07770	0.07267	0.06796	0.06356	0.05945	0.05560
28	0.08122	0.07577	0.07068	0.06594	0.06152	0.05739	0.05355	0.04996
29	0.07425	0.06910	0.06430	0.05984	0.05569	0.05183	0.04823	0.04489
30	0.06789	0.06302	0.05850	0.05430	0.05041	0.04680	0.04344	0.04033
31	0.06206	0.05747	0.05322	0.04928	0.04563	0.04226	0.03913	0.03624
32	0.05674	0.05241	0.04841	0.04472	0.04131	0.03816	0.03525	0.03256
33	0.05188	0.04780	0.04404	0.04058	0.03739	0.03445	0.03175	0.02926
34	0.04743	0.04359	0.04006	0.03682	0.03385	0.03111	0.02860	0.02629
35	0.04336	0.03975	0.03645	0.03342	0.03064	0.02809	0.02576	0.02362

Table 2

Present Value Of A Single Sum
(With Monthly Discounting)

Years	Annual Percentage Discount Rate							
	11.00	11.25	11.50	11.75	12.00	12.25	12.50	12.75
1	0.89628	0.89407	0.89185	0.88965	0.88745	0.88526	0.88307	0.88089
2	0.80332	0.79935	0.79540	0.79148	0.78757	0.78368	0.77981	0.77596
3	0.72001	0.71467	0.70938	0.70413	0.69892	0.69375	0.68862	0.68353
4	0.64533	0.63897	0.63267	0.62643	0.62026	0.61415	0.60810	0.60211
5	0.57840	0.57128	0.56425	0.55731	0.55045	0.54368	0.53699	0.53039
6	0.51841	0.51076	0.50323	0.49581	0.48850	0.48130	0.47420	0.46722
7	0.46464	0.45665	0.44880	0.44109	0.43352	0.42607	0.41875	0.41156
8	0.41645	0.40828	0.40027	0.39242	0.38472	0.37718	0.36979	0.36254
9	0.37326	0.36503	0.35698	0.34911	0.34142	0.33390	0.32655	0.31936
10	0.33454	0.32636	0.31838	0.31059	0.30299	0.29559	0.28836	0.28132
11	0.29985	0.29179	0.28394	0.27632	0.26889	0.26167	0.25464	0.24781
12	0.26875	0.26088	0.25324	0.24582	0.23863	0.23165	0.22487	0.21829
13	0.24087	0.23324	0.22585	0.21870	0.21177	0.20507	0.19857	0.19229
14	0.21589	0.20853	0.20143	0.19456	0.18794	0.18154	0.17535	0.16938
15	0.19350	0.18644	0.17964	0.17309	0.16678	0.16071	0.15485	0.14921
16	0.17343	0.16669	0.16021	0.15399	0.14801	0.14227	0.13674	0.13144
17	0.15544	0.14903	0.14289	0.13700	0.13135	0.12594	0.12075	0.11578
18	0.13932	0.13324	0.12744	0.12188	0.11657	0.11149	0.10663	0.10199
19	0.12487	0.11913	0.11365	0.10843	0.10345	0.09870	0.09416	0.08984
20	0.11192	0.10651	0.10136	0.09647	0.09181	0.08737	0.08315	0.07914
21	0.10031	0.09523	0.09040	0.08582	0.08147	0.07735	0.07343	0.06971
22	0.08991	0.08514	0.08062	0.07635	0.07230	0.06847	0.06484	0.06141
23	0.08058	0.07612	0.07191	0.06792	0.06417	0.06061	0.05726	0.05409
24	0.07222	0.06806	0.06413	0.06043	0.05694	0.05366	0.05057	0.04765
25	0.06473	0.06085	0.05719	0.05376	0.05053	0.04750	0.04465	0.04197
26	0.05802	0.05440	0.05101	0.04783	0.04485	0.04205	0.03943	0.03698
27	0.05200	0.04864	0.04549	0.04255	0.03980	0.03723	0.03482	0.03257
28	0.04661	0.04349	0.04057	0.03785	0.03532	0.03296	0.03075	0.02869
29	0.04177	0.03888	0.03618	0.03368	0.03134	0.02917	0.02715	0.02527
30	0.03744	0.03476	0.03227	0.02996	0.02782	0.02583	0.02398	0.02226
31	0.03356	0.03108	0.02878	0.02665	0.02469	0.02286	0.02117	0.01961
32	0.03008	0.02779	0.02567	0.02371	0.02191	0.02024	0.01870	0.01728
33	0.02696	0.02484	0.02289	0.02110	0.01944	0.01792	0.01651	0.01522
34	0.02416	0.02221	0.02042	0.01877	0.01725	0.01586	0.01458	0.01340
35	0.02166	0.01986	0.01821	0.01670	0.01531	0.01404	0.01288	0.01181

Table 2

Present Value Of A Single Sum
(With Monthly Discounting)

Annual Percentage Discount Rate

Years	13.00	13.25	13.50	13.75	14.00	14.25	14.50	14.75
1	0.87871	0.87654	0.87437	0.87222	0.87006	0.86792	0.86577	0.86364
2	0.77213	0.76832	0.76453	0.76076	0.75701	0.75328	0.74957	0.74587
3	0.67848	0.67346	0.66849	0.66355	0.65865	0.65378	0.64895	0.64416
4	0.59619	0.59032	0.58451	0.57876	0.57306	0.56743	0.56185	0.55632
5	0.52387	0.51744	0.51108	0.50480	0.49860	0.49248	0.48643	0.48046
6	0.46033	0.45355	0.44687	0.44030	0.43381	0.42743	0.42114	0.41495
7	0.40450	0.39756	0.39074	0.38403	0.37745	0.37097	0.36461	0.35836
8	0.35544	0.34847	0.34165	0.33496	0.32840	0.32197	0.31567	0.30950
9	0.31233	0.30545	0.29873	0.29216	0.28573	0.27945	0.27330	0.26729
10	0.27444	0.26774	0.26120	0.25482	0.24860	0.24254	0.23662	0.23085
11	0.24116	0.23468	0.22839	0.22226	0.21630	0.21050	0.20486	0.19937
12	0.21191	0.20571	0.19970	0.19386	0.18820	0.18270	0.17736	0.17218
13	0.18620	0.18031	0.17461	0.16909	0.16374	0.15857	0.15355	0.14870
14	0.16362	0.15805	0.15267	0.14748	0.14247	0.13762	0.13294	0.12842
15	0.14377	0.13854	0.13349	0.12864	0.12395	0.11944	0.11510	0.11091
16	0.12634	0.12143	0.11672	0.11220	0.10785	0.10367	0.09965	0.09579
17	0.11101	0.10644	0.10206	0.09786	0.09383	0.08997	0.08627	0.08273
18	0.09755	0.09330	0.08924	0.08536	0.08164	0.07809	0.07469	0.07145
19	0.08572	0.08178	0.07803	0.07445	0.07103	0.06778	0.06467	0.06170
20	0.07532	0.07168	0.06823	0.06494	0.06180	0.05882	0.05599	0.05329
21	0.06618	0.06283	0.05966	0.05664	0.05377	0.05105	0.04847	0.04602
22	0.05816	0.05508	0.05216	0.04940	0.04679	0.04431	0.04197	0.03975
23	0.05110	0.04828	0.04561	0.04309	0.04071	0.03846	0.03633	0.03433
24	0.04490	0.04232	0.03988	0.03758	0.03542	0.03338	0.03146	0.02965
25	0.03946	0.03709	0.03487	0.03278	0.03082	0.02897	0.02723	0.02560
26	0.03467	0.03251	0.03049	0.02859	0.02681	0.02514	0.02358	0.02211
27	0.03047	0.02850	0.02666	0.02494	0.02333	0.02182	0.02041	0.01910
28	0.02677	0.02498	0.02331	0.02175	0.02030	0.01894	0.01767	0.01649
29	0.02352	0.02190	0.02038	0.01897	0.01766	0.01644	0.01530	0.01424
30	0.02067	0.01919	0.01782	0.01655	0.01536	0.01427	0.01325	0.01230
31	0.01816	0.01682	0.01558	0.01443	0.01337	0.01238	0.01147	0.01062
32	0.01596	0.01475	0.01362	0.01259	0.01163	0.01075	0.00993	0.00918
33	0.01402	0.01293	0.01191	0.01098	0.01012	0.00933	0.00860	0.00792
34	0.01232	0.01133	0.01042	0.00958	0.00880	0.00810	0.00744	0.00684
35	0.01083	0.00993	0.00911	0.00835	0.00766	0.00703	0.00644	0.00591

Table 2

Present Value Of A Single Sum
(With Monthly Discounting)

				Annual Percentage Discount Rate				
Years	15.00	15.25	15.50	15.75	16.00	16.25	16.50	16.75
1	0.86151	0.85938	0.85727	0.85515	0.85305	0.85094	0.84885	0.84676
2	0.74220	0.73854	0.73490	0.73129	0.72769	0.72410	0.72054	0.71700
3	0.63941	0.63469	0.63001	0.62536	0.62075	0.61617	0.61163	0.60712
4	0.55086	0.54544	0.54008	0.53478	0.52953	0.52433	0.51918	0.51408
5	0.47457	0.46875	0.46300	0.45732	0.45171	0.44617	0.44070	0.43530
6	0.40884	0.40283	0.39691	0.39108	0.38533	0.37967	0.37409	0.36860
7	0.35222	0.34619	0.34026	0.33443	0.32870	0.32308	0.31755	0.31211
8	0.30344	0.29751	0.29169	0.28599	0.28040	0.27492	0.26955	0.26428
9	0.26142	0.25567	0.25006	0.24456	0.23919	0.23394	0.22881	0.22378
10	0.22521	0.21972	0.21437	0.20914	0.20404	0.19907	0.19422	0.18949
11	0.19402	0.18883	0.18377	0.17885	0.17406	0.16940	0.16486	0.16045
12	0.16715	0.16227	0.15754	0.15294	0.14848	0.14415	0.13994	0.13586
13	0.14400	0.13946	0.13505	0.13079	0.12666	0.12266	0.11879	0.11504
14	0.12406	0.11985	0.11578	0.11184	0.10805	0.10438	0.10084	0.09741
15	0.10688	0.10299	0.09925	0.09564	0.09217	0.08882	0.08559	0.08249
16	0.09208	0.08851	0.08508	0.08179	0.07862	0.07558	0.07266	0.06985
17	0.07933	0.07607	0.07294	0.06994	0.06707	0.06431	0.06167	0.05914
18	0.06834	0.06537	0.06253	0.05981	0.05721	0.05473	0.05235	0.05008
19	0.05888	0.05618	0.05360	0.05115	0.04881	0.04657	0.04444	0.04240
20	0.05072	0.04828	0.04595	0.04374	0.04163	0.03963	0.03772	0.03591
21	0.04370	0.04149	0.03939	0.03740	0.03552	0.03372	0.03202	0.03040
22	0.03765	0.03566	0.03377	0.03199	0.03030	0.02870	0.02718	0.02574
23	0.03243	0.03064	0.02895	0.02735	0.02584	0.02442	0.02307	0.02180
24	0.02794	0.02633	0.02482	0.02339	0.02205	0.02078	0.01958	0.01846
25	0.02407	0.02263	0.02128	0.02000	0.01881	0.01768	0.01662	0.01563
26	0.02074	0.01945	0.01824	0.01711	0.01604	0.01505	0.01411	0.01324
27	0.01787	0.01671	0.01564	0.01463	0.01369	0.01280	0.01198	0.01121
28	0.01539	0.01436	0.01340	0.01251	0.01167	0.01089	0.01017	0.00949
29	0.01326	0.01234	0.01149	0.01070	0.00996	0.00927	0.00863	0.00804
30	0.01142	0.01061	0.00985	0.00915	0.00849	0.00789	0.00733	0.00680
31	0.00984	0.00912	0.00844	0.00782	0.00725	0.00671	0.00622	0.00576
32	0.00848	0.00783	0.00724	0.00669	0.00618	0.00571	0.00528	0.00488
33	0.00730	0.00673	0.00621	0.00572	0.00527	0.00486	0.00448	0.00413
34	0.00629	0.00579	0.00532	0.00489	0.00450	0.00414	0.00380	0.00350
35	0.00542	0.00497	0.00456	0.00418	0.00384	0.00352	0.00323	0.00296

Table 3

Future Value Of One Per Period
(With Monthly Discounting)

Year	9.00	9.25	9.50	9.75	10.00	10.25	10.50	10.75
1	12.508	12.522	12.537	12.551	12.566	12.580	12.595	12.609
2	26.188	26.253	26.317	26.382	26.447	26.512	26.577	26.643
3	41.153	41.309	41.466	41.623	41.782	41.941	42.101	42.262
4	57.521	57.818	58.118	58.419	58.722	59.028	59.335	59.645
5	75.424	75.921	76.422	76.928	77.437	77.951	78.469	78.991
6	95.007	95.771	96.544	97.323	98.111	98.907	99.711	100.523
7	116.427	117.538	118.662	119.799	120.950	122.115	123.294	124.487
8	139.856	141.405	142.975	144.567	146.181	147.817	149.476	151.159
9	165.483	167.576	169.702	171.861	174.054	176.281	178.544	180.842
10	193.514	196.273	199.081	201.938	204.845	207.804	210.815	213.879
11	224.175	227.740	231.375	235.082	238.860	242.713	246.642	250.648
12	257.712	262.245	266.875	271.606	276.438	281.374	286.417	291.570
13	294.394	300.080	305.899	311.854	317.950	324.190	330.576	337.114
14	334.518	341.567	348.795	356.207	363.809	371.606	379.602	387.803
15	378.406	387.058	395.949	405.084	414.470	424.117	434.030	444.218
16	426.410	436.941	447.782	458.944	470.436	482.270	494.456	507.005
17	478.918	491.638	504.760	518.297	532.263	546.673	561.542	576.885
18	536.352	551.615	567.393	583.702	600.563	617.996	636.020	654.658
19	599.173	617.382	636.242	655.778	676.016	696.982	718.706	741.216
20	667.887	689.496	711.924	735.203	759.369	784.457	810.505	837.552
21	743.047	768.571	795.117	822.728	851.450	881.331	912.420	944.769
22	825.257	855.279	886.567	919.179	953.174	988.615	1025.567	1064.098
23	915.180	950.356	987.093	1025.465	1065.549	1107.427	1151.182	1196.905
24	1013.538	1054.610	1097.596	1142.590	1189.692	1239.005	1290.641	1344.715
25	1121.122	1168.927	1219.066	1271.659	1326.833	1384.723	1445.469	1509.220
26	1238.798	1294.279	1352.592	1413.891	1478.336	1546.099	1617.359	1692.308
27	1367.514	1431.730	1499.370	1570.626	1645.702	1724.815	1808.192	1896.077
28	1508.304	1582.449	1660.716	1743.345	1830.595	1922.735	2020.056	2122.863
29	1662.301	1747.716	1838.074	1933.678	2034.847	2141.923	2255.268	2375.267
30	1830.743	1928.934	2033.035	2143.420	2260.488	2384.664	2516.401	2656.182
31	2014.987	2127.645	2247.346	2374.551	2509.756	2653.488	2806.312	2968.828
32	2216.515	2345.537	2482.926	2629.252	2785.126	2951.200	3128.172	3316.790
33	2436.947	2584.459	2741.887	2909.927	3089.331	3280.901	3485.502	3704.057
34	2678.057	2846.444	3026.549	3219.224	3425.389	3646.031	3882.211	4135.069
35	2941.784	3133.717	3339.463	3560.063	3796.638	4050.396	4322.638	4614.768

Table 3

Future Value Of One Per Period
(With Monthly Discounting)

			Annual Percentage Interest Rate					
Year	11.00	11.25	11.50	11.75	12.00	12.25	12.50	12.75
1	12.624	12.638	12.653	12.668	12.683	12.697	12.712	12.727
2	26.709	26.774	26.841	26.907	26.973	27.040	27.107	27.174
3	42.423	42.585	42.748	42.912	43.077	43.242	43.409	43.576
4	59.956	60.270	60.585	60.903	61.223	61.544	61.868	62.195
5	79.518	80.049	80.585	81.125	81.670	82.219	82.773	83.331
6	101.344	102.172	103.010	103.855	104.710	105.573	106.445	107.326
7	125.695	126.917	128.154	129.405	130.672	131.954	133.252	134.566
8	152.864	154.593	156.347	158.125	159.927	161.755	163.609	165.488
9	183.177	185.549	187.958	190.406	192.893	195.419	197.985	200.592
10	216.998	220.172	223.403	226.692	230.039	233.446	236.913	240.444
11	254.733	258.898	263.146	267.478	271.896	276.401	280.997	285.683
12	296.834	302.213	307.708	313.324	319.062	324.925	330.917	337.040
13	343.807	350.659	357.674	364.856	372.209	379.738	387.448	395.342
14	396.216	404.846	413.698	422.780	432.097	441.656	451.464	461.527
15	454.690	465.453	476.516	487.889	499.580	511.600	523.957	536.662
16	519.930	533.241	546.951	561.074	575.622	590.609	606.049	621.957
17	592.719	609.061	625.927	643.337	661.308	679.859	699.012	718.785
18	673.932	693.864	714.480	735.804	757.861	780.678	804.284	828.707
19	764.542	788.716	813.771	839.740	866.659	894.565	923.496	953.492
20	865.638	894.806	925.101	956.568	989.255	1023.213	1058.494	1095.151
21	978.433	1013.467	1049.931	1087.888	1127.400	1168.537	1211.367	1255.965
22	1104.279	1146.187	1189.898	1235.496	1283.065	1332.696	1384.483	1438.525
23	1244.689	1294.633	1346.838	1401.413	1458.473	1518.134	1580.523	1645.771
24	1401.347	1460.667	1522.808	1587.911	1656.126	1727.608	1802.522	1881.040
25	1576.133	1646.374	1720.115	1797.542	1878.847	1964.233	2053.917	2148.123
26	1771.145	1854.084	1941.349	2033.175	2129.814	2231.529	2338.600	2451.321
27	1988.724	2086.406	2189.408	2298.036	2412.610	2533.471	2660.980	2795.518
28	2231.481	2346.254	2467.548	2595.750	2731.272	2874.550	3026.048	3186.258
29	2502.329	2636.891	2779.414	2930.392	3090.348	3259.839	3439.458	3629.834
30	2804.520	2961.964	3129.097	3306.543	3494.964	3695.068	3907.609	4133.391
31	3141.679	3325.553	3521.183	3729.351	3950.896	4186.710	4437.751	4705.039
32	3517.855	3732.223	3960.812	4204.604	4464.651	4742.078	5038.093	5353.986
33	3937.561	4187.077	4453.750	4738.807	5043.562	5369.431	5717.929	6090.685
34	4405.834	4695.826	5006.462	5339.271	5695.895	6078.100	6487.786	6927.000
35	4928.296	5264.853	5626.196	6014.217	6430.959	6878.624	7359.585	7876.403

Table 3

Future Value Of One Per Period
(With Monthly Discounting)

				Annual Percentage Interest Rate				
Year	13.00	13.25	13.50	13.75	14.00	14.25	14.50	14.75
1	12.741	12.756	12.771	12.786	12.801	12.816	12.831	12.845
2	27.242	27.309	27.377	27.445	27.513	27.582	27.650	27.719
3	43.743	43.912	44.081	44.252	44.423	44.595	44.767	44.941
4	62.523	62.853	63.186	63.521	63.858	64.197	64.539	64.882
5	83.894	84.462	85.035	85.613	86.195	86.782	87.375	87.972
6	108.216	109.115	110.024	110.941	111.868	112.805	113.751	114.708
7	135.895	137.240	138.602	139.981	141.376	142.788	144.218	145.664
8	167.394	169.327	171.287	173.274	175.290	177.334	179.407	181.509
9	203.242	205.933	208.667	211.446	214.269	217.137	220.052	223.013
10	244.037	247.695	251.419	255.210	259.069	262.998	266.998	271.071
11	290.463	295.339	300.312	305.385	310.560	315.838	321.223	326.716
12	343.298	349.694	356.230	362.911	369.740	376.720	383.854	391.147
13	403.426	411.705	420.183	428.866	437.758	446.866	456.196	465.751
14	471.853	482.450	493.323	504.482	515.935	527.689	539.753	552.135
15	549.726	563.159	576.972	591.177	605.786	620.811	636.264	652.158
16	638.347	655.236	672.640	690.574	709.056	728.105	747.738	767.974
17	739.202	760.283	782.052	804.532	827.749	851.727	876.494	902.076
18	853.977	880.125	907.184	935.186	964.167	994.164	1025.212	1057.351
19	984.595	1016.847	1050.294	1084.982	1120.959	1158.276	1196.987	1237.144
20	1133.242	1172.827	1213.965	1256.723	1301.166	1347.365	1395.392	1445.324
21	1302.408	1350.776	1401.152	1453.625	1508.286	1565.230	1624.558	1686.374
22	1494.924	1553.789	1615.233	1679.374	1746.337	1816.251	1889.252	1965.484
23	1714.014	1785.397	1860.072	1938.197	2019.939	2105.473	2194.984	2288.663
24	1963.345	2049.627	2140.087	2234.938	2334.401	2438.711	2548.114	2662.870
25	2247.092	2351.074	2460.334	2575.154	2695.826	2822.663	2955.993	3096.160
26	2570.005	2694.979	2826.593	2965.213	3111.227	3265.047	3427.107	3597.863
27	2937.490	3087.324	3245.473	3412.417	3588.665	3774.756	3971.260	4178.782
28	3355.701	3534.930	3724.535	3925.139	4137.404	4362.034	4599.776	4851.422
29	3831.638	4045.583	4272.427	4512.978	4768.093	5038.688	5325.734	5630.267
30	4373.270	4628.160	4899.036	5186.937	5492.971	5818.319	6164.242	6532.084
31	4989.665	5292.794	5615.674	5959.636	6326.103	6716.598	7132.748	7576.292
32	5691.142	6051.042	6435.274	6845.538	7283.657	7751.583	8251.407	8785.371
33	6489.446	6916.089	7372.629	7861.230	8384.214	8944.076	9543.497	10185.353
34	7397.941	7902.978	8444.658	9025.725	9649.130	10318.051	11035.907	11806.381
35	8431.839	9028.871	9670.711	10360.825	11102.951	11901.124	12759.693	13683.356

Table 3

Future Value Of One Per Period
(With Monthly Discounting)

			Annual Percentage Interest Rate					
Year	15.00	15.25	15.50	15.75	16.00	16.25	16.50	16.75
1	12.860	12.875	12.890	12.905	12.920	12.935	12.950	12.965
2	27.788	27.857	27.927	27.997	28.066	28.137	28.207	28.277
3	45.116	45.291	45.467	45.644	45.822	46.000	46.180	46.360
4	65.228	65.577	65.927	66.280	66.636	66.994	67.354	67.716
5	88.575	89.182	89.795	90.412	91.036	91.664	92.298	92.937
6	115.674	116.650	117.636	118.632	119.639	120.656	121.683	122.722
7	147.129	148.612	150.112	151.631	153.169	154.726	156.302	157.897
8	183.641	185.803	187.996	190.220	192.476	194.764	197.084	199.438
9	226.023	229.080	232.188	235.345	238.554	241.815	245.129	248.497
10	275.217	279.439	283.737	288.114	292.571	297.108	301.729	306.435
11	332.320	338.037	343.870	349.821	355.892	362.087	368.408	374.858
12	398.602	406.223	414.014	421.979	430.122	438.448	446.960	455.663
13	475.540	485.566	495.838	506.360	517.140	528.185	539.500	551.093
14	564.845	577.892	591.285	605.034	619.149	633.640	648.518	663.794
15	668.507	685.324	702.624	720.421	738.730	757.568	776.949	796.891
16	788.833	810.335	832.501	855.352	878.912	903.203	928.249	954.075
17	928.501	955.800	984.002	1013.139	1043.243	1074.349	1106.491	1139.705
18	1090.623	1125.067	1160.728	1197.652	1235.884	1275.474	1316.472	1358.931
19	1278.805	1322.030	1366.879	1413.418	1461.711	1511.829	1563.844	1617.831
20	1497.239	1551.221	1607.355	1665.730	1726.442	1789.586	1855.266	1923.586
21	1750.788	1817.913	1887.869	1960.780	2036.777	2115.996	2198.580	2284.676
22	2045.095	2128.242	2215.089	2305.806	2400.575	2499.583	2603.027	2711.115
23	2386.714	2489.349	2596.790	2709.274	2827.044	2950.361	3079.494	3214.728
24	2783.249	2909.541	3042.045	3181.081	3326.982	3480.099	3640.804	3809.485
25	3243.530	3398.486	3561.435	3732.804	3913.044	4102.630	4302.065	4511.878
26	3777.802	3967.435	4167.303	4377.979	4600.067	4834.208	5081.076	5341.388
27	4397.961	4629.477	4874.048	5132.435	5405.445	5693.933	5998.805	6321.020
28	5117.814	5399.845	5698.465	6014.682	6349.566	6704.253	7079.951	7477.942
29	5953.386	6296.264	6660.148	7046.366	7456.331	7891.547	8353.615	8844.240
30	6923.280	7339.358	7781.950	8252.798	8753.759	9286.814	9854.078	10457.807
31	8049.088	8553.127	9090.532	9663.579	10274.696	10926.485	11621.726	12363.391
32	9355.876	9965.497	10616.993	11313.320	12057.647	12853.371	13704.135	14613.841
33	10872.736	11608.965	12397.609	13242.497	14147.748	15117.783	16157.355	17271.571
34	12633.438	13521.344	14474.696	15498.443	16597.912	17778.842	19047.415	20410.287
35	14677.180	15746.633	16897.618	18136.504	19470.168	20906.030	22452.103	24117.038

Table 4

Present Value Of One Per Period
(With Monthly Discounting)

Years	Annual Percentage Interest Rate							
	9.00	9.25	9.50	9.75	10.00	10.25	10.50	10.75
1	11.4349	11.4198	11.4047	11.3896	11.3745	11.3595	11.3445	11.3295
2	21.8891	21.8343	21.7796	21.7251	21.6709	21.6168	21.5629	21.5091
3	31.4468	31.3320	31.2179	31.1043	30.9912	30.8788	30.7669	30.6556
4	40.1848	39.9937	39.8039	39.6154	39.4282	39.2421	39.0573	38.8738
5	48.1734	47.8930	47.6148	47.3390	47.0654	46.7940	46.5248	46.2578
6	55.4768	55.0968	54.7205	54.3478	53.9787	53.6131	53.2511	52.8925
7	62.1540	61.6666	61.1846	60.7080	60.2367	59.7706	59.3096	58.8537
8	68.2584	67.6580	67.0651	66.4796	65.9015	65.3306	64.7668	64.2100
9	73.8394	73.1220	72.4146	71.7172	71.0294	70.3511	69.6822	69.0226
10	78.9417	78.1050	77.2812	76.4700	75.6712	74.8845	74.1098	73.3468
11	83.6064	82.6494	81.7084	80.7830	79.8730	78.9780	78.0978	77.2320
12	87.8711	86.7938	85.7358	84.6969	83.6765	82.6743	81.6900	80.7230
13	91.7700	90.5733	89.3997	88.2486	87.1195	86.0120	84.9255	83.8596
14	95.3346	94.0202	92.7327	91.4716	90.2362	89.0259	87.8400	86.6779
15	98.5934	97.1636	95.7648	94.3964	93.0574	91.7473	90.4651	89.2102
16	101.5728	100.0303	98.5232	97.0505	95.6113	94.2046	92.8296	91.4855
17	104.2966	102.6447	101.0325	99.4590	97.9230	96.4235	94.9594	93.5298
18	106.7869	105.0289	103.3152	101.6446	100.0156	98.4271	96.8778	95.3666
19	109.0635	107.2032	105.3919	103.6279	101.9099	100.2363	98.6058	97.0170
20	111.1450	109.1862	107.2810	105.4278	103.6246	101.8700	100.1623	98.4999
21	113.0479	110.9946	108.9996	107.0610	105.1768	103.3451	101.5642	99.8324
22	114.7876	112.6438	110.5630	108.5431	106.5819	104.6772	102.8270	101.0295
23	116.3781	114.1478	111.9853	109.8881	107.8537	105.8799	103.9645	102.1052
24	117.8322	115.5194	113.2792	111.1086	109.0050	106.9660	104.9890	103.0717
25	119.1616	116.7703	114.4562	112.2161	110.0472	107.9467	105.9118	103.9401
26	120.3770	117.9111	115.5270	113.2212	110.9906	108.8322	106.7430	104.7203
27	121.4882	118.9515	116.5011	114.1332	111.8446	109.6318	107.4918	105.4214
28	122.5040	119.9003	117.3872	114.9609	112.6176	110.3539	108.1662	106.0513
29	123.4328	120.7655	118.1933	115.7120	113.3174	111.0058	108.7736	106.6173
30	124.2819	121.5546	118.9267	116.3935	113.9508	111.5945	109.3208	107.1259
31	125.0581	122.2743	119.5938	117.0120	114.5242	112.1261	109.8136	107.5828
32	125.7678	122.9305	120.2007	117.5732	115.0432	112.6061	110.2575	107.9933
33	126.4167	123.5291	120.7528	118.0826	115.5131	113.0396	110.6574	108.3622
34	127.0099	124.0749	121.2551	118.5447	115.9384	113.4309	111.0175	108.6937
35	127.5522	124.5727	121.7120	118.9641	116.3234	113.7843	111.3420	108.9915

Table 4

Present Value Of One Per Period
(With Monthly Discounting)

Years	Annual Percentage Interest Rate							
	11.00	11.25	11.50	11.75	12.00	12.25	12.50	12.75
1	11.3146	11.2997	11.2848	11.2699	11.2551	11.2403	11.2255	11.2108
2	21.4556	21.4023	21.3491	21.2962	21.2434	21.1908	21.1384	21.0862
3	30.5449	30.4347	30.3251	30.2160	30.1075	29.9995	29.8921	29.7853
4	38.6914	38.5103	38.3303	38.1516	37.9740	37.7975	37.6223	37.4482
5	45.9930	45.7304	45.4698	45.2114	44.9550	44.7008	44.4485	44.1983
6	52.5373	52.1856	51.8372	51.4922	51.1504	50.8119	50.4766	50.1444
7	58.4029	57.9570	57.5160	57.0799	56.6485	56.2218	55.7997	55.3823
8	63.6601	63.1170	62.5807	62.0509	61.5277	61.0109	60.5004	59.9962
9	68.3720	67.7304	67.0976	66.4734	65.8578	65.2505	64.6515	64.0605
10	72.5953	71.8551	71.1261	70.4079	69.7005	69.0037	68.3171	67.6408
11	76.3805	75.5428	74.7188	73.9082	73.1108	72.3261	71.5542	70.7946
12	79.7731	78.8399	77.9231	77.0223	76.1372	75.2674	74.4127	73.5727
13	82.8139	81.7877	80.7808	79.7927	78.8229	77.8711	76.9369	76.0199
14	85.5392	84.4233	83.3295	82.2574	81.2064	80.1761	79.1660	78.1756
15	87.9819	86.7796	85.6025	84.4501	83.3217	82.2166	81.1344	80.0745
16	90.1713	88.8863	87.6297	86.4008	85.1988	84.0230	82.8727	81.7472
17	92.1336	90.7699	89.4377	88.1363	86.8647	85.6221	84.4077	83.2207
18	93.8923	92.4539	91.0502	89.6803	88.3431	87.0377	85.7632	84.5187
19	95.4687	93.9595	92.4883	91.0539	89.6551	88.2909	86.9602	85.6621
20	96.8815	95.3056	93.7708	92.2759	90.8194	89.4003	88.0173	86.6693
21	98.1479	96.5091	94.9147	93.3630	91.8527	90.3824	88.9507	87.5565
22	99.2828	97.5852	95.9348	94.3302	92.7697	91.2518	89.7750	88.3380
23	100.3001	98.5472	96.8447	95.1907	93.5835	92.0214	90.5029	89.0264
24	101.2119	99.4073	97.6561	95.9562	94.3056	92.7027	91.1457	89.6329
25	102.0290	100.1764	98.3798	96.6372	94.9466	93.3059	91.7133	90.1671
26	102.7615	100.8639	99.0252	97.2431	95.5153	93.8398	92.2146	90.6376
27	103.4179	101.4786	99.6008	97.7821	96.0201	94.3125	92.6572	91.0522
28	104.0063	102.0282	100.1142	98.2616	96.4680	94.7309	93.0481	91.4173
29	104.5337	102.5196	100.5720	98.6883	96.8655	95.1014	93.3933	91.7390
30	105.0063	102.9589	100.9804	99.0678	97.2183	95.4293	93.6981	92.0223
31	105.4300	103.3517	101.3445	99.4055	97.5314	95.7196	93.9672	92.2719
32	105.8097	103.7028	101.6693	99.7059	97.8093	95.9766	94.2049	92.4917
33	106.1500	104.0168	101.9590	99.9731	98.0558	96.2040	94.4148	92.6854
34	106.4550	104.2975	102.2173	100.2109	98.2746	96.4054	94.6002	92.8560
35	106.7284	104.5485	102.4478	100.4224	98.4688	96.5837	94.7639	93.0063

Table 4

Present Value Of One Per Period
(With Monthly Discounting)

			Annual Percentage Interest Rate					
Years	13.00	13.25	13.50	13.75	14.00	14.25	14.50	14.75
1	11.1960	11.1814	11.1667	11.1521	11.1375	11.1229	11.1083	11.0938
2	21.0341	20.9822	20.9306	20.8791	20.8277	20.7766	20.7256	20.6748
3	29.6789	29.5731	29.4679	29.3631	29.2589	29.1552	29.0521	28.9494
4	37.2752	37.1034	36.9326	36.7630	36.5945	36.4272	36.2608	36.0956
5	43.9501	43.7039	43.4597	43.2174	42.9770	42.7386	42.5020	42.2674
6	49.8154	49.4895	49.1667	48.8469	48.5302	48.2164	47.9055	47.5976
7	54.9693	54.5609	54.1568	53.7571	53.3618	52.9706	52.5837	52.2009
8	59.4981	59.0061	58.5201	58.0399	57.5655	57.0969	56.6339	56.1765
9	63.4776	62.9025	62.3351	61.7754	61.2231	60.6782	60.1405	59.6100
10	66.9744	66.3179	65.6710	65.0335	64.4054	63.7864	63.1765	62.5753
11	70.0471	69.3116	68.5877	67.8754	67.1742	66.4841	65.8049	65.1363
12	72.7471	71.9357	71.1381	70.3540	69.5833	68.8255	68.0805	67.3480
13	75.1196	74.2358	73.3680	72.5160	71.6793	70.8576	70.0507	69.2581
14	77.2044	76.2519	75.3178	74.4016	73.5029	72.6213	71.7564	70.9078
15	79.0363	78.0192	77.0227	76.0464	75.0897	74.1521	73.2332	72.3325
16	80.6460	79.5682	78.5134	77.4809	76.4702	75.4806	74.5118	73.5630
17	82.0604	80.9260	79.8168	78.7322	77.6713	76.6337	75.6187	74.6256
18	83.3033	82.1162	80.9565	79.8235	78.7164	77.6345	76.5771	75.5434
19	84.3955	83.1594	81.9530	80.7754	79.6257	78.5031	77.4068	76.3360
20	85.3551	84.0738	82.8243	81.6056	80.4168	79.2570	78.1251	77.0205
21	86.1984	84.8754	83.5862	82.3298	81.1052	79.9112	78.7471	77.6117
22	86.9394	85.5779	84.2523	82.9614	81.7041	80.4791	79.2855	78.1223
23	87.5905	86.1938	84.8348	83.5124	82.2251	80.9720	79.7517	78.5632
24	88.1627	86.7336	85.3441	83.9929	82.6785	81.3997	80.1553	78.9440
25	88.6654	87.2067	85.7894	84.4120	83.0730	81.7710	80.5047	79.2729
26	89.1072	87.6215	86.1788	84.7775	83.4162	82.0932	80.8073	79.5570
27	89.4954	87.9850	86.5192	85.0964	83.7148	82.3729	81.0692	79.8023
28	89.8365	88.3037	86.8169	85.3745	83.9746	82.6156	81.2960	80.0141
29	90.1362	88.5830	87.0772	85.6171	84.2006	82.8263	81.4923	80.1971
30	90.3996	88.8278	87.3048	85.8286	84.3973	83.0091	81.6623	80.3551
31	90.6310	89.0424	87.5038	86.0132	84.5684	83.1678	81.8094	80.4916
32	90.8344	89.2305	87.6778	86.1741	84.7173	83.3055	81.9368	80.6095
33	91.0131	89.3954	87.8300	86.3145	84.8469	83.4251	82.0471	80.7112
34	91.1701	89.5399	87.9630	86.4369	84.9596	83.5288	82.1426	80.7992
35	91.3081	89.6666	88.0793	86.5437	85.0576	83.6189	82.2253	80.8751

Table 4

Present Value Of One Per Period
(With Monthly Discounting)

| | Annual Percentage Interest Rate | | | | | | | |
Years	15.00	15.25	15.50	15.75	16.00	16.25	16.50	16.75
1	11.0793	11.0648	11.0504	11.0360	11.0216	11.0073	10.9929	10.9786
2	20.6242	20.5738	20.5235	20.4735	20.4235	20.3738	20.3242	20.2748
3	28.8473	28.7456	28.6445	28.5439	28.4438	28.3442	28.2451	28.1465
4	35.9315	35.7684	35.6064	35.4454	35.2855	35.1266	34.9687	34.8118
5	42.0346	41.8036	41.5745	41.3472	41.1217	40.8980	40.6760	40.4558
6	47.2925	46.9902	46.6908	46.3942	46.1003	45.8091	45.5206	45.2348
7	51.8222	51.4475	51.0768	50.7101	50.3472	49.9882	49.6330	49.2815
8	55.7246	55.2780	54.8368	54.4009	53.9701	53.5444	53.1238	52.7081
9	59.0865	58.5699	58.0601	57.5570	57.0605	56.5705	56.0869	55.6095
10	61.9828	61.3989	60.8234	60.2560	59.6968	59.1456	58.6021	58.0664
11	64.4781	63.8301	63.1922	62.5641	61.9457	61.3368	60.7372	60.1467
12	66.6277	65.9194	65.2229	64.5378	63.8641	63.2014	62.5495	61.9083
13	68.4797	67.7150	66.9637	66.2257	65.5006	64.7881	64.0879	63.3999
14	70.0751	69.2580	68.4561	67.6691	66.8965	66.1382	65.3938	64.6629
15	71.4496	70.5841	69.7355	68.9034	68.0874	67.2871	66.5022	65.7323
16	72.6338	71.7237	70.8322	69.9589	69.1032	68.2648	67.4432	66.6379
17	73.6540	72.7031	71.7724	70.8615	69.9698	69.0967	68.2419	67.4047
18	74.5328	73.5447	72.5784	71.6334	70.7090	69.8047	68.9199	68.0540
19	75.2900	74.2680	73.2694	72.2935	71.3396	70.4071	69.4954	68.6038
20	75.9423	74.8896	73.8618	72.8580	71.8775	70.9197	69.9839	69.0694
21	76.5042	75.4238	74.3695	73.3407	72.3364	71.3559	70.3985	69.4636
22	76.9884	75.8829	74.8049	73.7535	72.7278	71.7271	70.7505	69.7974
23	77.4055	76.2774	75.1780	74.1064	73.0617	72.0430	71.0493	70.0800
24	77.7648	76.6164	75.4979	74.4083	73.3466	72.3117	71.3030	70.3194
25	78.0743	76.9078	75.7722	74.6665	73.5895	72.5404	71.5182	70.5220
26	78.3410	77.1582	76.0073	74.8872	73.7968	72.7351	71.7010	70.6936
27	78.5708	77.3734	76.2089	75.0760	73.9736	72.9007	71.8561	70.8389
28	78.7687	77.5583	76.3816	75.2374	74.1245	73.0416	71.9878	70.9619
29	78.9392	77.7172	76.5298	75.3755	74.2531	73.1615	72.0996	71.0661
30	79.0861	77.8538	76.6567	75.4935	74.3629	73.2636	72.1944	71.1543
31	79.2127	77.9712	76.7656	75.5945	74.4565	73.3504	72.2750	71.2290
32	79.3217	78.0721	76.8589	75.6808	74.5364	73.4243	72.3433	71.2923
33	79.4157	78.1587	76.9389	75.7546	74.6045	73.4872	72.4014	71.3459
34	79.4966	78.2332	77.0075	75.8178	74.6626	73.5407	72.4506	71.3912
35	79.5663	78.2973	77.0663	75.8717	74.7122	73.5862	72.4925	71.4296

Table 5

Monthly Mortgage Constants

Year	9.00	9.25	Annual Contract Interest Rate 9.50	9.75	10.00	10.25	10.50	10.75
1	0.08745	0.08757	0.08768	0.08780	0.08792	0.08803	0.08815	0.08827
2	0.04568	0.04580	0.04591	0.04603	0.04614	0.04626	0.04638	0.04649
3	0.03180	0.03192	0.03203	0.03215	0.03227	0.03238	0.03250	0.03262
4	0.02489	0.02500	0.02512	0.02524	0.02536	0.02548	0.02560	0.02572
5	0.02076	0.02088	0.02100	0.02112	0.02125	0.02137	0.02149	0.02162
6	0.01803	0.01815	0.01827	0.01840	0.01853	0.01865	0.01878	0.01891
7	0.01609	0.01622	0.01634	0.01647	0.01660	0.01673	0.01686	0.01699
8	0.01465	0.01478	0.01491	0.01504	0.01517	0.01531	0.01544	0.01557
9	0.01354	0.01368	0.01381	0.01394	0.01408	0.01421	0.01435	0.01449
10	0.01267	0.01280	0.01294	0.01308	0.01322	0.01335	0.01349	0.01363
11	0.01196	0.01210	0.01224	0.01238	0.01252	0.01266	0.01280	0.01295
12	0.01138	0.01152	0.01166	0.01181	0.01195	0.01210	0.01224	0.01239
13	0.01090	0.01104	0.01119	0.01133	0.01148	0.01163	0.01178	0.01192
14	0.01049	0.01064	0.01078	0.01093	0.01108	0.01123	0.01138	0.01154
15	0.01014	0.01029	0.01044	0.01059	0.01075	0.01090	0.01105	0.01121
16	0.00985	0.01000	0.01015	0.01030	0.01046	0.01062	0.01077	0.01093
17	0.00959	0.00974	0.00990	0.01005	0.01021	0.01037	0.01053	0.01069
18	0.00936	0.00952	0.00968	0.00984	0.01000	0.01016	0.01032	0.01049
19	0.00917	0.00933	0.00949	0.00965	0.00981	0.00998	0.01014	0.01031
20	0.00900	0.00916	0.00932	0.00949	0.00965	0.00982	0.00998	0.01015
21	0.00885	0.00901	0.00917	0.00934	0.00951	0.00968	0.00985	0.01002
22	0.00871	0.00888	0.00904	0.00921	0.00938	0.00955	0.00973	0.00990
23	0.00859	0.00876	0.00893	0.00910	0.00927	0.00944	0.00962	0.00979
24	0.00849	0.00866	0.00883	0.00900	0.00917	0.00935	0.00952	0.00970
25	0.00839	0.00856	0.00874	0.00891	0.00909	0.00926	0.00944	0.00962
26	0.00831	0.00848	0.00866	0.00883	0.00901	0.00919	0.00937	0.00955
27	0.00823	0.00841	0.00858	0.00876	0.00894	0.00912	0.00930	0.00949
28	0.00816	0.00834	0.00852	0.00870	0.00888	0.00906	0.00925	0.00943
29	0.00810	0.00828	0.00846	0.00864	0.00882	0.00901	0.00919	0.00938
30	0.00805	0.00823	0.00841	0.00859	0.00878	0.00896	0.00915	0.00933
31	0.00800	0.00818	0.00836	0.00855	0.00873	0.00892	0.00911	0.00930
32	0.00795	0.00813	0.00832	0.00851	0.00869	0.00888	0.00907	0.00926
33	0.00791	0.00810	0.00828	0.00847	0.00866	0.00885	0.00904	0.00923
34	0.00787	0.00806	0.00825	0.00844	0.00863	0.00882	0.00901	0.00920
35	0.00784	0.00803	0.00822	0.00841	0.00860	0.00879	0.00898	0.00918

Table 5

Monthly Mortgage Constants

Annual Contract Interest Rate

Year	11.00	11.25	11.50	11.75	12.00	12.25	12.50	12.75
1	0.08838	0.08850	0.08862	0.08873	0.08885	0.08897	0.08908	0.08920
2	0.04661	0.04672	0.04684	0.04696	0.04707	0.04719	0.04731	0.04742
3	0.03274	0.03286	0.03298	0.03310	0.03321	0.03333	0.03345	0.03357
4	0.02585	0.02597	0.02609	0.02621	0.02633	0.02646	0.02658	0.02670
5	0.02174	0.02187	0.02199	0.02212	0.02224	0.02237	0.02250	0.02263
6	0.01903	0.01916	0.01929	0.01942	0.01955	0.01968	0.01981	0.01994
7	0.01712	0.01725	0.01739	0.01752	0.01765	0.01779	0.01792	0.01806
8	0.01571	0.01584	0.01598	0.01612	0.01625	0.01639	0.01653	0.01667
9	0.01463	0.01476	0.01490	0.01504	0.01518	0.01533	0.01547	0.01561
10	0.01378	0.01392	0.01406	0.01420	0.01435	0.01449	0.01464	0.01478
11	0.01309	0.01324	0.01338	0.01353	0.01368	0.01383	0.01398	0.01413
12	0.01254	0.01268	0.01283	0.01298	0.01313	0.01329	0.01344	0.01359
13	0.01208	0.01223	0.01238	0.01253	0.01269	0.01284	0.01300	0.01315
14	0.01169	0.01185	0.01200	0.01216	0.01231	0.01247	0.01263	0.01279
15	0.01137	0.01152	0.01168	0.01184	0.01200	0.01216	0.01233	0.01249
16	0.01109	0.01125	0.01141	0.01157	0.01174	0.01190	0.01207	0.01223
17	0.01085	0.01102	0.01118	0.01135	0.01151	0.01168	0.01185	0.01202
18	0.01065	0.01082	0.01098	0.01115	0.01132	0.01149	0.01166	0.01183
19	0.01047	0.01064	0.01081	0.01098	0.01115	0.01133	0.01150	0.01167
20	0.01032	0.01049	0.01066	0.01084	0.01101	0.01119	0.01136	0.01154
21	0.01019	0.01036	0.01054	0.01071	0.01089	0.01106	0.01124	0.01142
22	0.01007	0.01025	0.01042	0.01060	0.01078	0.01096	0.01114	0.01132
23	0.00997	0.01015	0.01033	0.01051	0.01069	0.01087	0.01105	0.01123
24	0.00988	0.01006	0.01024	0.01042	0.01060	0.01079	0.01097	0.01116
25	0.00980	0.00998	0.01016	0.01035	0.01053	0.01072	0.01090	0.01109
26	0.00973	0.00991	0.01010	0.01028	0.01047	0.01066	0.01084	0.01103
27	0.00967	0.00985	0.01004	0.01023	0.01041	0.01060	0.01079	0.01098
28	0.00961	0.00980	0.00999	0.01018	0.01037	0.01056	0.01075	0.01094
29	0.00957	0.00975	0.00994	0.01013	0.01032	0.01052	0.01071	0.01090
30	0.00952	0.00971	0.00990	0.01009	0.01029	0.01048	0.01067	0.01087
31	0.00948	0.00968	0.00987	0.01006	0.01025	0.01045	0.01064	0.01084
32	0.00945	0.00964	0.00984	0.01003	0.01022	0.01042	0.01062	0.01081
33	0.00942	0.00961	0.00981	0.01000	0.01020	0.01039	0.01059	0.01079
34	0.00939	0.00959	0.00978	0.00998	0.01018	0.01037	0.01057	0.01077
35	0.00937	0.00956	0.00976	0.00996	0.01016	0.01035	0.01055	0.01075

Table 5

Monthly Mortgage Constants

Year	Annual Contract Interest Rate 13.00	13.25	13.50	13.75	14.00	14.25	14.50	14.75
1	0.08932	0.08943	0.08955	0.08967	0.08979	0.08990	0.09002	0.09014
2	0.04754	0.04766	0.04778	0.04789	0.04801	0.04813	0.04825	0.04837
3	0.03369	0.03381	0.03394	0.03406	0.03418	0.03430	0.03442	0.03454
4	0.02683	0.02695	0.02708	0.02720	0.02733	0.02745	0.02758	0.02770
5	0.02275	0.02288	0.02301	0.02314	0.02327	0.02340	0.02353	0.02366
6	0.02007	0.02021	0.02034	0.02047	0.02061	0.02074	0.02087	0.02101
7	0.01819	0.01833	0.01846	0.01860	0.01874	0.01888	0.01902	0.01916
8	0.01681	0.01695	0.01709	0.01723	0.01737	0.01751	0.01766	0.01780
9	0.01575	0.01590	0.01604	0.01619	0.01633	0.01648	0.01663	0.01678
10	0.01493	0.01508	0.01523	0.01538	0.01553	0.01568	0.01583	0.01598
11	0.01428	0.01443	0.01458	0.01473	0.01489	0.01504	0.01520	0.01535
12	0.01375	0.01390	0.01406	0.01421	0.01437	0.01453	0.01469	0.01485
13	0.01331	0.01347	0.01363	0.01379	0.01395	0.01411	0.01428	0.01444
14	0.01295	0.01311	0.01328	0.01344	0.01360	0.01377	0.01394	0.01410
15	0.01265	0.01282	0.01298	0.01315	0.01332	0.01349	0.01366	0.01383
16	0.01240	0.01257	0.01274	0.01291	0.01308	0.01325	0.01342	0.01359
17	0.01219	0.01236	0.01253	0.01270	0.01287	0.01305	0.01322	0.01340
18	0.01200	0.01218	0.01235	0.01253	0.01270	0.01288	0.01306	0.01324
19	0.01185	0.01203	0.01220	0.01238	0.01256	0.01274	0.01292	0.01310
20	0.01172	0.01189	0.01207	0.01225	0.01244	0.01262	0.01280	0.01298
21	0.01160	0.01178	0.01196	0.01215	0.01233	0.01251	0.01270	0.01288
22	0.01150	0.01169	0.01187	0.01205	0.01224	0.01243	0.01261	0.01280
23	0.01142	0.01160	0.01179	0.01197	0.01216	0.01235	0.01254	0.01273
24	0.01134	0.01153	0.01172	0.01191	0.01210	0.01229	0.01248	0.01267
25	0.01128	0.01147	0.01166	0.01185	0.01204	0.01223	0.01242	0.01261
26	0.01122	0.01141	0.01160	0.01180	0.01199	0.01218	0.01238	0.01257
27	0.01117	0.01137	0.01156	0.01175	0.01195	0.01214	0.01234	0.01253
28	0.01113	0.01132	0.01152	0.01171	0.01191	0.01210	0.01230	0.01250
29	0.01109	0.01129	0.01148	0.01168	0.01188	0.01207	0.01227	0.01247
30	0.01106	0.01126	0.01145	0.01165	0.01185	0.01205	0.01225	0.01244
31	0.01103	0.01123	0.01143	0.01163	0.01182	0.01202	0.01222	0.01242
32	0.01101	0.01121	0.01141	0.01160	0.01180	0.01200	0.01220	0.01241
33	0.01099	0.01119	0.01139	0.01159	0.01179	0.01199	0.01219	0.01239
34	0.01097	0.01117	0.01137	0.01157	0.01177	0.01197	0.01217	0.01238
35	0.01095	0.01115	0.01135	0.01155	0.01176	0.01196	0.01216	0.01236

Table 5

Monthly Mortgage Constants

	Annual Contract Interest Rate							
Year	15.00	15.25	15.50	15.75	16.00	16.25	16.50	16.75
1	0.09026	0.09038	0.09049	0.09061	0.09073	0.09085	0.09097	0.09109
2	0.04849	0.04861	0.04872	0.04884	0.04896	0.04908	0.04920	0.04932
3	0.03467	0.03479	0.03491	0.03503	0.03516	0.03528	0.03540	0.03553
4	0.02783	0.02796	0.02808	0.02821	0.02834	0.02847	0.02860	0.02873
5	0.02379	0.02392	0.02405	0.02419	0.02432	0.02445	0.02458	0.02472
6	0.02115	0.02128	0.02142	0.02155	0.02169	0.02183	0.02197	0.02211
7	0.01930	0.01944	0.01958	0.01972	0.01986	0.02000	0.02015	0.02029
8	0.01795	0.01809	0.01824	0.01838	0.01853	0.01868	0.01882	0.01897
9	0.01692	0.01707	0.01722	0.01737	0.01753	0.01768	0.01783	0.01798
10	0.01613	0.01629	0.01644	0.01660	0.01675	0.01691	0.01706	0.01722
11	0.01551	0.01567	0.01582	0.01598	0.01614	0.01630	0.01646	0.01663
12	0.01501	0.01517	0.01533	0.01549	0.01566	0.01582	0.01599	0.01615
13	0.01460	0.01477	0.01493	0.01510	0.01527	0.01543	0.01560	0.01577
14	0.01427	0.01444	0.01461	0.01478	0.01495	0.01512	0.01529	0.01546
15	0.01400	0.01417	0.01434	0.01451	0.01469	0.01486	0.01504	0.01521
16	0.01377	0.01394	0.01412	0.01429	0.01447	0.01465	0.01483	0.01501
17	0.01358	0.01375	0.01393	0.01411	0.01429	0.01447	0.01465	0.01484
18	0.01342	0.01360	0.01378	0.01396	0.01414	0.01433	0.01451	0.01469
19	0.01328	0.01346	0.01365	0.01383	0.01402	0.01420	0.01439	0.01458
20	0.01317	0.01335	0.01354	0.01373	0.01391	0.01410	0.01429	0.01448
21	0.01307	0.01326	0.01345	0.01364	0.01382	0.01401	0.01420	0.01440
22	0.01299	0.01318	0.01337	0.01356	0.01375	0.01394	0.01413	0.01433
23	0.01292	0.01311	0.01330	0.01349	0.01369	0.01388	0.01407	0.01427
24	0.01286	0.01305	0.01325	0.01344	0.01363	0.01383	0.01402	0.01422
25	0.01281	0.01300	0.01320	0.01339	0.01359	0.01379	0.01398	0.01418
26	0.01276	0.01296	0.01316	0.01335	0.01355	0.01375	0.01395	0.01415
27	0.01273	0.01292	0.01312	0.01332	0.01352	0.01372	0.01392	0.01412
28	0.01270	0.01289	0.01309	0.01329	0.01349	0.01369	0.01389	0.01409
29	0.01267	0.01287	0.01307	0.01327	0.01347	0.01367	0.01387	0.01407
30	0.01264	0.01284	0.01305	0.01325	0.01345	0.01365	0.01385	0.01405
31	0.01262	0.01283	0.01303	0.01323	0.01343	0.01363	0.01384	0.01404
32	0.01261	0.01281	0.01301	0.01321	0.01342	0.01362	0.01382	0.01403
33	0.01259	0.01279	0.01300	0.01320	0.01340	0.01361	0.01381	0.01402
34	0.01258	0.01278	0.01299	0.01319	0.01339	0.01360	0.01380	0.01401
35	0.01257	0.01277	0.01298	0.01318	0.01338	0.01359	0.01379	0.01400

Table 6

Remaining Mortgage Balance Percentage For 9.00 Percent

Age of loan	5	10	15	Original Loan Term 20	25	30	35	40
1	0.83417	0.93537	0.96695	0.98127	0.98884	0.99317	0.99575	0.99733
2	0.65278	0.86467	0.93079	0.96079	0.97664	0.98570	0.99110	0.99441
3	0.45438	0.78734	0.89125	0.93838	0.96329	0.97752	0.98601	0.99121
4	0.23737	0.70276	0.84799	0.91388	0.94869	0.96858	0.98045	0.98771
5		0.61024	0.80068	0.88707	0.93272	0.95880	0.97436	0.98389
6		0.50904	0.74893	0.85775	0.91526	0.94810	0.96770	0.97971
7		0.39835	0.69232	0.82568	0.89615	0.93640	0.96042	0.97513
8		0.27728	0.63041	0.79060	0.87525	0.92361	0.95246	0.97012
9		0.14485	0.56268	0.75223	0.85239	0.90961	0.94375	0.96465
10			0.48861	0.71026	0.82739	0.89430	0.93422	0.95866
11			0.40758	0.66435	0.80004	0.87755	0.92380	0.95211
12			0.31895	0.61414	0.77013	0.85923	0.91240	0.94495
13			0.22201	0.55922	0.73741	0.83919	0.89993	0.93711
14			0.11598	0.49914	0.70162	0.81728	0.88629	0.92854
15				0.43343	0.66248	0.79330	0.87137	0.91917
16				0.36155	0.61966	0.76708	0.85505	0.90891
17				0.28294	0.57282	0.73840	0.83720	0.89770
18				0.19694	0.52159	0.70703	0.81768	0.88543
19				0.10288	0.46556	0.67272	0.79632	0.87201
20					0.40427	0.63518	0.77297	0.85733
21					0.33723	0.59413	0.74742	0.84127
22					0.26390	0.54922	0.71947	0.82371
23					0.18369	0.50010	0.68890	0.80450
24					0.09596	0.44638	0.65547	0.78349
25						0.38761	0.61890	0.76051
26						0.32334	0.57890	0.73537
27						0.25303	0.53514	0.70788
28						0.17613	0.48728	0.67780
29						0.09201	0.43493	0.64491
30							0.37768	0.60893
31							0.31505	0.56957
32							0.24654	0.52652
33							0.17161	0.47943
34							0.08965	0.42793
35								0.37159
36								0.30997
37								0.24257
38								0.16884
39								0.08820
40								

Table 6

Remaining Mortgage Balance Percentage For 9.25 Percent

Age of loan	5	10	15	Original Loan Term 20	25	30	35	40
1	0.83506	0.93620	0.96765	0.98184	0.98929	0.99351	0.99600	0.99752
2	0.65421	0.86624	0.93217	0.96192	0.97754	0.98639	0.99162	0.99479
3	0.45590	0.78953	0.89327	0.94009	0.96466	0.97858	0.98682	0.99181
4	0.23844	0.70542	0.85062	0.91614	0.95054	0.97003	0.98155	0.98854
5		0.61319	0.80385	0.88989	0.93505	0.96064	0.97577	0.98495
6		0.51205	0.75257	0.86110	0.91807	0.95035	0.96944	0.98101
7		0.40115	0.69633	0.82953	0.89945	0.93907	0.96249	0.97670
8		0.27955	0.63467	0.79492	0.87903	0.92669	0.95488	0.97196
9		0.14621	0.56705	0.75696	0.85664	0.91313	0.94652	0.96677
10			0.49291	0.71534	0.83209	0.89825	0.93737	0.96108
11			0.41161	0.66970	0.80517	0.88193	0.92733	0.95485
12			0.32247	0.61966	0.77565	0.86405	0.91632	0.94800
13			0.22472	0.56478	0.74329	0.84443	0.90424	0.94050
14			0.11753	0.50461	0.70779	0.82292	0.89100	0.93228
15				0.43864	0.66888	0.79934	0.87649	0.92326
16				0.36629	0.62620	0.77348	0.86057	0.91337
17				0.28696	0.57941	0.74512	0.84311	0.90252
18				0.19997	0.52810	0.71403	0.82397	0.89063
19				0.10459	0.47184	0.67994	0.80299	0.87759
20					0.41015	0.64255	0.77998	0.86329
21					0.34250	0.60156	0.75474	0.84761
22					0.26832	0.55661	0.72707	0.83042
23					0.18698	0.50732	0.69673	0.81157
24					0.09780	0.45327	0.66346	0.79090
25						0.39400	0.62698	0.76823
26						0.32902	0.58698	0.74338
27						0.25776	0.54312	0.71613
28						0.17963	0.49502	0.68624
29						0.09395	0.44229	0.65348
30							0.38446	0.61755
31							0.32105	0.57815
32							0.25152	0.53495
33							0.17527	0.48757
34							0.09167	0.43563
35								0.37867
36								0.31621
37								0.24773
38								0.17264
39								0.09029
40								

Table 6

Remaining Mortgage Balance Percentage For 9.50 Percent

Age of loan	5	10	15	Original Loan Term 20	25	30	35	40
1	0.83596	0.93703	0.96834	0.98239	0.98972	0.99383	0.99625	0.99769
2	0.65563	0.86781	0.93353	0.96303	0.97841	0.98706	0.99212	0.99516
3	0.45741	0.79171	0.89527	0.94176	0.96599	0.97960	0.98758	0.99237
4	0.23952	0.70807	0.85322	0.91837	0.95233	0.97141	0.98260	0.98931
5		0.61612	0.80699	0.89265	0.93731	0.96241	0.97712	0.98594
6		0.51505	0.75617	0.86439	0.92081	0.95251	0.97109	0.98224
7		0.40395	0.70031	0.83332	0.90266	0.94163	0.96447	0.97817
8		0.28182	0.63890	0.79917	0.88272	0.92967	0.95719	0.97370
9		0.14757	0.57140	0.76163	0.86079	0.91653	0.94918	0.96878
10			0.49721	0.72036	0.83669	0.90208	0.94039	0.96338
11			0.41564	0.67500	0.81020	0.88619	0.93071	0.95744
12			0.32598	0.62513	0.78108	0.86873	0.92008	0.95091
13			0.22743	0.57032	0.74907	0.84954	0.90840	0.94373
14			0.11909	0.51007	0.71388	0.82844	0.89555	0.93584
15				0.44383	0.67520	0.80524	0.88143	0.92717
16				0.37103	0.63268	0.77975	0.86591	0.91763
17				0.29099	0.58595	0.75172	0.84885	0.90715
18				0.20301	0.53457	0.72091	0.83009	0.89563
19				0.10631	0.47809	0.68705	0.80948	0.88296
20					0.41601	0.64982	0.78681	0.86904
21					0.34777	0.60890	0.76190	0.85374
22					0.27275	0.56392	0.73452	0.83692
23					0.19029	0.51447	0.70442	0.81843
24					0.09964	0.46012	0.67133	0.79810
25						0.40037	0.63495	0.77575
26						0.33469	0.59497	0.75119
27						0.26250	0.55101	0.72419
28						0.18313	0.50270	0.69451
29						0.09590	0.44959	0.66189
30							0.39121	0.62603
31							0.32703	0.58660
32							0.25649	0.54327
33							0.17894	0.49563
34							0.09370	0.44327
35								0.38571
36								0.32244
37								0.25288
38								0.17643
39								0.09238
40								

Table 6

Remaining Mortgage Balance Percentage For 9.75 Percent

Age of loan	Original Loan Term							
	5	10	15	20	25	30	35	40
1	0.83685	0.93785	0.96902	0.98293	0.99013	0.99414	0.99647	0.99786
2	0.65705	0.86936	0.93487	0.96412	0.97925	0.98769	0.99259	0.99550
3	0.45893	0.79388	0.89725	0.94339	0.96727	0.98058	0.98831	0.99290
4	0.24060	0.71071	0.85579	0.92054	0.95406	0.97274	0.98359	0.99003
5		0.61905	0.81009	0.89537	0.93951	0.96411	0.97839	0.98688
6		0.51805	0.75974	0.86762	0.92347	0.95459	0.97266	0.98340
7		0.40675	0.70426	0.83705	0.90579	0.94411	0.96635	0.97956
8		0.28410	0.64312	0.80336	0.88632	0.93255	0.95939	0.97534
9		0.14894	0.57574	0.76624	0.86485	0.91982	0.95173	0.97068
10			0.50149	0.72533	0.84120	0.90579	0.94328	0.96555
11			0.41967	0.68025	0.81514	0.89032	0.93397	0.95990
12			0.32951	0.63057	0.78642	0.87328	0.92371	0.95367
13			0.23015	0.57583	0.75477	0.85451	0.91240	0.94680
14			0.12066	0.51550	0.71989	0.83381	0.89994	0.93924
15				0.44902	0.68145	0.81101	0.88621	0.93090
16				0.37576	0.63910	0.78588	0.87109	0.92171
17				0.29503	0.59242	0.75819	0.85441	0.91159
18				0.20607	0.54099	0.72768	0.83604	0.90043
19				0.10803	0.48431	0.69405	0.81580	0.88813
20					0.42186	0.65700	0.79349	0.87458
21					0.35303	0.61616	0.76890	0.85965
22					0.27718	0.57116	0.74181	0.84320
23					0.19360	0.52158	0.71195	0.82507
24					0.10150	0.46693	0.67905	0.80509
25						0.40671	0.64280	0.78307
26						0.34036	0.60285	0.75881
27						0.26723	0.55882	0.73207
28						0.18665	0.51030	0.70261
29						0.09785	0.45684	0.67014
30							0.39793	0.63436
31							0.33300	0.59494
32							0.26146	0.55149
33							0.18262	0.50361
34							0.09574	0.45085
35								0.39270
36								0.32863
37								0.25803
38								0.18022
39								0.09448
40								

Table 6

Remaining Mortgage Balance Percentage For 10.00 Percent

Age of loan	Original Loan Term							
	5	10	15	20	25	30	35	40
1	0.83773	0.93866	0.96968	0.98345	0.99053	0.99444	0.99669	0.99801
2	0.65847	0.87089	0.93619	0.96517	0.98007	0.98830	0.99303	0.99582
3	0.46044	0.79603	0.89919	0.94498	0.96851	0.98152	0.98900	0.99339
4	0.24167	0.71333	0.85832	0.92267	0.95574	0.97402	0.98453	0.99071
5		0.62197	0.81317	0.89802	0.94164	0.96574	0.97960	0.98776
6		0.52105	0.76329	0.87080	0.92606	0.95660	0.97416	0.98449
7		0.40955	0.70818	0.84072	0.90884	0.94649	0.96814	0.98087
8		0.28638	0.64731	0.80750	0.88983	0.93533	0.96150	0.97689
9		0.15031	0.58006	0.77079	0.86882	0.92300	0.95416	0.97248
10			0.50577	0.73024	0.84561	0.90938	0.94605	0.96761
11			0.42370	0.68545	0.81998	0.89433	0.93709	0.96223
12			0.33303	0.63596	0.79166	0.87771	0.92719	0.95629
13			0.23288	0.58130	0.76037	0.85934	0.91625	0.94972
14			0.12223	0.52091	0.72581	0.83906	0.90418	0.94247
15				0.45419	0.68762	0.81665	0.89083	0.93446
16				0.38049	0.64544	0.79189	0.87609	0.92561
17				0.29907	0.59885	0.76454	0.85981	0.91584
18				0.20913	0.54737	0.73432	0.84182	0.90504
19				0.10977	0.49050	0.70094	0.82194	0.89310
20					0.42768	0.66407	0.79999	0.87992
21					0.35828	0.62333	0.77574	0.86536
22					0.28162	0.57833	0.74894	0.84928
23					0.19692	0.52862	0.71934	0.83151
24					0.10336	0.47370	0.68665	0.81188
25						0.41303	0.65052	0.79019
26						0.34601	0.61062	0.76624
27						0.27197	0.56654	0.73977
28						0.19018	0.51784	0.71054
29						0.09982	0.46404	0.67824
30							0.40461	0.64256
31							0.33895	0.60314
32							0.26642	0.55960
33							0.18630	0.51150
34							0.09778	0.45836
35								0.39965
36								0.33480
37								0.26316
38								0.18402
39								0.09659
40								

Table 6

Remaining Mortgage Balance Percentage For 10.25 Percent

Age of loan	5	10	15	Original Loan Term 20	25	30	35	40
1	0.83861	0.93946	0.97034	0.98396	0.99092	0.99472	0.99689	0.99816
2	0.65989	0.87242	0.93749	0.96620	0.98085	0.98888	0.99345	0.99612
3	0.46196	0.79817	0.90111	0.94653	0.96971	0.98241	0.98965	0.99385
4	0.24276	0.71594	0.86082	0.92475	0.95737	0.97525	0.98543	0.99135
5		0.62488	0.81620	0.90063	0.94371	0.96731	0.98075	0.98858
6		0.52404	0.76679	0.87392	0.92857	0.95852	0.97558	0.98551
7		0.41235	0.71207	0.84433	0.91181	0.94879	0.96985	0.98211
8		0.28867	0.65147	0.81157	0.89325	0.93801	0.96351	0.97834
9		0.15169	0.58436	0.77528	0.87270	0.92608	0.95648	0.97417
10			0.51003	0.73510	0.84993	0.91286	0.94870	0.96955
11			0.42772	0.69060	0.82472	0.89822	0.94008	0.96444
12			0.33656	0.64131	0.79680	0.88201	0.93053	0.95877
13			0.23561	0.58673	0.76588	0.86405	0.91996	0.95250
14			0.12381	0.52629	0.73164	0.84417	0.90825	0.94555
15				0.45935	0.69372	0.82215	0.89529	0.93786
16				0.38522	0.65172	0.79776	0.88093	0.92934
17				0.30312	0.60521	0.77075	0.86503	0.91990
18				0.21220	0.55370	0.74085	0.84742	0.90945
19				0.11151	0.49666	0.70772	0.82792	0.89788
20					0.43349	0.67104	0.80633	0.88506
21					0.36353	0.63042	0.78241	0.87087
22					0.28606	0.58543	0.75592	0.85515
23					0.20025	0.53560	0.72659	0.83774
24					0.10523	0.48043	0.69410	0.81847
25						0.41932	0.65813	0.79712
26						0.35165	0.61828	0.77347
27						0.27671	0.57416	0.74729
28						0.19371	0.52530	0.71829
29						0.10179	0.47118	0.68618
30							0.41125	0.65061
31							0.34488	0.61122
32							0.27138	0.56760
33							0.18998	0.51930
34							0.09983	0.46580
35								0.40655
36								0.34094
37								0.26828
38								0.18781
39								0.09869
40								

Table 6

Remaining Mortgage Balance Percentage For 10.50 Percent

Age of loan	Original Loan Term							
	5	10	15	20	25	30	35	40
1	0.83949	0.94026	0.97098	0.98446	0.99129	0.99499	0.99709	0.99829
2	0.66130	0.87393	0.93877	0.96721	0.98161	0.98944	0.99385	0.99639
3	0.46347	0.80029	0.90300	0.94806	0.97087	0.98327	0.99026	0.99429
4	0.24384	0.71854	0.86329	0.92679	0.95895	0.97642	0.98627	0.99195
5		0.62778	0.81921	0.90319	0.94571	0.96882	0.98185	0.98935
6		0.52702	0.77027	0.87698	0.93102	0.96038	0.97693	0.98647
7		0.41515	0.71593	0.84788	0.91470	0.95100	0.97148	0.98327
8		0.29096	0.65561	0.81558	0.89659	0.94060	0.96542	0.97972
9		0.15308	0.58864	0.77971	0.87648	0.92905	0.95870	0.97577
10			0.51428	0.73990	0.85415	0.91622	0.95123	0.97139
11			0.43174	0.69569	0.82937	0.90199	0.94294	0.96653
12			0.34010	0.64662	0.80185	0.88618	0.93374	0.96113
13			0.23836	0.59214	0.77130	0.86863	0.92352	0.95514
14			0.12540	0.53165	0.73739	0.84915	0.91218	0.94849
15				0.46449	0.69973	0.82752	0.89959	0.94110
16				0.38994	0.65793	0.80351	0.88561	0.93290
17				0.30717	0.61152	0.77685	0.87009	0.92380
18				0.21528	0.55999	0.74725	0.85286	0.91369
19				0.11326	0.50279	0.71439	0.83373	0.90247
20					0.43928	0.67791	0.81250	0.89001
21					0.36877	0.63741	0.78892	0.87618
22					0.29050	0.59245	0.76275	0.86083
23					0.20359	0.54253	0.73369	0.84378
24					0.10711	0.48711	0.70142	0.82486
25						0.42558	0.66560	0.80385
26						0.35727	0.62584	0.78052
27						0.28144	0.58169	0.75462
28						0.19724	0.53268	0.72587
29						0.10377	0.47827	0.69395
30							0.41786	0.65852
31							0.35079	0.61918
32							0.27633	0.57550
33							0.19366	0.52701
34							0.10189	0.47317
35								0.41341
36								0.34705
37								0.27339
38								0.19160
39								0.10080
40								

Table 6

Remaining Mortgage Balance Percentage For 10.75 Percent

Age of loan	\	\	\	Original Loan Term \	\	\	\	\
	5	10	15	20	25	30	35	40
1	0.84037	0.94104	0.97161	0.98495	0.99165	0.99525	0.99727	0.99842
2	0.66271	0.87543	0.94002	0.96819	0.98235	0.98997	0.99423	0.99665
3	0.46498	0.80240	0.90486	0.94954	0.97200	0.98409	0.99084	0.99469
4	0.24492	0.72113	0.86573	0.92879	0.96048	0.97754	0.98708	0.99251
5		0.63067	0.82218	0.90569	0.94766	0.97026	0.98288	0.99008
6		0.53000	0.77371	0.87998	0.93339	0.96215	0.97822	0.98737
7		0.41795	0.71976	0.85137	0.91752	0.95313	0.97302	0.98436
8		0.29325	0.65972	0.81952	0.89984	0.94309	0.96724	0.98101
9		0.15447	0.59290	0.78408	0.88017	0.93192	0.96081	0.97728
10			0.51853	0.74464	0.85828	0.91948	0.95365	0.97313
11			0.43575	0.70074	0.83392	0.90564	0.94569	0.96851
12			0.34363	0.65188	0.80681	0.89023	0.93682	0.96337
13			0.24111	0.59750	0.77663	0.87308	0.92695	0.95765
14			0.12700	0.53698	0.74304	0.85400	0.91596	0.95128
15				0.46962	0.70566	0.83276	0.90374	0.94419
16				0.39466	0.66406	0.80912	0.89013	0.93630
17				0.31122	0.61776	0.78281	0.87499	0.92752
18				0.21837	0.56623	0.75353	0.85814	0.91775
19				0.11502	0.50887	0.72095	0.83938	0.90687
20					0.44504	0.68468	0.81851	0.89477
21					0.37400	0.64431	0.79527	0.88130
22					0.29494	0.59939	0.76941	0.86631
23					0.20694	0.54939	0.74064	0.84962
24					0.10900	0.49374	0.70861	0.83105
25						0.43181	0.67296	0.81038
26						0.36288	0.63328	0.78738
27						0.28616	0.58913	0.76178
28						0.20078	0.53998	0.73329
29						0.10576	0.48529	0.70157
30							0.42442	0.66628
31							0.35667	0.62700
32							0.28127	0.58328
33							0.19735	0.53463
34							0.10395	0.48047
35								0.42021
36								0.35313
37								0.27847
38								0.19539
39								0.10292
40								

Table 6

Remaining Mortgage Balance Percentage For 11.00 Percent

Age of loan	5	10	15	Original Loan Term 20	25	30	35	40
1	0.84125	0.94182	0.97224	0.98542	0.99199	0.99550	0.99744	0.99853
2	0.66412	0.87692	0.94126	0.96915	0.98305	0.99048	0.99458	0.99689
3	0.46650	0.80450	0.90670	0.95099	0.97308	0.98487	0.99139	0.99507
4	0.24601	0.72370	0.86814	0.93074	0.96196	0.97862	0.98783	0.99303
5		0.63355	0.82512	0.90814	0.94955	0.97165	0.98386	0.99075
6		0.53297	0.77711	0.88293	0.93570	0.96386	0.97944	0.98822
7		0.42076	0.72356	0.85480	0.92025	0.95518	0.97450	0.98538
8		0.29555	0.66381	0.82341	0.90301	0.94549	0.96898	0.98223
9		0.15586	0.59714	0.78839	0.88378	0.93468	0.96283	0.97870
10			0.52276	0.74932	0.86232	0.92263	0.95597	0.97477
11			0.43977	0.70573	0.83838	0.90917	0.94831	0.97038
12			0.34717	0.65709	0.81167	0.89416	0.93977	0.96548
13			0.24386	0.60283	0.78187	0.87741	0.93024	0.96002
14			0.12860	0.54228	0.74862	0.85872	0.91960	0.95393
15				0.47473	0.71152	0.83787	0.90774	0.94713
16				0.39937	0.67012	0.81461	0.89450	0.93954
17				0.31528	0.62394	0.78866	0.87973	0.93108
18				0.22146	0.57241	0.75970	0.86325	0.92164
19				0.11679	0.51493	0.72739	0.84487	0.91110
20					0.45078	0.69134	0.82435	0.89935
21					0.37922	0.65112	0.80147	0.88623
22					0.29937	0.60625	0.77593	0.87160
23					0.21029	0.55618	0.74744	0.85527
24					0.11090	0.50033	0.71565	0.83706
25						0.43800	0.68019	0.81673
26						0.36847	0.64062	0.79406
27						0.29089	0.59647	0.76876
28						0.20433	0.54721	0.74053
29						0.10775	0.49225	0.70904
30							0.43094	0.67390
31							0.36252	0.63469
32							0.28619	0.59095
33							0.20103	0.54215
34							0.10601	0.48770
35								0.42695
36								0.35917
37								0.28355
38								0.19917
39								0.10503
40								

Table 6

Remaining Mortgage Balance Percentage For 11.25 Percent

Age of loan	\ Original Loan Term							
	5	10	15	20	25	30	35	40
1	0.84212	0.94260	0.97285	0.98588	0.99232	0.99573	0.99760	0.99864
2	0.66552	0.87839	0.94248	0.97008	0.98374	0.99096	0.99491	0.99712
3	0.46801	0.80658	0.90851	0.95241	0.97413	0.98562	0.99191	0.99542
4	0.24709	0.72626	0.87051	0.93265	0.96339	0.97965	0.98855	0.99352
5		0.63642	0.82802	0.91054	0.95138	0.97297	0.98480	0.99139
6		0.53594	0.78049	0.88582	0.93794	0.96551	0.98059	0.98901
7		0.42356	0.72733	0.85816	0.92291	0.95715	0.97589	0.98635
8		0.29785	0.66786	0.82723	0.90610	0.94781	0.97064	0.98337
9		0.15726	0.60136	0.79264	0.88730	0.93736	0.96476	0.98004
10			0.52697	0.75394	0.86627	0.92567	0.95818	0.97632
11			0.44377	0.71067	0.84275	0.91259	0.95083	0.97215
12			0.35071	0.66226	0.81644	0.89797	0.94260	0.96749
13			0.24663	0.60812	0.78701	0.88161	0.93340	0.96228
14			0.13021	0.54756	0.75410	0.86332	0.92310	0.95645
15				0.47983	0.71729	0.84286	0.91159	0.94993
16				0.40407	0.67611	0.81997	0.89872	0.94264
17				0.31934	0.63006	0.79437	0.88432	0.93448
18				0.22456	0.57855	0.76574	0.86821	0.92536
19				0.11856	0.52094	0.73372	0.85019	0.91516
20					0.45650	0.69790	0.83004	0.90374
21					0.38442	0.65784	0.80750	0.89098
22					0.30381	0.61303	0.78229	0.87670
23					0.21365	0.56291	0.75410	0.86073
24					0.11280	0.50686	0.72256	0.84287
25						0.44416	0.68729	0.82289
26						0.37404	0.64784	0.80055
27						0.29560	0.60371	0.77556
28						0.20787	0.55436	0.74761
29						0.10975	0.49915	0.71634
30							0.43741	0.68137
31							0.36835	0.64226
32							0.29111	0.59851
33							0.20471	0.54958
34							0.10808	0.49485
35								0.43364
36								0.36518
37								0.28860
38								0.20295
39								0.10715
40								

Table 6

Remaining Mortgage Balance Percentage For 11.50 Percent

Age of loan	Original Loan Term							
	5	10	15	20	25	30	35	40
1	0.84298	0.94336	0.97345	0.98632	0.99264	0.99596	0.99775	0.99874
2	0.66693	0.87986	0.94367	0.97099	0.98440	0.99142	0.99523	0.99733
3	0.46952	0.80865	0.91029	0.95379	0.97515	0.98634	0.99240	0.99575
4	0.24818	0.72881	0.87286	0.93451	0.96478	0.98064	0.98923	0.99397
5		0.63929	0.83089	0.91289	0.95315	0.97425	0.98568	0.99198
6		0.53891	0.78383	0.88865	0.94011	0.96708	0.98169	0.98975
7		0.42636	0.73106	0.86147	0.92550	0.95904	0.97722	0.98725
8		0.30016	0.67190	0.83099	0.90911	0.95003	0.97221	0.98445
9		0.15866	0.60556	0.79682	0.89073	0.93993	0.96659	0.98130
10			0.53117	0.75851	0.87012	0.92860	0.96029	0.97777
11			0.44777	0.71555	0.84702	0.91590	0.95323	0.97382
12			0.35425	0.66738	0.82111	0.90166	0.94531	0.96939
13			0.24940	0.61337	0.79206	0.88569	0.93643	0.96442
14			0.13183	0.55281	0.75949	0.86779	0.92647	0.95884
15				0.48490	0.72297	0.84771	0.91530	0.95259
16				0.40877	0.68203	0.82520	0.90278	0.94559
17				0.32340	0.63611	0.79997	0.88875	0.93773
18				0.22767	0.58463	0.77167	0.87301	0.92892
19				0.12034	0.52691	0.73993	0.85536	0.91904
20					0.46219	0.70436	0.83557	0.90797
21					0.38962	0.66446	0.81339	0.89555
22					0.30825	0.61973	0.78851	0.88162
23					0.21701	0.56958	0.76061	0.86601
24					0.11471	0.51334	0.72934	0.84850
25						0.45028	0.69427	0.82887
26						0.37958	0.65494	0.80686
27						0.30031	0.61085	0.78219
28						0.21142	0.56142	0.75452
29						0.11175	0.50599	0.72349
30							0.44383	0.68870
31							0.37415	0.64969
32							0.29601	0.60596
33							0.20839	0.55692
34							0.11015	0.50193
35								0.44028
36								0.37115
37								0.29363
38								0.20672
39								0.10927
40								

Table 6

Remaining Mortgage Balance Percentage For 11.75 Percent

Age of loan	5	10	15	Original Loan Term 20	25	30	35	40
1	0.84385	0.94412	0.97404	0.98676	0.99295	0.99617	0.99789	0.99883
2	0.66833	0.88131	0.94485	0.97187	0.98503	0.99186	0.99553	0.99753
3	0.47104	0.81070	0.91205	0.95514	0.97613	0.98702	0.99286	0.99605
4	0.24927	0.73134	0.87517	0.93633	0.96612	0.98158	0.98987	0.99440
5		0.64213	0.83372	0.91519	0.95487	0.97547	0.98651	0.99254
6		0.54186	0.78713	0.89143	0.94222	0.96859	0.98273	0.99045
7		0.42916	0.73476	0.86472	0.92801	0.96086	0.97848	0.98810
8		0.30247	0.67590	0.83470	0.91203	0.95218	0.97371	0.98546
9		0.16007	0.60973	0.80095	0.89407	0.94242	0.96834	0.98249
10			0.53536	0.76302	0.87389	0.93144	0.96231	0.97915
11			0.45176	0.72038	0.85120	0.91911	0.95553	0.97540
12			0.35780	0.67245	0.82569	0.90524	0.94790	0.97118
13			0.25217	0.61858	0.79703	0.88966	0.93933	0.96644
14			0.13345	0.55802	0.76480	0.87214	0.92970	0.96112
15				0.48996	0.72858	0.85245	0.91888	0.95513
16				0.41345	0.68787	0.83031	0.90671	0.94840
17				0.32745	0.64210	0.80544	0.89303	0.94083
18				0.23079	0.59066	0.77747	0.87766	0.93233
19				0.12213	0.53284	0.74604	0.86037	0.92277
20					0.46785	0.71070	0.84095	0.91202
21					0.39479	0.67099	0.81911	0.89994
22					0.31267	0.62635	0.79457	0.88637
23					0.22037	0.57617	0.76698	0.87111
24					0.11662	0.51977	0.73597	0.85395
25						0.45637	0.70112	0.83467
26						0.38511	0.66194	0.81300
27						0.30500	0.61790	0.78864
28						0.21497	0.56840	0.76126
29						0.11376	0.51276	0.73048
30							0.45021	0.69589
31							0.37991	0.65700
32							0.30089	0.61329
33							0.21207	0.56416
34							0.11223	0.50893
35								0.44685
36								0.37708
37								0.29864
38								0.21048
39								0.11139
40								

Table 6

Remaining Mortgage Balance Percentage For 12.00 Percent

Age of loan				Original Loan Term				
	5	10	15	20	25	30	35	40
1	0.84471	0.94487	0.97461	0.98718	0.99325	0.99637	0.99803	0.99892
2	0.66972	0.88274	0.94601	0.97273	0.98564	0.99228	0.99581	0.99771
3	0.47255	0.81274	0.91377	0.95646	0.97707	0.98767	0.99330	0.99634
4	0.25036	0.73386	0.87745	0.93811	0.96741	0.98248	0.99048	0.99480
5		0.64497	0.83652	0.91744	0.95653	0.97663	0.98730	0.99306
6		0.54482	0.79040	0.89415	0.94427	0.97004	0.98372	0.99110
7		0.43196	0.73844	0.86791	0.93045	0.96261	0.97968	0.98889
8		0.30478	0.67988	0.83834	0.91488	0.95424	0.97513	0.98641
9		0.16148	0.61389	0.80501	0.89733	0.94481	0.97001	0.98360
10			0.53954	0.76746	0.87756	0.93418	0.96423	0.98045
11			0.45575	0.72515	0.85529	0.92220	0.95772	0.97689
12			0.36134	0.67747	0.83018	0.90871	0.95039	0.97288
13			0.25496	0.62375	0.80189	0.89350	0.94212	0.96836
14			0.13508	0.56321	0.77002	0.87637	0.93281	0.96327
15				0.49499	0.73410	0.85706	0.92232	0.95754
16				0.41813	0.69363	0.83530	0.91049	0.95107
17				0.33151	0.64802	0.81078	0.89717	0.94379
18				0.23391	0.59664	0.78316	0.88215	0.93558
19				0.12393	0.53873	0.75203	0.86524	0.92633
20					0.47348	0.71695	0.84617	0.91591
21					0.39995	0.67742	0.82469	0.90417
22					0.31710	0.63288	0.80049	0.89094
23					0.22374	0.58269	0.77321	0.87603
24					0.11854	0.52614	0.74248	0.85923
25						0.46241	0.70784	0.84030
26						0.39060	0.66882	0.81897
27						0.30969	0.62484	0.79493
28						0.21851	0.57529	0.76784
29						0.11577	0.51946	0.73732
30							0.45654	0.70293
31							0.38564	0.66418
32							0.30576	0.62051
33							0.21574	0.57130
34							0.11430	0.51585
35								0.45337
36								0.38297
37								0.30363
38								0.21424
39								0.11351
40								

Table 6

Remaining Mortgage Balance Percentage For 12.25 Percent

Age of loan	5	10	15	Original Loan Term 20	25	30	35	40
1	0.84557	0.94561	0.97518	0.98759	0.99354	0.99656	0.99815	0.99900
2	0.67112	0.88417	0.94715	0.97357	0.98623	0.99268	0.99607	0.99788
3	0.47406	0.81477	0.91548	0.95774	0.97799	0.98830	0.99371	0.99660
4	0.25146	0.73636	0.87970	0.93985	0.96867	0.98334	0.99105	0.99517
5		0.64780	0.83929	0.91965	0.95814	0.97775	0.98805	0.99354
6		0.54776	0.79364	0.89682	0.94625	0.97143	0.98465	0.99171
7		0.43475	0.74207	0.87104	0.93282	0.96429	0.98082	0.98964
8		0.30710	0.68382	0.84191	0.91765	0.95622	0.97648	0.98730
9		0.16289	0.61802	0.80901	0.90051	0.94711	0.97159	0.98465
10			0.54369	0.77185	0.88115	0.93682	0.96606	0.98167
11			0.45973	0.72987	0.85928	0.92520	0.95982	0.97829
12			0.36488	0.68245	0.83458	0.91207	0.95276	0.97448
13			0.25774	0.62888	0.80667	0.89723	0.94479	0.97018
14			0.13672	0.56836	0.77515	0.88047	0.93579	0.96532
15				0.50001	0.73954	0.86155	0.92562	0.95982
16				0.42279	0.69932	0.84016	0.91414	0.95362
17				0.33556	0.65388	0.81601	0.90116	0.94661
18				0.23703	0.60255	0.78872	0.88651	0.93869
19				0.12573	0.54457	0.75790	0.86995	0.92975
20					0.47908	0.72309	0.85125	0.91965
21					0.40509	0.68376	0.83012	0.90824
22					0.32152	0.63933	0.80626	0.89535
23					0.22711	0.58915	0.77930	0.88078
24					0.12047	0.53246	0.74884	0.86433
25						0.46842	0.71444	0.84575
26						0.39608	0.67558	0.82476
27						0.31436	0.63169	0.80105
28						0.22206	0.58210	0.77427
29						0.11779	0.52609	0.74401
30							0.46282	0.70983
31							0.39134	0.67122
32							0.31061	0.62761
33							0.21940	0.57835
34							0.11638	0.52269
35								0.45983
36								0.38882
37								0.30860
38								0.21799
39								0.11563
40								

Table 6

Remaining Mortgage Balance Percentage For 12.50 Percent

Age of loan				Original Loan Term				
	5	10	15	20	25	30	35	40
1	0.84642	0.94634	0.97574	0.98799	0.99381	0.99675	0.99827	0.99908
2	0.67251	0.88558	0.94826	0.97439	0.98680	0.99306	0.99632	0.99803
3	0.47557	0.81677	0.91715	0.95899	0.97887	0.98889	0.99410	0.99685
4	0.25255	0.73886	0.88192	0.94155	0.96988	0.98417	0.99159	0.99551
5		0.65062	0.84202	0.92180	0.95970	0.97882	0.98875	0.99400
6		0.55070	0.79684	0.89944	0.94817	0.97276	0.98554	0.99228
7		0.43755	0.74568	0.87411	0.93512	0.96590	0.98189	0.99034
8		0.30942	0.68774	0.84543	0.92034	0.95813	0.97777	0.98813
9		0.16431	0.62213	0.81296	0.90361	0.94933	0.97310	0.98564
10			0.54784	0.77618	0.88465	0.93937	0.96781	0.98282
11			0.46370	0.73453	0.86319	0.92809	0.96182	0.97962
12			0.36843	0.68737	0.83888	0.91531	0.95504	0.97600
13			0.26054	0.63396	0.81136	0.90085	0.94735	0.97190
14			0.13836	0.57348	0.78019	0.88447	0.93866	0.96726
15				0.50500	0.74490	0.86591	0.92881	0.96200
16				0.42744	0.70493	0.84491	0.91765	0.95604
17				0.33962	0.65967	0.82112	0.90502	0.94930
18				0.24016	0.60841	0.79417	0.89072	0.94167
19				0.12754	0.55037	0.76367	0.87452	0.93302
20					0.48465	0.72912	0.85617	0.92323
21					0.41022	0.69000	0.83540	0.91214
22					0.32593	0.64570	0.81188	0.89959
23					0.23048	0.59553	0.78524	0.88537
24					0.12240	0.53871	0.75508	0.86927
25						0.47438	0.72092	0.85103
26						0.40153	0.68224	0.83039
27						0.31903	0.63843	0.80701
28						0.22560	0.58883	0.78053
29						0.11981	0.53266	0.75055
30							0.46904	0.71659
31							0.39701	0.67814
32							0.31544	0.63460
33							0.22306	0.58529
34							0.11846	0.52946
35								0.46623
36								0.39463
37								0.31354
38								0.22172
39								0.11775
40								

Table 6

Remaining Mortgage Balance Percentage For 12.75 Percent

Age of loan	5	10	15	Original Loan Term 20	25	30	35	40
1	0.84728	0.94707	0.97629	0.98838	0.99408	0.99692	0.99838	0.99915
2	0.67390	0.88698	0.94936	0.97519	0.98735	0.99343	0.99655	0.99818
3	0.47708	0.81877	0.91880	0.96021	0.97971	0.98946	0.99447	0.99708
4	0.25365	0.74133	0.88411	0.94321	0.97105	0.98495	0.99210	0.99584
5		0.65343	0.84472	0.92391	0.96121	0.97984	0.98942	0.99442
6		0.55363	0.80001	0.90200	0.95004	0.97403	0.98637	0.99281
7		0.44034	0.74925	0.87713	0.93736	0.96744	0.98292	0.99099
8		0.31174	0.69163	0.84889	0.92296	0.95996	0.97899	0.98892
9		0.16574	0.62622	0.81684	0.90662	0.95147	0.97453	0.98657
10			0.55196	0.78045	0.88807	0.94183	0.96947	0.98390
11			0.46767	0.73914	0.86701	0.93088	0.96373	0.98087
12			0.37197	0.69224	0.84310	0.91846	0.95721	0.97743
13			0.26333	0.63901	0.81596	0.90435	0.94981	0.97353
14			0.14000	0.57857	0.78515	0.88834	0.94140	0.96909
15				0.50997	0.75017	0.87016	0.93186	0.96406
16				0.43208	0.71046	0.84953	0.92104	0.95835
17				0.34367	0.66539	0.82610	0.90874	0.95187
18				0.24329	0.61422	0.79951	0.89479	0.94451
19				0.12935	0.55613	0.76932	0.87894	0.93615
20					0.49018	0.73505	0.86096	0.92666
21					0.41532	0.69614	0.84054	0.91590
22					0.33033	0.65197	0.81736	0.90367
23					0.23386	0.60184	0.79105	0.88979
24					0.12433	0.54492	0.76118	0.87404
25						0.48030	0.72727	0.85615
26						0.40695	0.68878	0.83585
27						0.32367	0.64508	0.81280
28						0.22914	0.59547	0.78664
29						0.12183	0.53915	0.75693
30							0.47522	0.72321
31							0.40264	0.68493
32							0.32025	0.64148
33							0.22672	0.59215
34							0.12054	0.53614
35								0.47257
36								0.40039
37								0.31846
38								0.22545
39								0.11987
40								

Table 6

Remaining Mortgage Balance Percentage For 13.00 Percent

Age of loan	5	10	15	Original Loan Term 20	25	30	35	40
1	0.84813	0.94779	0.97682	0.98876	0.99433	0.99709	0.99849	0.99921
2	0.67529	0.88837	0.95045	0.97596	0.98788	0.99377	0.99677	0.99832
3	0.47859	0.82075	0.92043	0.96140	0.98053	0.99000	0.99481	0.99730
4	0.25474	0.74380	0.88627	0.94483	0.97218	0.98570	0.99258	0.99614
5		0.65622	0.84739	0.92597	0.96267	0.98082	0.99005	0.99481
6		0.55656	0.80315	0.90451	0.95184	0.97526	0.98717	0.99331
7		0.44314	0.75280	0.88008	0.93952	0.96893	0.98388	0.99160
8		0.31406	0.69550	0.85229	0.92551	0.96172	0.98015	0.98965
9		0.16717	0.63029	0.82065	0.90955	0.95353	0.97590	0.98744
10			0.55608	0.78466	0.89140	0.94420	0.97106	0.98492
11			0.47162	0.74369	0.87074	0.93358	0.96555	0.98205
12			0.37551	0.69707	0.84723	0.92150	0.95929	0.97878
13			0.26613	0.64401	0.82047	0.90775	0.95215	0.97506
14			0.14166	0.58363	0.79002	0.89211	0.94404	0.97084
15				0.51491	0.75536	0.87430	0.93480	0.96602
16				0.43671	0.71592	0.85403	0.92429	0.96054
17				0.34771	0.67104	0.83097	0.91233	0.95431
18				0.24643	0.61996	0.80473	0.89872	0.94722
19				0.13117	0.56184	0.77486	0.88323	0.93914
20					0.49568	0.74087	0.86560	0.92996
21					0.42040	0.70219	0.84554	0.91950
22					0.33473	0.65817	0.82270	0.90760
23					0.23723	0.60807	0.79672	0.89406
24					0.12627	0.55106	0.76715	0.87865
25						0.48618	0.73350	0.86111
26						0.41234	0.69520	0.84115
27						0.32831	0.65162	0.81844
28						0.23268	0.60202	0.79259
29						0.12385	0.54558	0.76317
30							0.48134	0.72970
31							0.40824	0.69160
32							0.32504	0.64824
33							0.23036	0.59890
34							0.12262	0.54275
35								0.47884
36								0.40612
37								0.32336
38								0.22917
39								0.12198
40								

Table 7

Annual Percentage Rate (APR)
Term Of Loan: 20 Years

Contract Rate	Percentage Points Charged							
	0.50	1.00	1.50	2.00	2.50	3.00	3.50	4.00
7.00	7.0648	7.1301	7.1960	7.2623	7.3291	7.3965	7.4644	7.5329
7.25	7.3155	7.3814	7.4479	7.5149	7.5824	7.6505	7.7191	7.7882
7.50	7.5661	7.6328	7.6999	7.7676	7.8358	7.9045	7.9738	8.0437
7.75	7.8168	7.8841	7.9519	8.0203	8.0892	8.1586	8.2286	8.2992
8.00	8.0675	8.1354	8.2040	8.2730	8.3426	8.4128	8.4835	8.5548
8.25	8.3181	8.3868	8.4560	8.5258	8.5961	8.6669	8.7384	8.8104
8.50	8.5688	8.6382	8.7081	8.7786	8.8496	8.9212	8.9934	9.0661
8.75	8.8195	8.8896	8.9602	9.0314	9.1031	9.1755	9.2484	9.3219
9.00	9.0702	9.1410	9.2123	9.2842	9.3567	9.4298	9.5035	9.5778
9.25	9.3209	9.3924	9.4645	9.5371	9.6104	9.6842	9.7586	9.8337
9.50	9.5717	9.6439	9.7167	9.7901	9.8641	9.9386	10.0138	10.0897
9.75	9.8224	9.8953	9.9689	10.0430	10.1178	10.1931	10.2691	10.3457
10.00	10.0731	10.1468	10.2211	10.2960	10.3715	10.4477	10.5244	10.6019
10.25	10.3239	10.3983	10.4734	10.5491	10.6253	10.7023	10.7798	10.8580
10.50	10.5746	10.6498	10.7257	10.8021	10.8792	10.9569	11.0353	11.1143
10.75	10.8254	10.9014	10.9780	11.0552	11.1331	11.2116	11.2908	11.3706
11.00	11.0761	11.1529	11.2303	11.3083	11.3870	11.4663	11.5464	11.6270
11.25	11.3269	11.4045	11.4827	11.5615	11.6410	11.7211	11.8020	11.8835
11.50	11.5777	11.6560	11.7350	11.8147	11.8950	11.9760	12.0577	12.1400
11.75	11.8285	11.9076	11.9874	12.0679	12.1490	12.2309	12.3134	12.3966
12.00	12.0793	12.1592	12.2399	12.3212	12.4031	12.4858	12.5692	12.6533
12.25	12.3301	12.4109	12.4923	12.5744	12.6573	12.7408	12.8250	12.9100
12.50	12.5809	12.6625	12.7448	12.8278	12.9114	12.9958	13.0810	13.1668
12.75	12.8317	12.9142	12.9973	13.0811	13.1657	13.2509	13.3369	13.4237
13.00	13.0826	13.1658	13.2498	13.3345	13.4199	13.5061	13.5929	13.6806
13.25	13.3334	13.4175	13.5024	13.5879	13.6742	13.7612	13.8490	13.9376
13.50	13.5843	13.6692	13.7549	13.8413	13.9285	14.0165	14.1052	14.1946
13.75	13.8351	13.9209	14.0075	14.0948	14.1829	14.2717	14.3613	14.4518
14.00	14.0860	14.1727	14.2601	14.3483	14.4373	14.5270	14.6176	14.7089
14.25	14.3368	14.4244	14.5128	14.6019	14.6917	14.7824	14.8739	14.9662
14.50	14.5877	14.6762	14.7654	14.8554	14.9462	15.0378	15.1302	15.2235
14.75	14.8386	14.9280	15.0181	15.1090	15.2007	15.2933	15.3866	15.4808
15.00	15.0895	15.1798	15.2708	15.3626	15.4553	15.5488	15.6431	15.7383
15.25	15.3404	15.4316	15.5235	15.6163	15.7099	15.8043	15.8996	15.9957
15.50	15.5913	15.6834	15.7763	15.8700	15.9645	16.0599	16.1562	16.2533
15.75	15.8422	15.9352	16.0290	16.1237	16.2192	16.3156	16.4128	16.5109
16.00	16.0931	16.1871	16.2818	16.3774	16.4739	16.5712	16.6694	16.7685
16.25	16.3441	16.4389	16.5346	16.6312	16.7286	16.8269	16.9261	17.0263
16.50	16.5950	16.6908	16.7875	16.8850	16.9834	17.0827	17.1829	17.2840
16.75	16.8459	16.9427	17.0403	17.1388	17.2382	17.3385	17.4397	17.5419

Table 7

Annual Percentage Rate (APR)
Term Of Loan: 20 Years

Contract Rate	4.50	5.00	5.50	6.00	6.50	7.00	7.50	8.00
7.00	7.6018	7.6714	7.7415	7.8121	7.8834	7.9552	8.0276	8.1007
7.25	7.8579	7.9282	7.9990	8.0704	8.1424	8.2149	8.2881	8.3619
7.50	8.1141	8.1850	8.2566	8.3287	8.4015	8.4748	8.5488	8.6233
7.75	8.3703	8.4420	8.5143	8.5872	8.6607	8.7348	8.8095	8.8849
8.00	8.6266	8.6991	8.7721	8.8458	8.9200	8.9949	9.0704	9.1466
8.25	8.8830	8.9562	9.0300	9.1044	9.1795	9.2551	9.3314	9.4084
8.50	9.1395	9.2134	9.2880	9.3632	9.4390	9.5155	9.5926	9.6704
8.75	9.3960	9.4707	9.5461	9.6221	9.6987	9.7760	9.8539	9.9325
9.00	9.6526	9.7281	9.8043	9.8811	9.9585	10.0366	10.1154	10.1948
9.25	9.9093	9.9856	10.0626	10.1402	10.2184	10.2973	10.3769	10.4572
9.50	10.1661	10.2432	10.3210	10.3994	10.4784	10.5582	10.6386	10.7198
9.75	10.4230	10.5009	10.5794	10.6587	10.7386	10.8192	10.9005	10.9825
10.00	10.6799	10.7586	10.8380	10.9181	10.9988	11.0803	11.1624	11.2453
10.25	10.9369	11.0165	11.0967	11.1776	11.2592	11.3415	11.4246	11.5083
10.50	11.1940	11.2744	11.3554	11.4372	11.5197	11.6029	11.6868	11.7715
10.75	11.4512	11.5324	11.6143	11.6969	11.7803	11.8644	11.9492	12.0347
11.00	11.7084	11.7905	11.8733	11.9568	12.0410	12.1260	12.2117	12.2982
11.25	11.9657	12.0487	12.1323	12.2167	12.3018	12.3877	12.4743	12.5617
11.50	12.2231	12.3069	12.3914	12.4767	12.5627	12.6495	12.7371	12.8254
11.75	12.4806	12.5653	12.6507	12.7369	12.8238	12.9115	13.0000	13.0893
12.00	12.7381	12.8237	12.9100	12.9971	13.0849	13.1736	13.2630	13.3533
12.25	12.9957	13.0822	13.1694	13.2574	13.3462	13.4358	13.5262	13.6174
12.50	13.2534	13.3408	13.4289	13.5179	13.6076	13.6981	13.7895	13.8817
12.75	13.5112	13.5995	13.6885	13.7784	13.8691	13.9606	14.0529	14.1461
13.00	13.7690	13.8582	13.9482	14.0390	14.1307	14.2231	14.3164	14.4106
13.25	14.0269	14.1171	14.2080	14.2998	14.3924	14.4858	14.5801	14.6753
13.50	14.2849	14.3760	14.4679	14.5606	14.6542	14.7486	14.8439	14.9401
13.75	14.5430	14.6350	14.7278	14.8215	14.9161	15.0115	15.1078	15.2050
14.00	14.8011	14.8941	14.9879	15.0826	15.1781	15.2745	15.3719	15.4701
14.25	15.0593	15.1532	15.2480	15.3437	15.4402	15.5377	15.6360	15.7353
14.50	15.3175	15.4125	15.5082	15.6049	15.7025	15.8009	15.9003	16.0006
14.75	15.5759	15.6718	15.7686	15.8662	15.9648	16.0643	16.1647	16.2661
15.00	15.8343	15.9312	16.0289	16.1276	16.2272	16.3278	16.4292	16.5317
15.25	16.0927	16.1906	16.2894	16.3891	16.4898	16.5913	16.6939	16.7974
15.50	16.3513	16.4502	16.5500	16.6507	16.7524	16.8550	16.9586	17.0632
15.75	16.6099	16.7098	16.8106	16.9124	17.0151	17.1188	17.2235	17.3292
16.00	16.8685	16.9695	17.0713	17.1742	17.2779	17.3827	17.4885	17.5953
16.25	17.1273	17.2292	17.3321	17.4360	17.5409	17.6467	17.7536	17.8615
16.50	17.3861	17.4891	17.5930	17.6980	17.8039	17.9108	18.0188	18.1278
16.75	17.6449	17.7490	17.8540	17.9600	18.0670	18.1750	18.2841	18.3942

Table 7

Annual Percentage Rate (APR)
Term Of Loan: 20 Years

Contract Rate	Percentage Points Charged							
	8.50	9.00	9.50	10.00	10.50	11.00	11.50	12.00
7.00	8.1743	8.2486	8.3235	8.3990	8.4752	8.5521	8.6296	8.7078
7.25	8.4363	8.5114	8.5871	8.6634	8.7405	8.8181	8.8965	8.9756
7.50	8.6985	8.7744	8.8509	8.9280	9.0059	9.0844	9.1636	9.2435
7.75	8.9609	9.0375	9.1148	9.1928	9.2715	9.3509	9.4309	9.5117
8.00	9.2234	9.3008	9.3790	9.4578	9.5373	9.6175	9.6985	9.7801
8.25	9.4860	9.5643	9.6433	9.7230	9.8033	9.8844	9.9662	10.0488
8.50	9.7488	9.8280	9.9078	9.9883	10.0696	10.1515	10.2342	10.3177
8.75	10.0118	10.0918	10.1725	10.2539	10.3360	10.4188	10.5024	10.5868
9.00	10.2749	10.3558	10.4373	10.5196	10.6026	10.6863	10.7709	10.8561
9.25	10.5382	10.6199	10.7023	10.7855	10.8694	10.9541	11.0395	11.1257
9.50	10.8016	10.8842	10.9675	11.0516	11.1364	11.2220	11.3084	11.3955
9.75	11.0652	11.1487	11.2329	11.3179	11.4036	11.4901	11.5774	11.6656
10.00	11.3290	11.4133	11.4984	11.5843	11.6710	11.7585	11.8467	11.9358
10.25	11.5928	11.6781	11.7642	11.8510	11.9386	12.0270	12.1163	12.2063
10.50	11.8569	11.9431	12.0301	12.1178	12.2064	12.2958	12.3860	12.4770
10.75	12.1211	12.2082	12.2961	12.3848	12.4744	12.5647	12.6559	12.7480
11.00	12.3854	12.4735	12.5624	12.6520	12.7425	12.8339	12.9261	13.0192
11.25	12.6499	12.7390	12.8288	12.9194	13.0109	13.1033	13.1965	13.2906
11.50	12.9146	13.0046	13.0954	13.1870	13.2795	13.3728	13.4671	13.5622
11.75	13.1794	13.2703	13.3621	13.4547	13.5482	13.6426	13.7379	13.8340
12.00	13.4444	13.5363	13.6290	13.7227	13.8172	13.9126	14.0089	14.1061
12.25	13.7095	13.8024	13.8961	13.9908	14.0863	14.1827	14.2801	14.3784
12.50	13.9747	14.0686	14.1634	14.2590	14.3556	14.4531	14.5515	14.6509
12.75	14.2401	14.3350	14.4308	14.5275	14.6251	14.7237	14.8232	14.9236
13.00	14.5056	14.6016	14.6984	14.7961	14.8948	14.9944	15.0950	15.1966
13.25	14.7713	14.8683	14.9661	15.0649	15.1647	15.2654	15.3670	15.4697
13.50	15.0371	15.1351	15.2341	15.3339	15.4347	15.5365	15.6393	15.7431
13.75	15.3031	15.4022	15.5021	15.6031	15.7050	15.8079	15.9117	16.0167
14.00	15.5692	15.6693	15.7704	15.8724	15.9754	16.0794	16.1844	16.2905
14.25	15.8355	15.9366	16.0388	16.1419	16.2460	16.3511	16.4572	16.5644
14.50	16.1019	16.2041	16.3073	16.4115	16.5167	16.6230	16.7303	16.8386
14.75	16.3684	16.4717	16.5760	16.6813	16.7877	16.8951	17.0035	17.1131
15.00	16.6351	16.7395	16.8449	16.9513	17.0588	17.1673	17.2769	17.3877
15.25	16.9019	17.0074	17.1139	17.2215	17.3301	17.4398	17.5506	17.6625
15.50	17.1688	17.2754	17.3831	17.4918	17.6015	17.7124	17.8244	17.9375
15.75	17.4359	17.5436	17.6524	17.7622	17.8732	17.9852	18.0984	18.2127
16.00	17.7031	17.8119	17.9218	18.0328	18.1450	18.2582	18.3725	18.4881
16.25	17.9704	18.0804	18.1915	18.3036	18.4169	18.5313	18.6469	18.7636
16.50	18.2378	18.3490	18.4612	18.5746	18.6890	18.8046	18.9214	19.0394
16.75	18.5054	18.6177	18.7311	18.8456	18.9613	19.0781	19.1961	19.3154

Table 7

Annual Percentage Rate (APR)
Term Of Loan: 25 Years

Contract Rate	Percentage Points Charged							
	0.50	1.00	1.50	2.00	2.50	3.00	3.50	4.00
7.00	7.0556	7.1117	7.1682	7.2251	7.2825	7.3404	7.3987	7.4575
7.25	7.3063	7.3631	7.4203	7.4780	7.5361	7.5947	7.6538	7.7133
7.50	7.5570	7.6145	7.6725	7.7309	7.7897	7.8491	7.9089	7.9693
7.75	7.8078	7.8660	7.9246	7.9838	8.0434	8.1036	8.1642	8.2253
8.00	8.0585	8.1174	8.1769	8.2368	8.2972	8.3581	8.4195	8.4814
8.25	8.3092	8.3689	8.4291	8.4898	8.5510	8.6127	8.6749	8.7376
8.50	8.5600	8.6205	8.6814	8.7429	8.8049	8.8673	8.9304	8.9939
8.75	8.8107	8.8720	8.9337	8.9960	9.0588	9.1221	9.1859	9.2503
9.00	9.0615	9.1236	9.1861	9.2491	9.3127	9.3768	9.4415	9.5067
9.25	9.3123	9.3751	9.4385	9.5023	9.5667	9.6317	9.6972	9.7632
9.50	9.5631	9.6267	9.6909	9.7556	9.8208	9.8866	9.9529	10.0199
9.75	9.8139	9.8783	9.9433	10.0088	10.0749	10.1416	10.2088	10.2766
10.00	10.0647	10.1300	10.1958	10.2622	10.3291	10.3966	10.4647	10.5333
10.25	10.3155	10.3816	10.4483	10.5155	10.5833	10.6517	10.7206	10.7902
10.50	10.5664	10.6333	10.7008	10.7689	10.8376	10.9068	10.9767	11.0471
10.75	10.8172	10.8850	10.9534	11.0223	11.0919	11.1620	11.2328	11.3042
11.00	11.0681	11.1367	11.2060	11.2758	11.3462	11.4173	11.4890	11.5613
11.25	11.3189	11.3885	11.4586	11.5293	11.6006	11.6726	11.7452	11.8184
11.50	11.5698	11.6402	11.7112	11.7828	11.8551	11.9280	12.0015	12.0757
11.75	11.8207	11.8920	11.9639	12.0364	12.1096	12.1834	12.2579	12.3330
12.00	12.0716	12.1438	12.2166	12.2900	12.3641	12.4389	12.5143	12.5904
12.25	12.3225	12.3956	12.4693	12.5437	12.6187	12.6945	12.7708	12.8479
12.50	12.5734	12.6474	12.7221	12.7974	12.8734	12.9501	13.0274	13.1055
12.75	12.8243	12.8992	12.9748	13.0511	13.1281	13.2057	13.2841	13.3631
13.00	13.0752	13.1511	13.2276	13.3049	13.3828	13.4614	13.5408	13.6208
13.25	13.3262	13.4030	13.4805	13.5587	13.6376	13.7172	13.7975	13.8786
13.50	13.5771	13.6549	13.7333	13.8125	13.8924	13.9730	14.0544	14.1365
13.75	13.8280	13.9068	13.9862	14.0664	14.1473	14.2289	14.3112	14.3944
14.00	14.0790	14.1587	14.2391	14.3203	14.4022	14.4848	14.5682	14.6524
14.25	14.3300	14.4106	14.4921	14.5742	14.6571	14.7408	14.8252	14.9104
14.50	14.5809	14.6626	14.7450	14.8282	14.9121	14.9968	15.0822	15.1685
14.75	14.8319	14.9146	14.9980	15.0822	15.1671	15.2528	15.3394	15.4267
15.00	15.0829	15.1666	15.2510	15.3362	15.4222	15.5090	15.5965	15.6849
15.25	15.3339	15.4186	15.5040	15.5902	15.6773	15.7651	15.8538	15.9433
15.50	15.5849	15.6706	15.7571	15.8443	15.9324	16.0213	16.1110	16.2016
15.75	15.8359	15.9226	16.0101	16.0985	16.1876	16.2776	16.3684	16.4601
16.00	16.0869	16.1747	16.2632	16.3526	16.4428	16.5339	16.6258	16.7185
16.25	16.3380	16.4267	16.5163	16.6068	16.6980	16.7902	16.8832	16.9771
16.50	16.5890	16.6788	16.7695	16.8610	16.9533	17.0466	17.1407	17.2357
16.75	16.8400	16.9309	17.0226	17.1152	17.2086	17.3030	17.3982	17.4944

Table 7

Annual Percentage Rate (APR)
Term Of Loan: 25 Years

Contract Rate	4.50	5.00	5.50	6.00	Percentage Points Charged 6.50	7.00	7.50	8.00
7.00	7.5168	7.5766	7.6368	7.6976	7.7589	7.8207	7.8831	7.9459
7.25	7.7734	7.8340	7.8950	7.9566	8.0187	8.0813	8.1445	8.2082
7.50	8.0301	8.0915	8.1533	8.2157	8.2786	8.3421	8.4061	8.4707
7.75	8.2869	8.3491	8.4118	8.4750	8.5387	8.6030	8.6679	8.7333
8.00	8.5439	8.6068	8.6703	8.7344	8.7989	8.8641	8.9298	8.9961
8.25	8.8009	8.8647	8.9290	8.9939	9.0593	9.1253	9.1919	9.2591
8.50	9.0580	9.1226	9.1878	9.2535	9.3198	9.3867	9.4542	9.5223
8.75	9.3152	9.3806	9.4467	9.5133	9.5805	9.6483	9.7167	9.7856
9.00	9.5725	9.6388	9.7057	9.7732	9.8413	9.9100	9.9793	10.0492
9.25	9.8299	9.8971	9.9649	10.0332	10.1022	10.1718	10.2420	10.3129
9.50	10.0873	10.1554	10.2241	10.2934	10.3633	10.4338	10.5050	10.5768
9.75	10.3449	10.4139	10.4835	10.5537	10.6245	10.6960	10.7681	10.8408
10.00	10.6026	10.6725	10.7430	10.8141	10.8859	10.9583	11.0313	11.1051
10.25	10.8604	10.9312	11.0026	11.0746	11.1474	11.2207	11.2948	11.3695
10.50	11.1182	11.1899	11.2623	11.3353	11.4090	11.4833	11.5583	11.6340
10.75	11.3762	11.4488	11.5221	11.5961	11.6707	11.7461	11.8221	11.8988
11.00	11.6342	11.7078	11.7821	11.8570	11.9326	12.0089	12.0860	12.1637
11.25	11.8923	11.9669	12.0421	12.1180	12.1947	12.2720	12.3500	12.4288
11.50	12.1505	12.2261	12.3023	12.3792	12.4568	12.5351	12.6142	12.6940
11.75	12.4088	12.4854	12.5626	12.6405	12.7191	12.7985	12.8786	12.9594
12.00	12.6672	12.7447	12.8229	12.9019	12.9815	13.0619	13.1431	13.2250
12.25	12.9257	13.0042	13.0834	13.1634	13.2440	13.3255	13.4077	13.4907
12.50	13.1843	13.2638	13.3440	13.4250	13.5067	13.5892	13.6725	13.7566
12.75	13.4429	13.5234	13.6047	13.6867	13.7695	13.8531	13.9374	14.0226
13.00	13.7016	13.7832	13.8655	13.9485	14.0324	14.1171	14.2025	14.2888
13.25	13.9604	14.0430	14.1264	14.2105	14.2954	14.3812	14.4677	14.5551
13.50	14.2193	14.3029	14.3873	14.4726	14.5586	14.6454	14.7331	14.8216
13.75	14.4783	14.5629	14.6484	14.7347	14.8218	14.9098	14.9986	15.0882
14.00	14.7373	14.8230	14.9096	14.9970	15.0852	15.1743	15.2642	15.3550
14.25	14.9964	15.0832	15.1709	15.2594	15.3487	15.4389	15.5300	15.6219
14.50	15.2556	15.3435	15.4322	15.5218	15.6123	15.7036	15.7958	15.8890
14.75	15.5149	15.6039	15.6937	15.7844	15.8760	15.9685	16.0618	16.1561
15.00	15.7742	15.8643	15.9552	16.0471	16.1398	16.2334	16.3280	16.4235
15.25	16.0336	16.1248	16.2169	16.3098	16.4037	16.4985	16.5942	16.6909
15.50	16.2931	16.3854	16.4786	16.5727	16.6677	16.7637	16.8606	16.9585
15.75	16.5526	16.6461	16.7404	16.8357	16.9319	17.0290	17.1271	17.2262
16.00	16.8122	16.9068	17.0023	17.0987	17.1961	17.2944	17.3937	17.4940
16.25	17.0719	17.1676	17.2642	17.3618	17.4604	17.5599	17.6604	17.7620
16.50	17.3316	17.4285	17.5263	17.6251	17.7248	17.8255	17.9273	18.0300
16.75	17.5914	17.6894	17.7884	17.8884	17.9893	18.0912	18.1942	18.2982

Table 7

Annual Percentage Rate (APR)
Term Of Loan: 25 Years

Contract Rate	8.50	9.00	9.50	10.00	10.50	11.00	11.50	12.00
7.00	8.0094	8.0733	8.1379	8.2030	8.2687	8.3349	8.4018	8.4693
7.25	8.2725	8.3373	8.4027	8.4687	8.5353	8.6024	8.6702	8.7386
7.50	8.5358	8.6015	8.6678	8.7347	8.8021	8.8702	8.9389	9.0083
7.75	8.7993	8.8659	8.9331	9.0008	9.0692	9.1383	9.2079	9.2782
8.00	9.0630	9.1305	9.1986	9.2673	9.3366	9.4065	9.4771	9.5484
8.25	9.3269	9.3953	9.4643	9.5339	9.6042	9.6751	9.7467	9.8189
8.50	9.5910	9.6603	9.7302	9.8008	9.8720	9.9439	10.0165	10.0897
8.75	9.8553	9.9255	9.9964	10.0679	10.1401	10.2130	10.2865	10.3608
9.00	10.1197	10.1909	10.2628	10.3353	10.4084	10.4823	10.5568	10.6321
9.25	10.3844	10.4565	10.5293	10.6028	10.6770	10.7519	10.8274	10.9037
9.50	10.6492	10.7223	10.7961	10.8706	10.9458	11.0217	11.0983	11.1756
9.75	10.9143	10.9884	11.0632	11.1386	11.2148	11.2918	11.3694	11.4478
10.00	11.1795	11.2546	11.3304	11.4069	11.4841	11.5621	11.6408	11.7203
10.25	11.4449	11.5210	11.5978	11.6753	11.7536	11.8327	11.9125	11.9930
10.50	11.7105	11.7876	11.8654	11.9440	12.0234	12.1035	12.1844	12.2660
10.75	11.9762	12.0544	12.1333	12.2129	12.2933	12.3745	12.4565	12.5393
11.00	12.2422	12.3214	12.4013	12.4820	12.5635	12.6458	12.7289	12.8128
11.25	12.5083	12.5885	12.6696	12.7514	12.8340	12.9174	13.0016	13.0866
11.50	12.7746	12.8559	12.9380	13.0209	13.1046	13.1891	13.2745	13.3607
11.75	13.0410	13.1235	13.2066	13.2907	13.3755	13.4611	13.5476	13.6350
12.00	13.3077	13.3912	13.4755	13.5606	13.6466	13.7334	13.8210	13.9096
12.25	13.5745	13.6591	13.7445	13.8308	13.9179	14.0058	14.0947	14.1844
12.50	13.8415	13.9272	14.0137	14.1011	14.1894	14.2785	14.3685	14.4595
12.75	14.1086	14.1954	14.2831	14.3717	14.4611	14.5514	14.6426	14.7348
13.00	14.3759	14.4639	14.5527	14.6424	14.7330	14.8245	14.9169	15.0103
13.25	14.6434	14.7325	14.8225	14.9134	15.0051	15.0979	15.1915	15.2861
13.50	14.9110	15.0013	15.0924	15.1845	15.2775	15.3714	15.4663	15.5621
13.75	15.1788	15.2702	15.3625	15.4558	15.5500	15.6451	15.7413	15.8384
14.00	15.4467	15.5393	15.6328	15.7273	15.8227	15.9191	16.0165	16.1148
14.25	15.7148	15.8086	15.9033	15.9990	16.0956	16.1933	16.2919	16.3915
14.50	15.9830	16.0780	16.1739	16.2708	16.3687	16.4676	16.5675	16.6685
14.75	16.2514	16.3476	16.4447	16.5429	16.6420	16.7421	16.8433	16.9456
15.00	16.5199	16.6173	16.7157	16.8151	16.9155	17.0169	17.1194	17.2229
15.25	16.7886	16.8872	16.9868	17.0874	17.1891	17.2918	17.3956	17.5005
15.50	17.0573	17.1572	17.2581	17.3600	17.4629	17.5669	17.6720	17.7782
15.75	17.3263	17.4274	17.5295	17.6327	17.7369	17.8422	17.9486	18.0561
16.00	17.5953	17.6977	17.8011	17.9055	18.0110	18.1177	18.2254	18.3343
16.25	17.8645	17.9681	18.0728	18.1785	18.2853	18.3933	18.5024	18.6126
16.50	18.1338	18.2387	18.3446	18.4517	18.5598	18.6691	18.7795	18.8911
16.75	18.4033	18.5094	18.6166	18.7250	18.8344	18.9450	19.0568	19.1698

Table 7

Annual Percentage Rate (APR)
Term Of Loan: 30 Years

Contract Rate	Percentage Points Charged							
	0.50	1.00	1.50	2.00	2.50	3.00	3.50	4.00
7.00	7.0497	7.0999	7.1504	7.2014	7.2527	7.3045	7.3568	7.4094
7.25	7.3005	7.3514	7.4027	7.4545	7.5066	7.5592	7.6123	7.6658
7.50	7.5513	7.6029	7.6551	7.7076	7.7606	7.8140	7.8679	7.9222
7.75	7.8020	7.8545	7.9074	7.9608	8.0146	8.0688	8.1236	8.1787
8.00	8.0528	8.1061	8.1599	8.2140	8.2687	8.3238	8.3793	8.4354
8.25	8.3037	8.3578	8.4123	8.4673	8.5228	8.5788	8.6352	8.6921
8.50	8.5545	8.6094	8.6648	8.7207	8.7770	8.8338	8.8911	8.9489
8.75	8.8053	8.8611	8.9173	8.9740	9.0313	9.0890	9.1472	9.2059
9.00	9.0561	9.1128	9.1699	9.2275	9.2856	9.3442	9.4033	9.4629
9.25	9.3070	9.3645	9.4225	9.4810	9.5399	9.5994	9.6595	9.7200
9.50	9.5579	9.6162	9.6751	9.7345	9.7944	9.8548	9.9157	9.9772
9.75	9.8087	9.8680	9.9278	9.9880	10.0489	10.1102	10.1721	10.2345
10.00	10.0596	10.1198	10.1805	10.2417	10.3034	10.3657	10.4285	10.4919
10.25	10.3105	10.3716	10.4332	10.4953	10.5580	10.6212	10.6850	10.7494
10.50	10.5614	10.6234	10.6859	10.7490	10.8127	10.8769	10.9416	11.0070
10.75	10.8124	10.8753	10.9387	11.0028	11.0674	11.1325	11.1983	11.2647
11.00	11.0633	11.1271	11.1916	11.2565	11.3221	11.3883	11.4551	11.5224
11.25	11.3142	11.3790	11.4444	11.5104	11.5769	11.6441	11.7119	11.7803
11.50	11.5652	11.6309	11.6973	11.7642	11.8318	11.9000	11.9688	12.0382
11.75	11.8161	11.8829	11.9502	12.0182	12.0867	12.1559	12.2257	12.2962
12.00	12.0671	12.1348	12.2032	12.2721	12.3417	12.4119	12.4828	12.5543
12.25	12.3181	12.3868	12.4561	12.5261	12.5967	12.6679	12.7399	12.8124
12.50	12.5691	12.6388	12.7091	12.7801	12.8517	12.9240	12.9970	13.0707
12.75	12.8201	12.8908	12.9622	13.0342	13.1068	13.1802	13.2543	13.3290
13.00	13.0711	13.1428	13.2152	13.2883	13.3620	13.4364	13.5115	13.5874
13.25	13.3221	13.3949	13.4683	13.5424	13.6172	13.6927	13.7689	13.8458
13.50	13.5731	13.6469	13.7214	13.7966	13.8724	13.9490	14.0263	14.1044
13.75	13.8242	13.8990	13.9745	14.0508	14.1277	14.2054	14.2838	14.3630
14.00	14.0752	14.1511	14.2277	14.3050	14.3830	14.4618	14.5413	14.6216
14.25	14.3262	14.4032	14.4809	14.5593	14.6384	14.7183	14.7989	14.8804
14.50	14.5773	14.6553	14.7341	14.8135	14.8938	14.9748	15.0566	15.1392
14.75	14.8284	14.9075	14.9873	15.0679	15.1492	15.2314	15.3143	15.3980
15.00	15.0794	15.1596	15.2405	15.3222	15.4047	15.4880	15.5720	15.6569
15.25	15.3305	15.4118	15.4938	15.5766	15.6602	15.7446	15.8298	15.9159
15.50	15.5816	15.6639	15.7471	15.8310	15.9158	16.0013	16.0877	16.1749
15.75	15.8327	15.9161	16.0004	16.0855	16.1713	16.2580	16.3456	16.4340
16.00	16.0838	16.1683	16.2537	16.3399	16.4269	16.5148	16.6036	16.6932
16.25	16.3349	16.4206	16.5071	16.5944	16.6826	16.7716	16.8615	16.9523
16.50	16.5860	16.6728	16.7604	16.8489	16.9383	17.0285	17.1196	17.2116
16.75	16.8371	16.9250	17.0138	17.1035	17.1940	17.2854	17.3777	17.4709

Table 7

Annual Percentage Rate (APR)
Term Of Loan: 30 Years

Contract Rate	Percentage Points Charged							
	4.50	5.00	5.50	6.00	6.50	7.00	7.50	8.00
7.00	7.4625	7.5161	7.5701	7.6246	7.6796	7.7350	7.7910	7.8474
7.25	7.7197	7.7741	7.8290	7.8844	7.9402	7.9965	8.0534	8.1107
7.50	7.9770	8.0323	8.0880	8.1442	8.2010	8.2582	8.3159	8.3742
7.75	8.2344	8.2905	8.3472	8.4043	8.4619	8.5201	8.5787	8.6379
8.00	8.4919	8.5489	8.6065	8.6645	8.7230	8.7821	8.8417	8.9018
8.25	8.7495	8.8074	8.8659	8.9248	8.9843	9.0443	9.1049	9.1660
8.50	9.0073	9.0661	9.1254	9.1853	9.2457	9.3067	9.3682	9.4303
8.75	9.2651	9.3249	9.3851	9.4460	9.5074	9.5693	9.6318	9.6949
9.00	9.5231	9.5837	9.6450	9.7068	9.7691	9.8320	9.8955	9.9596
9.25	9.7811	9.8428	9.9050	9.9677	10.0310	10.0950	10.1595	10.2246
9.50	10.0393	10.1019	10.1651	10.2288	10.2931	10.3581	10.4236	10.4897
9.75	10.2976	10.3611	10.4253	10.4900	10.5554	10.6213	10.6879	10.7551
10.00	10.5559	10.6205	10.6856	10.7514	10.8178	10.8848	10.9524	11.0206
10.25	10.8144	10.8800	10.9461	11.0129	11.0803	11.1483	11.2170	11.2864
10.50	11.0730	11.1396	11.2067	11.2746	11.3430	11.4121	11.4819	11.5523
10.75	11.3317	11.3993	11.4675	11.5363	11.6059	11.6760	11.7469	11.8184
11.00	11.5904	11.6591	11.7283	11.7983	11.8688	11.9401	12.0120	12.0847
11.25	11.8493	11.9190	11.9893	12.0603	12.1320	12.2043	12.2774	12.3511
11.50	12.1083	12.1790	12.2504	12.3225	12.3952	12.4687	12.5429	12.6178
11.75	12.3673	12.4391	12.5116	12.5848	12.6586	12.7332	12.8085	12.8846
12.00	12.6265	12.6994	12.7729	12.8472	12.9222	12.9979	13.0743	13.1515
12.25	12.8857	12.9597	13.0344	13.1097	13.1859	13.2627	13.3403	13.4187
12.50	13.1450	13.2201	13.2959	13.3724	13.4497	13.5277	13.6064	13.6860
12.75	13.4044	13.4806	13.5575	13.6352	13.7136	13.7928	13.8727	13.9535
13.00	13.6639	13.7412	13.8193	13.8981	13.9776	14.0580	14.1391	14.2211
13.25	13.9235	14.0019	14.0811	14.1611	14.2418	14.3233	14.4057	14.4888
13.50	14.1832	14.2627	14.3431	14.4242	14.5061	14.5888	14.6724	14.7567
13.75	14.4429	14.5236	14.6051	14.6874	14.7705	14.8544	14.9392	15.0248
14.00	14.7027	14.7846	14.8672	14.9507	15.0350	15.1201	15.2061	15.2930
14.25	14.9626	15.0456	15.1294	15.2141	15.2996	15.3860	15.4732	15.5613
14.50	15.2225	15.3067	15.3917	15.4776	15.5643	15.6519	15.7404	15.8298
14.75	15.4826	15.5679	15.6541	15.7412	15.8292	15.9180	16.0077	16.0984
15.00	15.7426	15.8292	15.9166	16.0049	16.0941	16.1842	16.2752	16.3671
15.25	16.0028	16.0906	16.1792	16.2687	16.3591	16.4504	16.5427	16.6359
15.50	16.2630	16.3520	16.4418	16.5326	16.6242	16.7168	16.8104	16.9049
15.75	16.5233	16.6135	16.7045	16.7965	16.8894	16.9833	17.0781	17.1739
16.00	16.7836	16.8750	16.9673	17.0606	17.1547	17.2499	17.3460	17.4431
16.25	17.0440	17.1366	17.2302	17.3247	17.4201	17.5165	17.6139	17.7124
16.50	17.3045	17.3983	17.4931	17.5889	17.6856	17.7833	17.8820	17.9817
16.75	17.5650	17.6601	17.7561	17.8531	17.9511	18.0501	18.1502	18.2512

Table 7

Annual Percentage Rate (APR)
Term Of Loan: 30 Years

Contract Rate	Percentage Points Charged							
	8.50	9.00	9.50	10.00	10.50	11.00	11.50	12.00
7.00	7.9043	7.9618	8.0197	8.0782	8.1372	8.1968	8.2569	8.3176
7.25	8.1685	8.2269	8.2858	8.3453	8.4052	8.4658	8.5269	8.5886
7.50	8.4330	8.4923	8.5522	8.6126	8.6735	8.7351	8.7972	8.8599
7.75	8.6976	8.7579	8.8188	8.8801	8.9421	9.0047	9.0678	9.1315
8.00	8.9625	9.0238	9.0856	9.1480	9.2110	9.2745	9.3387	9.4035
8.25	9.2277	9.2899	9.3527	9.4161	9.4801	9.5447	9.6100	9.6758
8.50	9.4930	9.5562	9.6201	9.6845	9.7495	9.8152	9.8815	9.9485
8.75	9.7585	9.8228	9.8877	9.9532	10.0193	10.0860	10.1534	10.2214
9.00	10.0243	10.0896	10.1555	10.2221	10.2892	10.3571	10.4256	10.4947
9.25	10.2903	10.3566	10.4236	10.4912	10.5595	10.6284	10.6980	10.7683
9.50	10.5565	10.6239	10.6920	10.7607	10.8300	10.9001	10.9708	11.0422
9.75	10.8229	10.8914	10.9605	11.0303	11.1008	11.1720	11.2439	11.3165
10.00	11.0895	11.1591	11.2293	11.3003	11.3719	11.4442	11.5172	11.5910
10.25	11.3563	11.4270	11.4984	11.5704	11.6432	11.7167	11.7909	11.8658
10.50	11.6234	11.6952	11.7676	11.8408	11.9147	11.9894	12.0648	12.1410
10.75	11.8906	11.9635	12.0371	12.1115	12.1866	12.2624	12.3390	12.4164
11.00	12.1580	12.2320	12.3068	12.3824	12.4586	12.5357	12.6135	12.6921
11.25	12.4256	12.5008	12.5768	12.6535	12.7309	12.8092	12.8882	12.9681
11.50	12.6934	12.7698	12.8469	12.9248	13.0035	13.0830	13.1632	13.2444
11.75	12.9614	13.0389	13.1172	13.1963	13.2762	13.3570	13.4385	13.5209
12.00	13.2295	13.3082	13.3878	13.4681	13.5492	13.6312	13.7140	13.7977
12.25	13.4978	13.5778	13.6585	13.7401	13.8225	13.9057	13.9898	14.0748
12.50	13.7663	13.8475	13.9295	14.0123	14.0959	14.1804	14.2658	14.3521
12.75	14.0350	14.1174	14.2006	14.2846	14.3696	14.4554	14.5420	14.6296
13.00	14.3038	14.3874	14.4719	14.5572	14.6434	14.7305	14.8185	14.9074
13.25	14.5728	14.6577	14.7434	14.8300	14.9175	15.0059	15.0952	15.1855
13.50	14.8420	14.9281	15.0151	15.1029	15.1917	15.2815	15.3721	15.4637
13.75	15.1113	15.1986	15.2869	15.3761	15.4662	15.5572	15.6492	15.7422
14.00	15.3807	15.4694	15.5589	15.6494	15.7408	15.8332	15.9266	16.0209
14.25	15.6503	15.7402	15.8311	15.9229	16.0156	16.1094	16.2041	16.2999
14.50	15.9201	16.0113	16.1034	16.1966	16.2906	16.3857	16.4818	16.5790
14.75	16.1899	16.2824	16.3759	16.4704	16.5658	16.6623	16.7598	16.8583
15.00	16.4599	16.5538	16.6486	16.7444	16.8412	16.9390	17.0379	17.1378
15.25	16.7301	16.8252	16.9213	17.0185	17.1167	17.2159	17.3162	17.4175
15.50	17.0003	17.0968	17.1943	17.2928	17.3923	17.4929	17.5946	17.6974
15.75	17.2707	17.3685	17.4673	17.5672	17.6681	17.7701	17.8732	17.9775
16.00	17.5412	17.6403	17.7405	17.8418	17.9441	18.0475	18.1520	18.2577
16.25	17.8118	17.9123	18.0138	18.1165	18.2202	18.3250	18.4310	18.5381
16.50	18.0825	18.1844	18.2873	18.3913	18.4964	18.6027	18.7101	18.8187
16.75	18.3534	18.4566	18.5608	18.6663	18.7728	18.8805	18.9893	19.0994

Table 8

Mortgage Pricing As A Percent of Loan Amount
(30 Year Term And 9 Year Prepayment)

Required Percentage Yield	Net Percentage Contract Rate							
	9.00	9.25	9.50	9.75	10.00	10.25	10.50	10.75
7.00	1.12871	1.14502	1.16138	1.17776	1.19419	1.21065	1.22713	1.24365
7.25	1.11151	1.12763	1.14380	1.16000	1.17624	1.19251	1.20882	1.22515
7.50	1.09464	1.11058	1.12656	1.14258	1.15864	1.17473	1.19085	1.20700
7.75	1.07809	1.09385	1.10965	1.12549	1.14137	1.15728	1.17322	1.18919
8.00	1.06186	1.07745	1.09307	1.10873	1.12443	1.14017	1.15593	1.17173
8.25	1.04595	1.06135	1.07680	1.09229	1.10782	1.12338	1.13897	1.15459
8.50	1.03033	1.04557	1.06085	1.07616	1.09152	1.10691	1.12233	1.13778
8.75	1.01502	1.03009	1.04520	1.06034	1.07553	1.09075	1.10600	1.12129
9.00	1.00000	1.01490	1.02984	1.04482	1.05984	1.07490	1.08998	1.10510
9.25	0.98527	1.00000	1.01478	1.02960	1.04445	1.05934	1.07427	1.08922
9.50	0.97081	0.98538	1.00000	1.01466	1.02935	1.04408	1.05885	1.07364
9.75	0.95663	0.97104	0.98550	1.00000	1.01454	1.02911	1.04371	1.05835
10.00	0.94272	0.95698	0.97128	0.98562	1.00000	1.01442	1.02887	1.04335
10.25	0.92907	0.94318	0.95732	0.97151	0.98574	1.00000	1.01430	1.02863
10.50	0.91568	0.92963	0.94363	0.95767	0.97174	0.98585	1.00000	1.01418
10.75	0.90254	0.91635	0.93019	0.94408	0.95801	0.97197	0.98597	1.00000
11.00	0.88965	0.90331	0.91701	0.93075	0.94453	0.95835	0.97220	0.98608
11.25	0.87701	0.89052	0.90407	0.91767	0.93130	0.94498	0.95868	0.97243
11.50	0.86460	0.87796	0.89138	0.90483	0.91832	0.93185	0.94542	0.95902
11.75	0.85242	0.86565	0.87892	0.89223	0.90559	0.91898	0.93240	0.94586
12.00	0.84047	0.85356	0.86669	0.87987	0.89308	0.90634	0.91962	0.93295
12.25	0.82874	0.84169	0.85469	0.86773	0.88081	0.89393	0.90708	0.92027
12.50	0.81723	0.83005	0.84291	0.85582	0.86877	0.88175	0.89477	0.90782
12.75	0.80594	0.81862	0.83136	0.84413	0.85694	0.86980	0.88268	0.89561
13.00	0.79485	0.80741	0.82001	0.83265	0.84534	0.85806	0.87082	0.88361
13.25	0.78397	0.79640	0.80887	0.82139	0.83395	0.84654	0.85917	0.87184
13.50	0.77329	0.78559	0.79794	0.81033	0.82276	0.83523	0.84774	0.86028
13.75	0.76281	0.77499	0.78721	0.79948	0.81178	0.82413	0.83651	0.84893
14.00	0.75252	0.76458	0.77668	0.78882	0.80101	0.81323	0.82549	0.83778
14.25	0.74242	0.75435	0.76634	0.77836	0.79042	0.80253	0.81467	0.82684
14.50	0.73250	0.74432	0.75618	0.76809	0.78003	0.79202	0.80404	0.81610
14.75	0.72277	0.73447	0.74622	0.75800	0.76983	0.78170	0.79360	0.80554
15.00	0.71321	0.72480	0.73643	0.74810	0.75982	0.77157	0.78336	0.79518
15.25	0.70383	0.71530	0.72682	0.73838	0.74998	0.76162	0.77330	0.78501
15.50	0.69462	0.70598	0.71738	0.72883	0.74032	0.75185	0.76341	0.77501
15.75	0.68557	0.69683	0.70812	0.71946	0.73084	0.74225	0.75371	0.76520
16.00	0.67669	0.68784	0.69902	0.71025	0.72152	0.73283	0.74418	0.75556
16.25	0.66797	0.67901	0.69009	0.70121	0.71237	0.72358	0.73482	0.74609
16.50	0.65941	0.67034	0.68132	0.69233	0.70339	0.71449	0.72562	0.73679
16.75	0.65100	0.66183	0.67270	0.68361	0.69457	0.70556	0.71659	0.72765

Table 8

Mortgage Pricing As A Percent of Loan Amount
(30 Year Term And 9 Year Prepayment)

Required Percentage Yield	Net Percentage Contract Rate							
	11.00	11.25	11.50	11.75	12.00	12.25	12.50	12.75
7.00	1.26019	1.27676	1.29335	1.30996	1.32660	1.34325	1.35991	1.37659
7.25	1.24151	1.25789	1.27430	1.29073	1.30718	1.32364	1.34013	1.35663
7.50	1.22318	1.23938	1.25561	1.27186	1.28813	1.30441	1.32072	1.33704
7.75	1.20519	1.22122	1.23727	1.25334	1.26943	1.28554	1.30167	1.31782
8.00	1.18755	1.20340	1.21928	1.23517	1.25109	1.26703	1.28298	1.29895
8.25	1.17024	1.18592	1.20162	1.21735	1.23309	1.24886	1.26464	1.28044
8.50	1.15326	1.16877	1.18430	1.19986	1.21543	1.23103	1.24665	1.26228
8.75	1.13660	1.15194	1.16730	1.18269	1.19810	1.21354	1.22899	1.24445
9.00	1.12025	1.13543	1.15063	1.16585	1.18110	1.19637	1.21165	1.22696
9.25	1.10421	1.11922	1.13426	1.14932	1.16441	1.17952	1.19464	1.20979
9.50	1.08847	1.10332	1.11820	1.13311	1.14803	1.16298	1.17795	1.19293
9.75	1.07302	1.08772	1.10244	1.11719	1.13196	1.14675	1.16156	1.17639
10.00	1.05786	1.07241	1.08697	1.10157	1.11618	1.13082	1.14548	1.16016
10.25	1.04299	1.05738	1.07179	1.08623	1.10070	1.11518	1.12969	1.14422
10.50	1.02839	1.04263	1.05689	1.07119	1.08550	1.09984	1.11420	1.12857
10.75	1.01406	1.02815	1.04227	1.05641	1.07058	1.08477	1.09898	1.11321
11.00	1.00000	1.01395	1.02792	1.04192	1.05594	1.06998	1.08405	1.09814
11.25	0.98620	1.00000	1.01383	1.02768	1.04156	1.05547	1.06939	1.08333
11.50	0.97265	0.98631	1.00000	1.01371	1.02745	1.04122	1.05500	1.06880
11.75	0.95935	0.97288	0.98642	1.00000	1.01360	1.02722	1.04087	1.05453
12.00	0.94630	0.95969	0.97310	0.98654	1.00000	1.01349	1.02700	1.04053
12.25	0.93349	0.94674	0.96001	0.97332	0.98665	1.00000	1.01337	1.02677
12.50	0.92091	0.93403	0.94717	0.96034	0.97354	0.98676	1.00000	1.01326
12.75	0.90856	0.92155	0.93456	0.94760	0.96067	0.97376	0.98687	1.00000
13.00	0.89644	0.90929	0.92218	0.93509	0.94803	0.96099	0.97397	0.98698
13.25	0.88454	0.89726	0.91002	0.92281	0.93562	0.94845	0.96131	0.97419
13.50	0.87285	0.88545	0.89809	0.91074	0.92343	0.93614	0.94887	0.96162
13.75	0.86138	0.87386	0.88636	0.89890	0.91146	0.92405	0.93666	0.94929
14.00	0.85011	0.86247	0.87485	0.88727	0.89971	0.91217	0.92466	0.93717
14.25	0.83905	0.85128	0.86355	0.87585	0.88817	0.90051	0.91288	0.92527
14.50	0.82818	0.84030	0.85245	0.86463	0.87683	0.88906	0.90131	0.91358
14.75	0.81752	0.82952	0.84155	0.85361	0.86570	0.87781	0.88994	0.90210
15.00	0.80704	0.81893	0.83084	0.84279	0.85476	0.86676	0.87878	0.89082
15.25	0.79675	0.80852	0.82033	0.83216	0.84402	0.85590	0.86781	0.87974
15.50	0.78664	0.79831	0.81000	0.82172	0.83347	0.84524	0.85704	0.86886
15.75	0.77672	0.78827	0.79986	0.81147	0.82310	0.83477	0.84645	0.85816
16.00	0.76697	0.77842	0.78989	0.80139	0.81292	0.82448	0.83606	0.84766
16.25	0.75740	0.76873	0.78010	0.79150	0.80292	0.81437	0.82584	0.83734
16.50	0.74799	0.75922	0.77049	0.78178	0.79309	0.80444	0.81580	0.82719
16.75	0.73875	0.74988	0.76104	0.77223	0.78344	0.79468	0.80594	0.81723

Table 8

Mortgage Pricing As A Percent of Loan Amount
(30 Year Term And 9 Year Prepayment)

Required Percentage Yield	13.00	13.25	13.50	13.75	14.00	14.25	14.50	14.75
7.00	1.39329	1.40999	1.42671	1.44344	1.46018	1.47692	1.49367	1.51043
7.25	1.37314	1.38967	1.40620	1.42275	1.43931	1.45588	1.47245	1.48903
7.50	1.35337	1.36972	1.38608	1.40245	1.41883	1.43522	1.45162	1.46802
7.75	1.33398	1.35015	1.36633	1.38253	1.39874	1.41495	1.43118	1.44741
8.00	1.31494	1.33094	1.34695	1.36298	1.37901	1.39506	1.41111	1.42717
8.25	1.29626	1.31209	1.32793	1.34379	1.35966	1.37553	1.39142	1.40731
8.50	1.27793	1.29359	1.30927	1.32496	1.34066	1.35637	1.37208	1.38781
8.75	1.25994	1.27544	1.29095	1.30647	1.32201	1.33755	1.35311	1.36867
9.00	1.24228	1.25761	1.27296	1.28833	1.30370	1.31909	1.33448	1.34988
9.25	1.22495	1.24012	1.25531	1.27052	1.28573	1.30096	1.31619	1.33144
9.50	1.20794	1.22296	1.23799	1.25303	1.26809	1.28316	1.29824	1.31333
9.75	1.19124	1.20610	1.22098	1.23587	1.25078	1.26569	1.28062	1.29555
10.00	1.17485	1.18956	1.20429	1.21902	1.23378	1.24854	1.26331	1.27810
10.25	1.15876	1.17332	1.18790	1.20249	1.21709	1.23170	1.24633	1.26096
10.50	1.14297	1.15738	1.17181	1.18625	1.20070	1.21517	1.22965	1.24413
10.75	1.12746	1.14173	1.15601	1.17030	1.18461	1.19894	1.21327	1.22761
11.00	1.11224	1.12636	1.14050	1.15465	1.16882	1.18300	1.19719	1.21139
11.25	1.09730	1.11128	1.12527	1.13928	1.15331	1.16734	1.18139	1.19545
11.50	1.08262	1.09646	1.11032	1.12419	1.13808	1.15198	1.16589	1.17981
11.75	1.06822	1.08192	1.09564	1.10937	1.12312	1.13688	1.15066	1.16444
12.00	1.05407	1.06764	1.08122	1.09482	1.10843	1.12206	1.13570	1.14935
12.25	1.04018	1.05362	1.06707	1.08053	1.09401	1.10750	1.12101	1.13453
12.50	1.02655	1.03985	1.05316	1.06650	1.07985	1.09321	1.10658	1.11997
12.75	1.01315	1.02632	1.03951	1.05272	1.06593	1.07917	1.09241	1.10567
13.00	1.00000	1.01304	1.02610	1.03918	1.05227	1.06538	1.07850	1.09163
13.25	0.98708	1.00000	1.01293	1.02588	1.03885	1.05183	1.06482	1.07783
13.50	0.97440	0.98719	1.00000	1.01283	1.02567	1.03852	1.05139	1.06428
13.75	0.96194	0.97461	0.98730	1.00000	1.01272	1.02545	1.03820	1.05096
14.00	0.94970	0.96225	0.97482	0.98740	1.00000	1.01261	1.02524	1.03788
14.25	0.93768	0.95011	0.96256	0.97502	0.98750	1.00000	1.01251	1.02503
14.50	0.92587	0.93819	0.95052	0.96287	0.97523	0.98761	1.00000	1.01241
14.75	0.91428	0.92647	0.93869	0.95092	0.96317	0.97543	0.98771	1.00000
15.00	0.90288	0.91497	0.92707	0.93919	0.95132	0.96347	0.97563	0.98781
15.25	0.89169	0.90366	0.91565	0.92766	0.93968	0.95172	0.96377	0.97583
15.50	0.88070	0.89256	0.90443	0.91633	0.92824	0.94017	0.95211	0.96406
15.75	0.86989	0.88164	0.89341	0.90520	0.91700	0.92882	0.94065	0.95250
16.00	0.85928	0.87092	0.88258	0.89426	0.90596	0.91767	0.92939	0.94113
16.25	0.84885	0.86039	0.87194	0.88351	0.89510	0.90671	0.91833	0.92996
16.50	0.83860	0.85004	0.86149	0.87295	0.88444	0.89594	0.90745	0.91898
16.75	0.82854	0.83986	0.85121	0.86257	0.87396	0.88535	0.89676	0.90819

Table 8

Mortgage Pricing As A Percent of Loan Amount
(30 Year Term And 9 Year Prepayment)

Required Percentage Yield	Net Percentage Contract Rate							
	15.00	15.25	15.50	15.75	16.00	16.25	16.50	16.75
7.00	1.52720	1.54396	1.56074	1.57751	1.59429	1.61107	1.62786	1.64464
7.25	1.50562	1.52221	1.53880	1.55540	1.57200	1.58861	1.60521	1.62182
7.50	1.48443	1.50085	1.51727	1.53370	1.55012	1.56655	1.58299	1.59942
7.75	1.46364	1.47989	1.49614	1.51239	1.52865	1.54491	1.56117	1.57743
8.00	1.44324	1.45931	1.47539	1.49147	1.50756	1.52365	1.53975	1.55584
8.25	1.42321	1.43911	1.45503	1.47094	1.48686	1.50279	1.51872	1.53465
8.50	1.40355	1.41929	1.43503	1.45079	1.46654	1.48230	1.49807	1.51383
8.75	1.38424	1.39982	1.41541	1.43100	1.44659	1.46219	1.47779	1.49340
9.00	1.36530	1.38071	1.39614	1.41157	1.42701	1.44245	1.45789	1.47334
9.25	1.34669	1.36195	1.37722	1.39249	1.40777	1.42306	1.43834	1.45364
9.50	1.32843	1.34353	1.35865	1.37377	1.38889	1.40402	1.41915	1.43429
9.75	1.31050	1.32545	1.34041	1.35538	1.37035	1.38532	1.40031	1.41529
10.00	1.29289	1.30769	1.32250	1.33732	1.35214	1.36697	1.38180	1.39664
10.25	1.27561	1.29026	1.30492	1.31959	1.33426	1.34894	1.36362	1.37831
10.50	1.25863	1.27314	1.28765	1.30217	1.31670	1.33124	1.34577	1.36032
10.75	1.24196	1.25633	1.27070	1.28507	1.29946	1.31385	1.32824	1.34264
11.00	1.22560	1.23982	1.25404	1.26828	1.28252	1.29677	1.31103	1.32528
11.25	1.20952	1.22360	1.23769	1.25179	1.26589	1.28000	1.29411	1.30823
11.50	1.19374	1.20768	1.22163	1.23559	1.24955	1.26352	1.27750	1.29149
11.75	1.17824	1.19204	1.20586	1.21968	1.23351	1.24734	1.26119	1.27503
12.00	1.16301	1.17668	1.19036	1.20405	1.21775	1.23145	1.24516	1.25887
12.25	1.14806	1.16159	1.17514	1.18870	1.20226	1.21583	1.22941	1.24299
12.50	1.13337	1.14678	1.16019	1.17362	1.18705	1.20049	1.21394	1.22740
12.75	1.11894	1.13222	1.14551	1.15881	1.17211	1.18543	1.19875	1.21207
13.00	1.10477	1.11792	1.13108	1.14425	1.15743	1.17062	1.18382	1.19702
13.25	1.09085	1.10387	1.11691	1.12996	1.14301	1.15608	1.16915	1.18222
13.50	1.07717	1.09007	1.10299	1.11591	1.12884	1.14179	1.15473	1.16769
13.75	1.06373	1.07652	1.08931	1.10211	1.11492	1.12774	1.14057	1.15340
14.00	1.05053	1.06320	1.07587	1.08855	1.10125	1.11395	1.12665	1.13937
14.25	1.03757	1.05011	1.06267	1.07523	1.08781	1.10039	1.11298	1.12557
14.50	1.02482	1.03725	1.04969	1.06214	1.07460	1.08706	1.09954	1.11202
14.75	1.01230	1.02462	1.03694	1.04928	1.06162	1.07397	1.08633	1.09870
15.00	1.00000	1.01220	1.02441	1.03663	1.04886	1.06110	1.07335	1.08561
15.25	0.98791	1.00000	1.01210	1.02421	1.03633	1.04846	1.06059	1.07274
15.50	0.97603	0.98801	1.00000	1.01200	1.02401	1.03603	1.04806	1.06009
15.75	0.96436	0.97623	0.98811	1.00000	1.01190	1.02381	1.03573	1.04766
16.00	0.95288	0.96465	0.97642	0.98821	1.00000	1.01180	1.02362	1.03544
16.25	0.94161	0.95326	0.96493	0.97661	0.98830	1.00000	1.01171	1.02342
16.50	0.93052	0.94208	0.95364	0.96522	0.97680	0.98840	1.00000	1.01161
16.75	0.91963	0.93108	0.94254	0.95402	0.96550	0.97699	0.98849	1.00000

Table 8

Mortgage Pricing As A Percent of Loan Amount
(30 Year Term And 12 Year Prepayment)

Required Percentage Yield	Net Percentage Contract Rate							
	9.00	9.25	9.50	9.75	10.00	10.25	10.50	10.75
7.00	1.15426	1.17390	1.19360	1.21337	1.23319	1.25307	1.27300	1.29298
7.25	1.13329	1.15264	1.17206	1.19154	1.21108	1.23067	1.25031	1.27001
7.50	1.11283	1.13190	1.15104	1.17024	1.18949	1.20881	1.22817	1.24758
7.75	1.09286	1.11166	1.13052	1.14944	1.16843	1.18747	1.20656	1.22569
8.00	1.07338	1.09190	1.11050	1.12915	1.14787	1.16664	1.18546	1.20433
8.25	1.05436	1.07262	1.09095	1.10934	1.12780	1.14630	1.16486	1.18347
8.50	1.03580	1.05381	1.07188	1.09001	1.10820	1.12645	1.14475	1.16310
8.75	1.01768	1.03544	1.05325	1.07114	1.08908	1.10707	1.12512	1.14322
9.00	1.00000	1.01751	1.03508	1.05271	1.07040	1.08815	1.10595	1.12380
9.25	0.98274	1.00000	1.01733	1.03472	1.05217	1.06967	1.08723	1.10484
9.50	0.96588	0.98291	1.00000	1.01715	1.03436	1.05163	1.06895	1.08632
9.75	0.94943	0.96622	0.98308	1.00000	1.01698	1.03401	1.05110	1.06824
10.00	0.93337	0.94993	0.96656	0.98325	1.00000	1.01681	1.03366	1.05057
10.25	0.91768	0.93402	0.95042	0.96689	0.98342	1.00000	1.01663	1.03332
10.50	0.90236	0.91848	0.93467	0.95091	0.96722	0.98358	1.00000	1.01647
10.75	0.88740	0.90331	0.91928	0.93531	0.95140	0.96755	0.98375	1.00000
11.00	0.87279	0.88848	0.90424	0.92007	0.93595	0.95188	0.96787	0.98391
11.25	0.85852	0.87401	0.88956	0.90518	0.92085	0.93658	0.95236	0.96820
11.50	0.84458	0.85986	0.87521	0.89063	0.90610	0.92163	0.93721	0.95284
11.75	0.83096	0.84605	0.86120	0.87641	0.89169	0.90702	0.92240	0.93783
12.00	0.81765	0.83255	0.84751	0.86253	0.87760	0.89274	0.90792	0.92316
12.25	0.80466	0.81936	0.83413	0.84896	0.86384	0.87878	0.89378	0.90882
12.50	0.79195	0.80647	0.82105	0.83569	0.85039	0.86515	0.87996	0.89481
12.75	0.77954	0.79388	0.80827	0.82273	0.83725	0.85182	0.86644	0.88112
13.00	0.76742	0.78157	0.79579	0.81006	0.82440	0.83879	0.85323	0.86773
13.25	0.75556	0.76954	0.78358	0.79768	0.81184	0.82605	0.84032	0.85464
13.50	0.74398	0.75778	0.77165	0.78558	0.79956	0.81360	0.82770	0.84184
13.75	0.73266	0.74629	0.75999	0.77374	0.78756	0.80143	0.81535	0.82932
14.00	0.72159	0.73505	0.74858	0.76218	0.77582	0.78953	0.80328	0.81708
14.25	0.71076	0.72407	0.73744	0.75086	0.76435	0.77789	0.79148	0.80512
14.50	0.70018	0.71333	0.72654	0.73980	0.75313	0.76650	0.77993	0.79341
14.75	0.68984	0.70283	0.71588	0.72899	0.74215	0.75537	0.76864	0.78196
15.00	0.67973	0.69256	0.70545	0.71841	0.73142	0.74448	0.75760	0.77076
15.25	0.66983	0.68252	0.69526	0.70806	0.72092	0.73383	0.74679	0.75981
15.50	0.66016	0.67269	0.68529	0.69794	0.71065	0.72341	0.73623	0.74909
15.75	0.65070	0.66308	0.67553	0.68804	0.70060	0.71322	0.72589	0.73860
16.00	0.64144	0.65369	0.66599	0.67836	0.69077	0.70325	0.71577	0.72834
16.25	0.63239	0.64449	0.65666	0.66888	0.68116	0.69349	0.70587	0.71830
16.50	0.62353	0.63550	0.64752	0.65961	0.67175	0.68394	0.69618	0.70847
16.75	0.61487	0.62670	0.63859	0.65054	0.66254	0.67459	0.68670	0.69885

Table 8

Mortgage Pricing As A Percent of Loan Amount
(30 Year Term And 12 Year Prepayment)

Required Percentage Yield	Net Percentage Contract Rate							
	11.00	11.25	11.50	11.75	12.00	12.25	12.50	12.75
7.00	1.31300	1.33307	1.35317	1.37331	1.39348	1.41369	1.43392	1.45418
7.25	1.28974	1.30952	1.32934	1.34920	1.36909	1.38901	1.40896	1.42893
7.50	1.26704	1.28654	1.30608	1.32566	1.34527	1.36491	1.38458	1.40429
7.75	1.24488	1.26410	1.28337	1.30268	1.32201	1.34139	1.36079	1.38022
8.00	1.22324	1.24220	1.26120	1.28024	1.29931	1.31841	1.33755	1.35671
8.25	1.20212	1.22082	1.23955	1.25833	1.27714	1.29598	1.31485	1.33376
8.50	1.18150	1.19994	1.21842	1.23693	1.25549	1.27407	1.29269	1.31134
8.75	1.16136	1.17955	1.19777	1.21604	1.23434	1.25268	1.27105	1.28944
9.00	1.14170	1.15964	1.17762	1.19564	1.21369	1.23178	1.24990	1.26805
9.25	1.12249	1.14019	1.15793	1.17571	1.19352	1.21137	1.22925	1.24716
9.50	1.10374	1.12120	1.13870	1.15624	1.17382	1.19143	1.20907	1.22675
9.75	1.08542	1.10265	1.11992	1.13723	1.15457	1.17195	1.18936	1.20681
10.00	1.06753	1.08453	1.10157	1.11865	1.13577	1.15292	1.17011	1.18732
10.25	1.05005	1.06683	1.08365	1.10050	1.11740	1.13433	1.15129	1.16828
10.50	1.03298	1.04954	1.06613	1.08277	1.09945	1.11616	1.13290	1.14968
10.75	1.01630	1.03264	1.04902	1.06545	1.08191	1.09840	1.11493	1.13149
11.00	1.00000	1.01613	1.03230	1.04852	1.06477	1.08105	1.09737	1.11372
11.25	0.98408	1.00000	1.01597	1.03197	1.04802	1.06410	1.08021	1.09635
11.50	0.96851	0.98424	1.00000	1.01580	1.03165	1.04752	1.06343	1.07937
11.75	0.95331	0.96883	0.98439	1.00000	1.01564	1.03132	1.04703	1.06277
12.00	0.93844	0.95377	0.96914	0.98455	1.00000	1.01548	1.03100	1.04655
12.25	0.92392	0.93905	0.95423	0.96945	0.98471	1.00000	1.01533	1.03068
12.50	0.90972	0.92467	0.93966	0.95469	0.96976	0.98486	1.00000	1.01517
12.75	0.89584	0.91060	0.92541	0.94026	0.95514	0.97006	0.98501	1.00000
13.00	0.88227	0.89685	0.91148	0.92614	0.94085	0.95559	0.97036	0.98517
13.25	0.86900	0.88340	0.89785	0.91234	0.92687	0.94143	0.95603	0.97066
13.50	0.85603	0.87026	0.88453	0.89885	0.91320	0.92759	0.94201	0.95647
13.75	0.84334	0.85740	0.87151	0.88565	0.89983	0.91405	0.92830	0.94259
14.00	0.83093	0.84483	0.85877	0.87274	0.88676	0.90081	0.91489	0.92901
14.25	0.81880	0.83253	0.84630	0.86012	0.87397	0.88785	0.90177	0.91572
14.50	0.80694	0.82050	0.83411	0.84777	0.86145	0.87518	0.88894	0.90272
14.75	0.79533	0.80874	0.82219	0.83568	0.84921	0.86278	0.87638	0.89001
15.00	0.78397	0.79723	0.81052	0.82386	0.83723	0.85064	0.86409	0.87756
15.25	0.77286	0.78597	0.79911	0.81229	0.82552	0.83877	0.85206	0.86538
15.50	0.76200	0.77495	0.78794	0.80098	0.81405	0.82715	0.84029	0.85346
15.75	0.75136	0.76417	0.77701	0.78990	0.80282	0.81578	0.82877	0.84180
16.00	0.74096	0.75362	0.76632	0.77906	0.79184	0.80465	0.81750	0.83038
16.25	0.73077	0.74329	0.75585	0.76845	0.78109	0.79376	0.80646	0.81920
16.50	0.72081	0.73318	0.74560	0.75806	0.77056	0.78309	0.79566	0.80825
16.75	0.71105	0.72329	0.73558	0.74790	0.76026	0.77265	0.78508	0.79754

Table 8

Mortgage Pricing As A Percent of Loan Amount
(30 Year Term And 12 Year Prepayment)

Required Percentage Yield	Net Percentage Contract Rate							
	13.00	13.25	13.50	13.75	14.00	14.25	14.50	14.75
7.00	1.47446	1.49477	1.51510	1.53544	1.55581	1.57619	1.59658	1.61698
7.25	1.44894	1.46896	1.48901	1.50907	1.52916	1.54925	1.56937	1.58949
7.50	1.42401	1.44376	1.46353	1.48332	1.50313	1.52295	1.54279	1.56264
7.75	1.39967	1.41915	1.43865	1.45817	1.47771	1.49726	1.51683	1.53641
8.00	1.37590	1.39511	1.41435	1.43360	1.45288	1.47217	1.49147	1.51080
8.25	1.35269	1.37164	1.39061	1.40961	1.42862	1.44766	1.46670	1.48577
8.50	1.33001	1.34871	1.36743	1.38617	1.40493	1.42371	1.44251	1.46132
8.75	1.30786	1.32631	1.34478	1.36328	1.38179	1.40032	1.41886	1.43743
9.00	1.28623	1.30443	1.32266	1.34091	1.35918	1.37746	1.39577	1.41408
9.25	1.26510	1.28306	1.30105	1.31905	1.33708	1.35513	1.37319	1.39127
9.50	1.24445	1.26218	1.27993	1.29770	1.31549	1.33331	1.35114	1.36898
9.75	1.22428	1.24177	1.25929	1.27683	1.29440	1.31198	1.32958	1.34720
10.00	1.20456	1.22183	1.23913	1.25644	1.27378	1.29114	1.30851	1.32590
10.25	1.18530	1.20235	1.21942	1.23651	1.25363	1.27077	1.28792	1.30509
10.50	1.16648	1.18331	1.20016	1.21704	1.23394	1.25085	1.26779	1.28475
10.75	1.14808	1.16470	1.18134	1.19800	1.21468	1.23139	1.24811	1.26486
11.00	1.13010	1.14651	1.16294	1.17939	1.19587	1.21236	1.22888	1.24541
11.25	1.11252	1.12872	1.14495	1.16120	1.17747	1.19376	1.21007	1.22640
11.50	1.09534	1.11134	1.12736	1.14341	1.15948	1.17557	1.19168	1.20781
11.75	1.07855	1.09435	1.11017	1.12602	1.14189	1.15778	1.17370	1.18963
12.00	1.06213	1.07773	1.09336	1.10902	1.12469	1.14039	1.15611	1.17185
12.25	1.04607	1.06148	1.07692	1.09239	1.10788	1.12338	1.13891	1.15446
12.50	1.03037	1.04560	1.06085	1.07613	1.09143	1.10675	1.12209	1.13745
12.75	1.01502	1.03006	1.04513	1.06022	1.07534	1.09048	1.10564	1.12081
13.00	1.00000	1.01486	1.02975	1.04467	1.05960	1.07456	1.08954	1.10454
13.25	0.98531	1.00000	1.01471	1.02945	1.04421	1.05899	1.07379	1.08861
13.50	0.97095	0.98546	1.00000	1.01456	1.02915	1.04376	1.05839	1.07303
13.75	0.95690	0.97124	0.98561	1.00000	1.01442	1.02885	1.04331	1.05779
14.00	0.94315	0.95733	0.97153	0.98575	1.00000	1.01427	1.02856	1.04287
14.25	0.92970	0.94371	0.95775	0.97181	0.98589	1.00000	1.01413	1.02827
14.50	0.91654	0.93039	0.94427	0.95817	0.97209	0.98603	1.00000	1.01399
14.75	0.90367	0.91736	0.93107	0.94481	0.95858	0.97237	0.98617	1.00000
15.00	0.89107	0.90460	0.91816	0.93175	0.94536	0.95899	0.97264	0.98631
15.25	0.87874	0.89212	0.90552	0.91896	0.93241	0.94589	0.95939	0.97291
15.50	0.86667	0.87990	0.89315	0.90644	0.91974	0.93307	0.94642	0.95979
15.75	0.85485	0.86793	0.88104	0.89418	0.90734	0.92052	0.93372	0.94694
16.00	0.84329	0.85623	0.86919	0.88218	0.89519	0.90823	0.92128	0.93436
16.25	0.83197	0.84476	0.85758	0.87043	0.88330	0.89619	0.90911	0.92204
16.50	0.82088	0.83354	0.84622	0.85893	0.87166	0.88441	0.89718	0.90998
16.75	0.81003	0.82255	0.83509	0.84766	0.86025	0.87287	0.88550	0.89816

Table 8

Mortgage Pricing As A Percent of Loan Amount
(30 Year Term And 12 Year Prepayment)

Required Percentage Yield	Net Percentage Contract Rate							
	15.00	15.25	15.50	15.75	16.00	16.25	16.50	16.75
7.00	1.63740	1.65782	1.67826	1.69870	1.71915	1.73960	1.76006	1.78052
7.25	1.60963	1.62978	1.64993	1.67010	1.69027	1.71044	1.73063	1.75081
7.50	1.58250	1.60238	1.62226	1.64216	1.66205	1.68196	1.70187	1.72179
7.75	1.55601	1.57562	1.59523	1.61486	1.63449	1.65413	1.67378	1.69343
8.00	1.53013	1.54947	1.56883	1.58819	1.60757	1.62694	1.64633	1.66572
8.25	1.50484	1.52393	1.54303	1.56214	1.58125	1.60038	1.61951	1.63865
8.50	1.48014	1.49898	1.51782	1.53668	1.55554	1.57442	1.59330	1.61218
8.75	1.45600	1.47459	1.49319	1.51180	1.53042	1.54905	1.56768	1.58632
9.00	1.43242	1.45076	1.46912	1.48749	1.50587	1.52425	1.54265	1.56105
9.25	1.40937	1.42748	1.44560	1.46373	1.48187	1.50002	1.51818	1.53634
9.50	1.38684	1.40472	1.42261	1.44050	1.45841	1.47633	1.49425	1.51219
9.75	1.36483	1.38247	1.40013	1.41780	1.43548	1.45317	1.47087	1.48858
10.00	1.34331	1.36073	1.37817	1.39561	1.41307	1.43053	1.44801	1.46549
10.25	1.32228	1.33948	1.35669	1.37392	1.39116	1.40840	1.42566	1.44292
10.50	1.30172	1.31870	1.33570	1.35271	1.36973	1.38676	1.40380	1.42085
10.75	1.28161	1.29839	1.31517	1.33197	1.34878	1.36560	1.38243	1.39927
11.00	1.26196	1.27852	1.29510	1.31169	1.32830	1.34491	1.36153	1.37816
11.25	1.24274	1.25910	1.27548	1.29186	1.30826	1.32467	1.34109	1.35752
11.50	1.22395	1.24011	1.25628	1.27247	1.28867	1.30488	1.32110	1.33733
11.75	1.20557	1.22154	1.23751	1.25350	1.26951	1.28552	1.30155	1.31758
12.00	1.18760	1.20337	1.21916	1.23495	1.25076	1.26658	1.28242	1.29826
12.25	1.17002	1.18560	1.20120	1.21681	1.23243	1.24806	1.26370	1.27936
12.50	1.15283	1.16822	1.18363	1.19905	1.21449	1.22994	1.24539	1.26086
12.75	1.13601	1.15122	1.16644	1.18168	1.19694	1.21220	1.22748	1.24277
13.00	1.11955	1.13458	1.14963	1.16469	1.17977	1.19485	1.20995	1.22506
13.25	1.10345	1.11831	1.13318	1.14806	1.16296	1.17787	1.19280	1.20773
13.50	1.08770	1.10238	1.11708	1.13179	1.14652	1.16126	1.17601	1.19077
13.75	1.07229	1.08680	1.10133	1.11587	1.13043	1.14499	1.15957	1.17417
14.00	1.05720	1.07155	1.08591	1.10028	1.11467	1.12908	1.14349	1.15792
14.25	1.04244	1.05662	1.07082	1.08503	1.09926	1.11349	1.12775	1.14201
14.50	1.02799	1.04201	1.05605	1.07010	1.08416	1.09824	1.11233	1.12643
14.75	1.01385	1.02771	1.04159	1.05548	1.06939	1.08331	1.09724	1.11118
15.00	1.00000	1.01371	1.02743	1.04117	1.05492	1.06869	1.08246	1.09625
15.25	0.98645	1.00000	1.01357	1.02716	1.04076	1.05437	1.06800	1.08163
15.50	0.97317	0.98658	1.00000	1.01344	1.02689	1.04035	1.05383	1.06731
15.75	0.96018	0.97344	0.98671	1.00000	1.01330	1.02662	1.03995	1.05329
16.00	0.94746	0.96057	0.97370	0.98684	1.00000	1.01317	1.02636	1.03955
16.25	0.93499	0.94797	0.96095	0.97395	0.98697	1.00000	1.01304	1.02610
16.50	0.92279	0.93562	0.94847	0.96133	0.97421	0.98710	1.00000	1.01291
16.75	0.91084	0.92353	0.93624	0.94896	0.96170	0.97446	0.98722	1.00000

Table 8

Mortgage Pricing As A Percent of Loan Amount
(30 Year Term And 30 Year Prepayment)

Required Percentage Yield	Net Percentage Contract Rate							
	9.00	9.25	9.50	9.75	10.00	10.25	10.50	10.75
7.00	1.20941	1.23654	1.26387	1.29137	1.31906	1.34691	1.37492	1.40309
7.25	1.17949	1.20596	1.23261	1.25943	1.28643	1.31359	1.34091	1.36839
7.50	1.15075	1.17657	1.20257	1.22874	1.25508	1.28158	1.30824	1.33504
7.75	1.12313	1.14833	1.17370	1.19925	1.22495	1.25082	1.27683	1.30299
8.00	1.09657	1.12117	1.14595	1.17089	1.19599	1.22124	1.24664	1.27218
8.25	1.07102	1.09505	1.11925	1.14361	1.16812	1.19279	1.21760	1.24254
8.50	1.04644	1.06992	1.09356	1.11736	1.14131	1.16541	1.18965	1.21403
8.75	1.02278	1.04573	1.06884	1.09210	1.11551	1.13906	1.16275	1.18658
9.00	1.00000	1.02244	1.04503	1.06777	1.09066	1.11369	1.13686	1.16015
9.25	0.97806	1.00000	1.02210	1.04434	1.06673	1.08925	1.11191	1.13469
9.50	0.95691	0.97838	1.00000	1.02176	1.04367	1.06570	1.08787	1.11016
9.75	0.93653	0.95754	0.97870	1.00000	1.02144	1.04300	1.06470	1.08651
10.00	0.91687	0.93745	0.95816	0.97901	1.00000	1.02111	1.04235	1.06371
10.25	0.89791	0.91806	0.93835	0.95877	0.97932	1.00000	1.02080	1.04171
10.50	0.87962	0.89936	0.91923	0.93923	0.95937	0.97962	1.00000	1.02049
10.75	0.86196	0.88130	0.90077	0.92038	0.94011	0.95996	0.97992	1.00000
11.00	0.84490	0.86386	0.88295	0.90217	0.92151	0.94096	0.96053	0.98021
11.25	0.82843	0.84702	0.86573	0.88458	0.90354	0.92262	0.94181	0.96110
11.50	0.81251	0.83074	0.84910	0.86758	0.88618	0.90489	0.92371	0.94263
11.75	0.79712	0.81501	0.83302	0.85115	0.86939	0.88775	0.90621	0.92478
12.00	0.78224	0.79979	0.81746	0.83526	0.85316	0.87117	0.88929	0.90752
12.25	0.76785	0.78507	0.80242	0.81988	0.83746	0.85514	0.87293	0.89081
12.50	0.75392	0.77083	0.78786	0.80501	0.82227	0.83963	0.85709	0.87465
12.75	0.74043	0.75704	0.77377	0.79061	0.80756	0.82461	0.84176	0.85901
13.00	0.72738	0.74370	0.76013	0.77667	0.79332	0.81007	0.82692	0.84386
13.25	0.71473	0.73076	0.74691	0.76317	0.77953	0.79599	0.81254	0.82919
13.50	0.70247	0.71824	0.73411	0.75008	0.76616	0.78234	0.79861	0.81497
13.75	0.69060	0.70609	0.72169	0.73740	0.75321	0.76911	0.78511	0.80119
14.00	0.67908	0.69432	0.70966	0.72510	0.74065	0.75629	0.77202	0.78783
14.25	0.66791	0.68290	0.69799	0.71318	0.72846	0.74385	0.75932	0.77487
14.50	0.65707	0.67182	0.68666	0.70160	0.71664	0.73178	0.74700	0.76230
14.75	0.64656	0.66106	0.67567	0.69037	0.70517	0.72006	0.73504	0.75010
15.00	0.63634	0.65062	0.66500	0.67947	0.69404	0.70869	0.72343	0.73825
15.25	0.62643	0.64048	0.65464	0.66888	0.68322	0.69765	0.71216	0.72675
15.50	0.61680	0.63064	0.64457	0.65860	0.67272	0.68692	0.70121	0.71558
15.75	0.60744	0.62107	0.63479	0.64861	0.66251	0.67650	0.69057	0.70472
16.00	0.59834	0.61177	0.62528	0.63889	0.65259	0.66637	0.68023	0.69416
16.25	0.58950	0.60272	0.61604	0.62945	0.64294	0.65652	0.67017	0.68390
16.50	0.58089	0.59393	0.60705	0.62026	0.63356	0.64694	0.66039	0.67392
16.75	0.57252	0.58537	0.59830	0.61133	0.62443	0.63762	0.65088	0.66421

Table 8

Mortgage Pricing As A Percent of Loan Amount
(30 Year Term And 30 Year Prepayment)

Required Percentage Yield	Net Percentage Contract Rate							
	11.00	11.25	11.50	11.75	12.00	12.25	12.50	12.75
7.00	1.43141	1.45988	1.48848	1.51722	1.54608	1.57507	1.60417	1.63338
7.25	1.39601	1.42377	1.45167	1.47969	1.50784	1.53611	1.56449	1.59298
7.50	1.36199	1.38907	1.41629	1.44363	1.47110	1.49868	1.52637	1.55416
7.75	1.32930	1.35573	1.38229	1.40898	1.43578	1.46270	1.48973	1.51685
8.00	1.29786	1.32367	1.34960	1.37566	1.40183	1.42811	1.45450	1.48098
8.25	1.26762	1.29283	1.31816	1.34361	1.36917	1.39484	1.42061	1.44648
8.50	1.23853	1.26316	1.28791	1.31277	1.33775	1.36283	1.38801	1.41328
8.75	1.21053	1.23460	1.25879	1.28309	1.30750	1.33201	1.35663	1.38133
9.00	1.18357	1.20710	1.23075	1.25451	1.27838	1.30235	1.32641	1.35056
9.25	1.15759	1.18061	1.20375	1.22698	1.25033	1.27377	1.29730	1.32093
9.50	1.13257	1.15509	1.17772	1.20046	1.22329	1.24623	1.26925	1.29237
9.75	1.10844	1.13049	1.15263	1.17489	1.19724	1.21968	1.24222	1.26484
10.00	1.08518	1.10676	1.12845	1.15023	1.17211	1.19409	1.21615	1.23830
10.25	1.06274	1.08387	1.10511	1.12645	1.14788	1.16940	1.19100	1.21269
10.50	1.04109	1.06179	1.08259	1.10349	1.12449	1.14557	1.16673	1.18798
10.75	1.02018	1.04047	1.06086	1.08134	1.10191	1.12257	1.14331	1.16413
11.00	1.00000	1.01989	1.03987	1.05994	1.08011	1.10036	1.12069	1.14110
11.25	0.98050	1.00000	1.01959	1.03928	1.05905	1.07890	1.09884	1.11885
11.50	0.96166	0.98078	1.00000	1.01931	1.03870	1.05817	1.07772	1.09735
11.75	0.94345	0.96221	0.98106	1.00000	1.01902	1.03813	1.05731	1.07656
12.00	0.92583	0.94424	0.96274	0.98133	1.00000	1.01875	1.03757	1.05647
12.25	0.90880	0.92687	0.94503	0.96327	0.98160	1.00000	1.01848	1.03702
12.50	0.89231	0.91005	0.92788	0.94580	0.96379	0.98186	1.00000	1.01821
12.75	0.87635	0.89378	0.91129	0.92888	0.94655	0.96430	0.98212	1.00000
13.00	0.86090	0.87802	0.89522	0.91250	0.92986	0.94729	0.96480	0.98237
13.25	0.84593	0.86275	0.87965	0.89664	0.91369	0.93082	0.94802	0.96529
13.50	0.83142	0.84796	0.86457	0.88126	0.89803	0.91486	0.93177	0.94874
13.75	0.81737	0.83362	0.84995	0.86636	0.88284	0.89940	0.91601	0.93269
14.00	0.80374	0.81972	0.83578	0.85191	0.86812	0.88440	0.90074	0.91714
14.25	0.79052	0.80624	0.82203	0.83790	0.85384	0.86985	0.88592	0.90205
14.50	0.77769	0.79315	0.80869	0.82431	0.83999	0.85574	0.87155	0.88742
14.75	0.76524	0.78046	0.79575	0.81111	0.82654	0.84204	0.85760	0.87321
15.00	0.75316	0.76813	0.78318	0.79830	0.81349	0.82874	0.84405	0.85942
15.25	0.74142	0.75616	0.77098	0.78586	0.80081	0.81583	0.83090	0.84603
15.50	0.73002	0.74454	0.75913	0.77378	0.78850	0.80328	0.81812	0.83302
15.75	0.71894	0.73324	0.74761	0.76204	0.77654	0.79109	0.80571	0.82038
16.00	0.70818	0.72226	0.73641	0.75063	0.76491	0.77925	0.79364	0.80810
16.25	0.69771	0.71158	0.72552	0.73953	0.75360	0.76773	0.78191	0.79615
16.50	0.68752	0.70120	0.71494	0.72874	0.74260	0.75652	0.77050	0.78453
16.75	0.67762	0.69109	0.70464	0.71824	0.73190	0.74562	0.75940	0.77323

Table 8

Mortgage Pricing As A Percent of Loan Amount
(30 Year Term And 30 Year Prepayment)

Required Percentage Yield	Net Percentage Contract Rate							
	13.00	13.25	13.50	13.75	14.00	14.25	14.50	14.75
7.00	1.66270	1.69212	1.72164	1.75125	1.78095	1.81074	1.84060	1.87054
7.25	1.62157	1.65027	1.67906	1.70793	1.73690	1.76595	1.79507	1.82427
7.50	1.58206	1.61005	1.63814	1.66632	1.69458	1.72291	1.75133	1.77982
7.75	1.54408	1.57140	1.59882	1.62632	1.65390	1.68156	1.70929	1.73709
8.00	1.50757	1.53424	1.56101	1.58786	1.61478	1.64179	1.66887	1.69601
8.25	1.47245	1.49850	1.52464	1.55086	1.57717	1.60354	1.62999	1.65650
8.50	1.43865	1.46411	1.48965	1.51527	1.54097	1.56674	1.59258	1.61849
8.75	1.40613	1.43101	1.45597	1.48101	1.50613	1.53132	1.55657	1.58189
9.00	1.37481	1.39913	1.42354	1.44802	1.47258	1.49721	1.52190	1.54666
9.25	1.34464	1.36843	1.39230	1.41625	1.44027	1.46435	1.48850	1.51272
9.50	1.31557	1.33885	1.36220	1.38563	1.40913	1.43269	1.45632	1.48001
9.75	1.28754	1.31033	1.33319	1.35612	1.37911	1.40218	1.42530	1.44849
10.00	1.26052	1.28283	1.30521	1.32766	1.35017	1.37275	1.39539	1.41809
10.25	1.23446	1.25630	1.27822	1.30020	1.32225	1.34436	1.36654	1.38877
10.50	1.20931	1.23070	1.25217	1.27371	1.29531	1.31697	1.33869	1.36047
10.75	1.18503	1.20599	1.22703	1.24814	1.26930	1.29053	1.31182	1.33316
11.00	1.16158	1.18213	1.20276	1.22344	1.24419	1.26500	1.28586	1.30678
11.25	1.13893	1.15908	1.17930	1.19959	1.21993	1.24033	1.26079	1.28130
11.50	1.11704	1.13681	1.15664	1.17654	1.19649	1.21650	1.23656	1.25668
11.75	1.09589	1.11528	1.13473	1.15425	1.17383	1.19346	1.21314	1.23287
12.00	1.07543	1.09446	1.11355	1.13270	1.15191	1.17118	1.19049	1.20986
12.25	1.05564	1.07432	1.09306	1.11186	1.13071	1.14962	1.16858	1.18759
12.50	1.03649	1.05483	1.07323	1.09169	1.11020	1.12877	1.14739	1.16605
12.75	1.01795	1.03596	1.05403	1.07216	1.09035	1.10858	1.12686	1.14520
13.00	1.00000	1.01769	1.03545	1.05326	1.07112	1.08903	1.10699	1.12500
13.25	0.98261	1.00000	1.01744	1.03494	1.05250	1.07010	1.08775	1.10544
13.50	0.96577	0.98285	1.00000	1.01720	1.03445	1.05175	1.06910	1.08649
13.75	0.94944	0.96624	0.98309	1.00000	1.01696	1.03397	1.05102	1.06812
14.00	0.93360	0.95012	0.96670	0.98332	1.00000	1.01672	1.03349	1.05030
14.25	0.91825	0.93449	0.95080	0.96715	0.98355	1.00000	1.01649	1.03303
14.50	0.90335	0.91933	0.93537	0.95146	0.96759	0.98377	1.00000	1.01627
14.75	0.88889	0.90462	0.92040	0.93623	0.95211	0.96803	0.98399	1.00000
15.00	0.87485	0.89033	0.90586	0.92144	0.93707	0.95274	0.96845	0.98421
15.25	0.86122	0.87646	0.89175	0.90708	0.92247	0.93789	0.95336	0.96887
15.50	0.84798	0.86298	0.87804	0.89314	0.90828	0.92347	0.93870	0.95397
15.75	0.83511	0.84989	0.86471	0.87958	0.89450	0.90946	0.92446	0.93950
16.00	0.82260	0.83716	0.85176	0.86641	0.88110	0.89584	0.91062	0.92543
16.25	0.81044	0.82478	0.83917	0.85360	0.86808	0.88260	0.89715	0.91175
16.50	0.79861	0.81275	0.82692	0.84115	0.85541	0.86972	0.88406	0.89844
16.75	0.78711	0.80104	0.81501	0.82903	0.84309	0.85719	0.87132	0.88550

Table 8

Mortgage Pricing As A Percent of Loan Amount
(30 Year Term And 30 Year Prepayment)

Required Percentage Yield	Net Percentage Contract Rate							
	15.00	15.25	15.50	15.75	16.00	16.25	16.50	16.75
7.00	1.90056	1.93064	1.96079	1.99100	2.02127	2.05160	2.08198	2.11242
7.25	1.85354	1.88288	1.91229	1.94175	1.97127	2.00085	2.03048	2.06016
7.50	1.80838	1.83700	1.86569	1.89444	1.92324	1.95210	1.98101	2.00996
7.75	1.76497	1.79290	1.82090	1.84896	1.87707	1.90524	1.93345	1.96171
8.00	1.72323	1.75050	1.77784	1.80523	1.83268	1.86018	1.88773	1.91532
8.25	1.68308	1.70972	1.73642	1.76318	1.78999	1.81684	1.84375	1.87070
8.50	1.64446	1.67049	1.69657	1.72271	1.74891	1.77515	1.80144	1.82777
8.75	1.60728	1.63272	1.65821	1.68376	1.70936	1.73501	1.76071	1.78644
9.00	1.57147	1.59635	1.62128	1.64626	1.67129	1.69637	1.72149	1.74665
9.25	1.53699	1.56132	1.58570	1.61013	1.63461	1.65914	1.68371	1.70832
9.50	1.50376	1.52756	1.55142	1.57532	1.59927	1.62327	1.64731	1.67139
9.75	1.47173	1.49503	1.51837	1.54177	1.56521	1.58870	1.61222	1.63579
10.00	1.44084	1.46365	1.48651	1.50941	1.53236	1.55535	1.57839	1.60146
10.25	1.41105	1.43339	1.45577	1.47820	1.50068	1.52319	1.54575	1.56834
10.50	1.38230	1.40418	1.42611	1.44808	1.47010	1.49216	1.51425	1.53639
10.75	1.35455	1.37599	1.39748	1.41901	1.44058	1.46220	1.48385	1.50554
11.00	1.32775	1.34876	1.36983	1.39093	1.41208	1.43327	1.45449	1.47575
11.25	1.30186	1.32246	1.34312	1.36381	1.38455	1.40532	1.42613	1.44698
11.50	1.27684	1.29705	1.31731	1.33760	1.35794	1.37832	1.39873	1.41917
11.75	1.25266	1.27248	1.29236	1.31227	1.33222	1.35221	1.37224	1.39229
12.00	1.22927	1.24873	1.26823	1.28777	1.30735	1.32697	1.34662	1.36630
12.25	1.20665	1.22575	1.24489	1.26407	1.28329	1.30255	1.32184	1.34116
12.50	1.18476	1.20351	1.22231	1.24114	1.26001	1.27892	1.29786	1.31683
12.75	1.16357	1.18199	1.20045	1.21894	1.23748	1.25604	1.27465	1.29328
13.00	1.14305	1.16115	1.17928	1.19745	1.21566	1.23390	1.25217	1.27047
13.25	1.12318	1.14096	1.15877	1.17663	1.19452	1.21244	1.23040	1.24838
13.50	1.10392	1.12139	1.13891	1.15645	1.17404	1.19165	1.20930	1.22698
13.75	1.08525	1.10243	1.11965	1.13690	1.15419	1.17150	1.18885	1.20623
14.00	1.06716	1.08405	1.10098	1.11794	1.13494	1.15197	1.16903	1.18612
14.25	1.04960	1.06622	1.08287	1.09955	1.11627	1.13302	1.14980	1.16661
14.50	1.03257	1.04892	1.06530	1.08171	1.09816	1.11464	1.13114	1.14768
14.75	1.01605	1.03213	1.04825	1.06440	1.08058	1.09679	1.11304	1.12931
15.00	1.00000	1.01583	1.03169	1.04759	1.06352	1.07947	1.09546	1.11147
15.25	0.98442	1.00000	1.01562	1.03127	1.04694	1.06265	1.07839	1.09415
15.50	0.96928	0.98462	1.00000	1.01541	1.03085	1.04631	1.06181	1.07733
15.75	0.95457	0.96968	0.98483	1.00000	1.01520	1.03044	1.04570	1.06098
16.00	0.94028	0.95516	0.97008	0.98502	1.00000	1.01500	1.03004	1.04509
16.25	0.92638	0.94104	0.95574	0.97046	0.98522	1.00000	1.01481	1.02964
16.50	0.91286	0.92731	0.94179	0.95630	0.97084	0.98541	1.00000	1.01462
16.75	0.89971	0.91395	0.92822	0.94252	0.95685	0.97121	0.98559	1.00000

INDEX